A Geography
of Human Life

A Geography of Human Life
English Edition

Tsunesaburo Makiguchi

Edited by Dayle M. Bethel

Published by Caddo Gap Press
3145 Geary Boulevard PMB 275
San Francisco, California 94118 U.S.A.
Alan H. Jones, Publisher
Heather L. Hazuka, Cover Design & Page Layout

ISBN 1-880192-42-X

Price - $29.95

Library of Congress Cataloging-in-Publication Data

Makiguchi, Tsunesaburo, 1871-1944.
 [Jinsei chirigaku. English]
 A geography of human life / Tsunesaburo Makiguchi ; edited by Dayle M. Bethel ; translators, Katsusuke Hori ... [et al.].— English ed.
    p. cm.
Includes bibliographical references and index.
 ISBN 1-880192-42-X (alk. paper)
1. Human geography. I. Bethel, Dayle M., 1923- II. Title.
 GF41 .M33513 2002
 304.2—dc21
                              2002005592

Contents

Acknowledgements vii
Preface ix
Editor's Introduction xiii
Foreword xxxiii

A Geography of Human Life

Foreward to the First Edition 3
Preface to the First Edition 5

Introduction

Chapter 1
Earth and Human Life 11

Chapter 2
Our Homeland as a Base for Observing the World 17

Chapter 3
Interacting with the Earth 25

Part 1: The Earth as the Base for Human Life

Chapter 4
The Firmament 37

Chapter 5
The Earth 43

Chapter 6
Islands 51

Chapter 7
Peninsulas and Capes 57

Chapter 8
Isthmuses, Mountains and Valleys, Plains 61

Chapter 9
Rivers 69

Chapter 10
Lakes and Marshes 85

Chapter 11
Seas and Oceans 93

Chapter 12
Inland Seas and Straits 109

Chapter 13
Harbors and Ports 117

Chapter 14
The Seashore 125

Part 2: Nature as a Medium Between Humans and the Earth

Chapter 15
The Inanimate World 133

Chapter 16
The Atmosphere 139

Chapter 17
Climate 143

Chapter 18
The Earth's Vegetation 157

Chapter 19
Animals 165

Chapter 20
The Human Species 169

Part 3: The Phenomenon of Human Life on the Earth

Chapter 21
Society 179

Chapter 22
The Functions of Society 187

Chapter 23
The Location of Industry I 199

Chapter 24
The Location of Industry II 209

Chapter 25
The Location of Industry III 221

Chapter 26
The State 235

Chapter 27
The Phenomenon of Cities 259

Chapter 28
Customs, Temperament, and Geography 273

Chapter 29
Competition for Survival 281

Chapter 30
On Civilization and the Earth 291

Appendix
The Concept of Geography 295

Afterword
Geographic Education in the Twentieth Century 301

Index 307

vi   A Geography of Human Life ─────────────────────

An original 1903 edition of *Human Geography*, thick and well worn. The title in Japanese, *Jinsei Chiragaku*, runs down the center, and on the right is the imprimatur of the leading geographer of Makiguchi's day, Shigetaka Shiga.

Acknowledgements

I wish to express appreciation to Daisaku Ikeda, president of Soka Gakkai International, and to members of his staff, particularly Hiromu Yamaguchi, Director of Soka Gakkai's International Publications Department, for the support and assistance which have made the translating and editing of this book possible. I wish to acknowledge, also, the part played by Tomiya Akiyama of Soka Gakkai's International Bureau in initiating the project. It is more than fifteen years ago now, when we were engrossed in the work of translating an English version of Makiguchi's Theory of Value Creating Pedagogy, that Mr. Akiyama, half in jest, suggested that our next project must be the translating and editing of Makiguchi's first book, *Jinsei Chirigaku* (A Geography of Human Life), published in 1903. His untimely death ruled out his participation in this project, but I am sure he would be pleased that another aspect of Makiguchi's thought and scholarship is being made available in the English language.

For their painstaking work and untiring efforts during all stages of the difficult task of translating the old style language in which the book was written, I must express special appreciation to the members of the translation team: Katsusuke Hori, Satomi Nishida, Yukiko Summerville, and Mariko Takano. Their commitment to the project, their cooperation and creative suggestions during the uncertainties and perplexities of its early period, and often their sense of humor, helped to make the task of editing a joy and not only hard work. The assistance and creative ideas of Celine Shinbutsu have been particularly valuable in the later stages of editing the manuscript.

For taking time in his busy schedule to review and comment on the manuscript we are indebted to Dr. Andrew A. Nazzaro, Professor of Geography at Eastern Michigan University. His Afterword provides an insightful evaluation of Makiguchi's work as a geographer and places it in historical context.

Finally, I must acknowledge the contribution of my wife, Miyoko Shimizu Bethel, who served as co-editor, and who brought her own unique skills as typist, researcher, and general coordinator to the project. Her support and encouragement have been a constant source of strength and inspiration.

Preface

Makiguchi's last major work, *Soka Kyoikugaku Taikei* (A Theory of Value-Creating Pedagogy), translated during the 1980s and published in English by Iowa State University Press in 1989, was perceived by him as a step toward the design of a system of education which could draw forth and activate the creative powers resident in every human being. It is a significant work of scholarship and has been recognized as such by leading educators and educational philosophers in the English speaking world. However, that book represents but one segment of the productivity of Makiguchi's far-ranging and creative mind. His earlier publications, particularly his first work, *Jinsei Chirigaku* (A Geography of Human Life), published in 1903 when he was 32 years of age, and *Kyodoka* (Community Studies), published nine years later, are equally significant contributions to scholarship in the social sciences. We thus offer this translation of *A Geography of Human Life* as a further step toward making Makiguchi's work available in the English language.

A Geography of Human Life in the original is a partially edited collection of ideas, insights which occurred to Makiguchi from time to time, notes gleaned from his readings and discussions with other scholars, reports and comments on his observations, discoveries, and research which he accumulated while he was teaching geography in elementary and junior high schools. He indicates that it was not his intention, initially, to publish this material. The decision to publish came about as a result of two factors. The first was his deepening realization of the deplorable state of Japanese education, particularly the teaching of geography. Among his notes was the observation that:

> No other subject is taught in as pitiful and ridiculous a way in Japanese schools as geography. Not only in elementary schools but in junior high schools as well, students are made to memorize the names of mountains, rivers, lakes, cities, and population figures without any theoretical framework or relationship whatever. It is impossible for students to retain this factual mish mash for long, so all they have left after examinations are fragmented bits of useless knowledge. It is no wonder that students generally think of geography as the least interesting and the most disliked of all their subjects. This certainly is not true geography.

The other factor which convinced Makiguchi that he should publish his material was a deepening understanding of the significance of the earth for human life and the importance of place as a fundamental organizing concept for education. He became convinced that these insights held a key to the solution of many of the problems facing his society.[1]

These convictions about geography and the earth and a growing sense of urgency in sharing his insights and understandings with others created for Makiguchi a frustrating dilemma. He came to realize that publication was the answer to wide communication of his ideas. At the same time, limitations of both time and resources made it impossible for him to do a thorough job of editing the material he had accumulated. Thus, the manuscript which he finally got together was only partially edited; it contains excessive repetition of some of the material and the sources of quotations and references to the works of other scholars are often inadequate or lacking altogether.

A further consideration is that Makiguchi, conscious of his lack of formal training in geography, sought and received the advice and assistance from a well-known geographer, Shigetaka Shiga. Makiguchi relied heavily on notes taken during interviews with Shiga, as well as on Shiga's writings, in the final preparation of the manuscript for publication.[2] Moreover, Shiga indicates, in comments in a foreword he contributed to the first edition of the book, that he reduced Makiguchi's original 2,000 page manuscript to approximately half that length and in the process included some additional information and comments of his own. While Makiguchi frequently acknowledges his debt to Shiga, it is difficult in some instances to distinguish between Makiguchi's ideas and views and ideas or examples contributed by Shiga.

Makiguchi recognized the rough nature of his work, but his conviction as to the significance of the ideas he wanted to convey led him to proceed with publication. Included in the preface to early editions of the book is an apology to his readers for its errors and flaws and a request for their understanding and suggestions for corrections.

The first edition of *A Geography of Human Life*, consisting of approximately 1,100 pages, was revised by Makiguchi several times and went through numerous printings in the ensuing years. The book was approved by the Ministry of Education and during the early decades of the century was widely used as a text in Japanese schools for teachers seeking certification to teach geography. By the middle of the century, however, it had fallen into disuse and was little known in Japan during the post-war era, even to many members of Soka Gakkai, the Buddhist lay organization for peace, culture and education that considers Makiguchi as its founder. Between the years 1971 and 1980, a revision of the 5th (1905) edition of the book was published by Seikyo Press in five volumes with a total of 1,392 pages. The Seikyo Press revision sought to make the book more accessible and readable by adding commentary and explanations, further information on scholars and sources cited by Makiguchi, and phonetic symbols to aid in the reading of difficult Chinese characters. Some changes in the numbering of chapters were also included in this revision. In the course of the work of translation, the editorial staff used as the basis for this English edition both Seikyo Press's revised edition and a reprint of a 1908 edition published by Daisan Bunmei Publishing Company in 1976.

As will be expected, in view of the above explanation, this English edition of the book is not a direct translation of the original Japanese material. To the extent possible, repetition has been eliminated and dated and extraneous material omitted. In some cases, ideas, concepts, perceptions, and points of view which in the original are spread over several pages or chapters have been summarized in an attempt to provide a coherent statement of what we believe was Makiguchi's original intent and meaning.

Notes

[1] Makiguchi is recognized today as one of the first scholars in the world, and the first in Japan, to approach the discipline of geography in terms of the relationship between human beings and the earth.

[2] Another person who influenced Makiguchi's thinking was Kanzo Uchimura, a Christian theologian and founder of Mukyokai (non-church) Christianity in Japan. It has been observed that whereas Shiga's influence strengthened Makiguchi's nationalist leanings, his association with Uchimura nurtured in him a cosmopolitan outlook.

Makiguchi at the pinnacle of his career as an educator and geographer: "Education is the key factor influencing the destiny of society."

Editor's Introduction

Makiguchi's Life and Work in Historical Context

The scholarly writings of Tsunesaburo Makiguchi, taken together, provide a unique perception of industrial society from the viewpoint of one who lived and worked in Japan during the early years of the twentieth century. Makiguchi was enamored with modernization. He shared the high expectations of industrialism and the potential abundance it promised which was prevalent throughout much of the world at that time. However, like his American contemporaries, Lewis Mumford and John Dewey, Makiguchi foresaw the dangers and tragic consequences of the social and educational policies taking shape in industrial societies. He warned against tendencies he observed developing in his own society: reckless disregard for the environment, the sacrifice of traditional values in pursuit of profits, the isolating of children and young people day after day in schools, severing their ties with the natural environment as well as with their families and communities and forcing them to learn masses of fragmented, unrelated facts. Makiguchi feared that the ultimate outcome of such policies would be disastrous for Japan, and he worked tirelessly during the first four decades of the century, both through education and through his writing, in formulating and promoting what he believed was a more constructive and sustainable approach to industrial development.

The provocative ideas and proposals contained in Makiguchi's writings bring into focus some interesting questions: "Were the conditions we now observe in the world inevitable?" or perhaps the question should rather be: "Was industrial society inevitable?" "Will the 21st Century be a better century from the standpoint of human well-being than the 20th Century?" "Will human beings have some part in consciously determining what kinds of societies will characterize the 21st Century, and if so, what kinds of societies will they shape?" "Or will they simply be swept along by a tide of humanly uncontrollable cultural change?"

As people around the world attempt to take stock of the century that has just ended, they are increasingly raising such questions. They are also seeking new information, new insights, and new intellectual tools with which to carry on a constructive yet critical analysis of the human situation and an exploration of the prospects for a more humane society in the new century. Makiguchi's writings can, we believe, make a significant contribution to such inquiry and sociohistorical analysis, and it is this belief which has prompted our efforts to undertake the translation of his writings into English.

An Overview

The earth, for Makiguchi, was a miracle. Life was a miracle, and he saw life vibrating and pulsating through all phenomena. A major goal which began to motivate him early in his professional career was to call his fellows, particularly young people, to an awareness of and appreciation for the earth and for the life pulsating through it. Thus, in *A Geography of Human Life,* we are confronted with what to Makiguchi was the ultimate question:

> We are born of the earth; we live on the earth; we are inspired by the earth... The earth is our home... How then can we observe, and make contact with, our surroundings? (Chapter 3, p. 25)

In our interaction with our environment, we should

> ... regard people, animals, trees, rivers, rocks, or stones in the same light as ourselves and realize that we have much in common with them all. Such interaction causes us to feel, if not consciously think, "if I were in their (or its) place, what would I feel... or do?" Sympathetic interactions occur, therefore, when you regard or feel another person or object that you are in contact with as a part of yourself or as one of your kind. You share experience with that person or object and are able to place yourself in the position of that person or object.[1] (Chapter 3, p. 29)

Again,

> It is our nature as human beings to form societies. No one can live totally alone. It is through association in society that we can provide

not only for our basic needs and security, but for everything that makes our lives fulfilling and rewarding. This realization leads to the universalization of sympathetic feelings which were initially toward a specific individual or object. Growing awareness of our indebtedness to our society gives rise to feelings of appreciation and a sense of social responsibility within us. Beginning in our very personal relationships... our sympathetic concern and appreciation expands to include the larger society and, ultimately, the whole world. (Chapter 3, pp. 29-30)

Perhaps more than any thing else, it was this reverence for nature, this sense of wonder and appreciation for life, this sense of being intimately connected with both our natural and social environments, that Makiguchi longed to communicate to his students and fellow beings. The development of such awareness and appreciation upon the part of human beings was, he believed, of crucial importance both for nature's sake and for the development of persons of moral character.

Makiguchi tells us in the foreword of the book that the desire and compulsion to share these insights with his fellows became so strong that "they occupied my whole being. I could not think of anything else. I could not even work to make a living."[2] In the process of trying to respond to this inner compulsion and to free himself from it, the collection of ideas, insights, and personal feelings which he had jotted down over a period of some ten years came together under the title, *A Geography of Human Life*.

As the passages referred to above suggest, Makiguchi was convinced that the development of a sense of interdependence and interrelatedness with the natural world, of which he perceived humans a part, is a central aspect of what it means to be a human being. Not only is this holistic orientation *A Geography of Human Life*'s most pervasive theme, it became the central theme of Makiguchi's life. Consider the following, for example:

> ... being aware of the rich variety of phenomena that influence my life, I cannot help thinking of the way the whole earth operates. I look around and, although my eyes can reach only a few kilometers in any direction, my heart and mind are filled with excitement and wonder and curiosity about the earth and about the relationship between the earth and our lives on the earth. I begin to realize that if we would seek deeper understanding of this relationship, we must prepare ourselves to make observations and inquiries into several different aspects of the planet, such as its topography, dimensions, movements, and structure. (Chapter 5, p. 43)

Such was Makiguchi's invitation to young people in particular, and to all his contemporaries in general, to join him in a journey to explore the wonders of the earth and life born of the earth. *A Geography of Human Life* is something like a "ship's log" or diary of that journey. But it was also intended as a handbook or travel guide for others who are motivated to take the journey themselves.

Before embarking on this journey of discovery, Makiguchi explained that the method of inquiry to be used was that of participant observation. But what was to be the scope of that observation? Here, again, we can let him speak for himself:

> I arrived at a conviction that the natural beginning point of understanding the world we live in and our relationship to it is that community of persons, land, and culture, which gave us birth; that community, in fact, which gave us our very lives and started us on the path toward becoming the persons we are. In other words, that community which has given us our rootedness as human beings. The importance of this rootedness and personal identity given us by our native cultural community, our homeland, can scarcely be overemphasized. (Chapter 1, p. 14)

> If we think seriously about it, we can see that every aspect of this universe can be observed in this small area of our homeland. And because our homeland is the place where we live, where we walk, where we see and hear and gain impressions, it is possible for us to observe all these things directly. Thus, it is possible for us to explain the general nature of complex phenomena anywhere in the world through use of examples which we can find in abundance even in the most remote village or hamlet. (Chapter 2, p. 20)

> Let me stress my basic position again; every aspect of the entire universe can be found in the small, limited area of our home community. But we have to be sensitive to these untold riches all around us and we must learn how to be effective observers. (Chapter 2, p. 21)

Makiguchi writes that with this wealth of information and examples all around us:

> ...it is astounding that so many people, and teachers in particular, neglect this kind of basic and profound observation and just stick to books, using all their energy in memorizing. They read, forget what they have read, so start to read again, forgetting, reading, forgetting, reading... and on and on. (Chapter 2, p. 20)

He suggests that it might help in understanding the principle with which he is concerned to consider the famous people whom we look up to and who have made great contributions to human culture. Invariably, we find that these great geniuses of human history, Dante, John Louis Agassiz, Peter the Great, and many others, arrived at the discoveries for which we remember them in very simple surroundings and through the power of their own observations.

At this point, Makiguchi comes to one of his deepest convictions. When we consider such persons of genius, he says, we tend to believe that their great accomplishments were possible entirely because of their innate natural talents. "But," we think, "I can't be like that. It's impossible." Thus we tend to see a wide difference between these great people of history and "ordinary people like us." To this Makiguchi responds,

> I am convinced... that in the beginning of life there is very little difference between people. Every person has inborn natural talents and potential. Then why do these differences come about? I believe it hinges upon whether or not a person learns to see and grasp the true nature of phenomena with penetrating insight and understanding. The "geniuses" I cited above honed their vision to a high degree simply through direct observation of the marvels of nature and the world around them.
>
> The natural world can inspire us, foster our wisdom, and family, friends, neighbors and community groups can nurture us in so many ways. This immediate, direct experience available to us through the natural and social environments of our homelands can foster compassion, goodwill, friendship, kindness, sincerity, and humble hearts. (Chapter 2, pp.20-21)

Thus, one of Makiguchi's enduring themes is that at birth every person possesses potential for greatness and goodness. But it was one of the tragedies of contemporary life in his day, he observed, that in most people this inborn potential remained dormant and undeveloped. Most people "see" only on a surface level. They never develop the capacity for direct and intimate communication with natural phenomena. They tend to become a slave to books. Unfortunately, with such surface understanding, even after reading thousands of books, they remain ignorant of the really important insights and understandings they need for living fully and creatively. Their lives become stunted and their potential greatness lies unchallenged and unrealized.

Can anything be more important, then, than discovering how to plan educational experiences which will enable every person to develop the deeper understanding of life and nature which is so important for living a fulfilling and rewarding life? Both *A Geography of Human Life* and *A Theory of Value-Creating Pedagogy* three decades later sought to clarify and provide answers to that question. While he did not deny the importance and the place of books and other kinds of second-hand materials in human learning, he maintained that children can achieve the full potential of their humanness only through direct, active, communication with their immediate environment.

From this brief overview of Makiguchi's writings, the two related concerns which preoccupied him become clear: the developing of persons of moral character and the developing of social institutions capable of nurturing persons of character. He saw that the two must go together. In other words, good institutions can only be created by persons of good moral character, but good institutions are a prerequisite for a society of persons of character to develop.

Makiguchi offered his vision of a good society, which could nurture good, happy persons, as a model for the development of an industrial system in his country. At the time he was writing *A Geography of Human Life*, the American version of the Western model of industrialism was sweeping the earth. The contrast between that type of industrialism and the type that Makiguchi proposed is sharp and clear. It is especially clear in the respective views of the two models toward nature. A basic tenet of the American model, what Alvin Toffler labels "indust reality," is that "nature is an object waiting to be exploited" (Toffler, 1981, p. 99). For Makiguchi, on the other hand, to be human meant to live in harmony with the earth. To live as a human being meant to love and understand and appreciate the earth. ". . .it is through our spiritual interaction with the earth that the characteristics which we think of as truly human are ignited and nurtured within us" (Chapter 3, p. 25). Makiguchi envisioned an industrial society developing in his country upon a basis of interdependence and interconnectedness between human beings and the earth. It was to the realization of such a society that he directed his life and his work.

Education as Means to Personal and Social Transformation

Education, then, is a key factor in the development both of healthy, happy individuals and of good societies. Education is of central importance because for both conditions to be present, the growth of persons of good moral character is indispensable. This, in turn, according to Makiguchi, depends on whether those persons develop a realization of their interdependence and interconnectedness with the natural and social phenomena in their environment. Such realization and awareness can develop in a person's life only through direct, first-hand experience upon the part of each person with that phenomena. What is needed, therefore, are educational structures and teacher guides capable of enabling every child and youth to have this kind and quality of learning experience.

Six general propositions are stated or implicitly assumed in *A Geography of Human Life*:

◆ The earth is perceived as a unity and all phenomena on the earth, including human beings, are perceived as interconnected and interdependent.

◆ Education must be associated with a specific place, a "community," a localized environment, which students can experience directly.

◆ Curriculum consists of the natural and social systems within that environment. Books and other second-hand material are used *in support* of the direct, personal experiencing of phenomena by the learner, but never in place of direct experience.

◆ Direct experience learning implies and requires that learning take place in the midst of the phenomena, natural and social, which constitute the curriculum. Classrooms are for planning, reflecting on, comparing perceptions of phenomena experienced with fellow learners and with books and other second-hand material. (Makiguchi in later life systematized this element in a proposal for a "half-day school system").

◆ Learning cannot be imposed, but must grow out of each learner's own curiosity, questions, and explorations stemming from personal interests and motivation. Expressed another way, learning must be a process of elicitation, of drawing out, and not, as in the education of Makiguchi's day, and still today for the most part, by inculcation or putting in.

◆ Guidance of the learner in this community-based learning interaction occurs under the guidance of parents, educators (teacher-guides), and other adults in their varied community roles and specialties.[3]

During recent decades, evidence has been accumulating from many sources which point to the wisdom and the relevancy for education and society of the kind of educational principles and policies which Makiguchi proposed: the moral growth of individuals, interconnectedness with nature and with other individuals, education as a dialogue with a place through direct interaction with natural phenomena, the indispensability of community and "human scale" social structures within which this kind of education can be carried on and the nurture of persons of moral character occur.

Ron Miller and David Orr, two of the most articulate contemporary advocates of educational and social transformation, have written extensively about the need for a kind of educational and social policy very similar to that proposed in *A Geography of Human Life* and Makiguchi's other writings. The essence of their views and concerns are expressed in the following observation by Miller in a review of Orr's *Ecological Literacy*:

> Education in a post-industrial society, argues Orr, will need to extend beyond the classical liberal arts of the modern age. "Ecological literacy" is a morally and experientially engaged way of knowing, involving a sense of wonder and respect for life and the realization that all human activities have consequences for the larger ecosystem. Orr maintains that ecological literacy cannot be achieved by adding "environmental education" to our standardized compartmentalized curriculum, but entails radical educational as well as economic, political and cultural transformation. He asserts that "a great deal of what passes for knowledge is little more than abstraction piled on top of abstraction, disconnected from tangible experience, real problems, and the places where we live and work." Agreeing with Thoreau, Whitehead, and Dewey, Orr argues that an ecological education would immerse the learner in the natural world and the local community; it would engage the learner in conversation, in dialogue with the surrounding environment. Ecological literacy involves the whole body and feelings, not only the intellect; it cultivates a sense of place, not a rootless abstract intelligence; and it is most concerned with wholeness, connection, and relationship, rather than fragmenting knowledge into discrete specialties. (Miller, 1993, p. 5)

Elsewhere, Orr has stressed the importance of wonder in the learning experience of children. Referring to an observation by Rachel Carson in her book, *The Sense of Wonder*, that *feeling* is more important in learning than *knowing*, Orr writes:

> Feelings... begin early in life in the exploration of nature, generally with the companionship of an adult. The sense of wonder is rooted in

the trust that the world is, on balance, a friendly place full of
interesting life "beyond the boundaries of human existence." Wonder
cannot be taught. . . it can only be felt and those early feelings must
be encouraged, supported, legitimized by a caring and knowledgeable adult. My hunch is that the sense of wonder is fragile; once
crushed it rarely blossoms again but is replaced by varying shades of
cynicism and disappointment in the world. (Orr, 1993, p. 33)

Orr, writing in the closing days of the twentieth century, holds that we must develop this kind of education and approach to nature in order for human civilization to survive on the earth. A similar note is sounded by Catherine Burton, co-founder of the EarthBank Association:

Where is the focal point of human activity in this emerging planetary awareness? It would appear that person and planet find each
other in those naturally occurring ecological domains—called
bioregions—that are like cells of the planetary skin. These
bioregions transcend arbitrary political boundaries, reconnecting
human beings with the biosphere. . .To know our bioregion is to
know and connect with our home planet. It is to breathe with the
earth and to know ourselves as part of the sacred web of life. To
know this place—where its water comes from, its trees, its wildlife,
its food, its energy, its wisdom and its spirit is to know ourselves as
whole. (Burton, 1984)

It was precisely these spiritual insights and realities which so obsessed Makiguchi at the beginning of the century and which he
sought, in *A Geography of Human Life*, to share with his countrymen.

A Critical Analysis

Some of the attitudes and points of view expressed in *A Geography of Human Life* have led critics to charge that Makiguchi naively
accepted, without qualification, prevailing popular attitudes and
points of view extant in the world at the time he wrote, attitudes
toward race, modernization, technology, and international relations.
For example, he noted that most of the taxes collected in Japan were
being spent on the military, and he appears to have condoned this as
being necessary "if we want the secure and prosperous development
of our own country" (Chapter 26, p. 236). In another instance,
Makiguchi wrote that "state intervention poses no threat"[4] (Chapter
26, p. 241).

A further criticism which has been leveled at *A Geography of
Human Life* is that Makiguchi interpreted social phenomena purely
in subjective terms and that his understanding of the individual, of

society, and of the relationship between the individual and society was naive and simplistic. Makiguchi had, it is charged, a naive faith in government and the goodness of government. This, for example, is the conclusion of Koichi Mori, a scholar who has made one of the most thorough critical studies of Makiguchi's life and writings. Mori argues that Makiguchi's purpose of study—and the purpose of his life—was the realization of the common people's happiness. However,

> Makiguchi understood happiness as subjective so that he did not have any concrete idea about how the common people's happiness could be realized... Makiguchi valued "goodness" highly because individuals cannot become happy as long as there is confrontation between society and individuals. (Mori, 1977, p. 202)

Mori carries his criticism of what he believed to be Makiguchi's limited grasp of social phenomena and of scientific method further in the following passage:

> From the time he was teaching in Hokkaido, Makiguchi had thought that the purpose of education was to lead the students to be able to live a "happy community life" without conflicting with society... Makiguchi presented his thought of "happy community life" and his understanding of society as an organism in order to explain his thought of the harmony of individuals and society. But he did not talk about the confrontation of gains between individuals and society ... Makiguchi optimistically dreamed that social gain became identical with individual gain. However, if he had the ability to analyze society scientifically and to look through the reality of society at that time, he would never have dreamed such a thing. (Mori, 1977, p.207)

How are we to interpret such criticisms of Makiguchi's writings? What are we to make of views and attitudes expressed in the book which in some cases would be untenable today, and in others appear to conflict with statements elsewhere in the book and with Makiguchi's overall aims and goals?

Any attempt to make an objective and realistic evaluation of *A Geography of Human Life* must begin, I believe, by recognizing that we, today, cannot accept some of the views he held. We cannot today, for instance, share his opinion that native peoples lacked the capability to effectively manage the land areas they occupied (Chapter 20, pp. 170-172). It is became increasingly clear as we approached the end of the century that some native peoples have demonstrated wise and capable management of the earth and its resources, while it has been the advanced, "civilized," peoples who have brought the earth's ecosystem to the brink of collapse. Similarly, he failed to appreciate it seems, at the time he wrote, the destructive power of institutions, the tendency of bureaucracies to perpetuate themselves, and the capability of social elites to use institutions and bureaucracies for their own ends at the expense of the well-being of society as a whole. His views in some of these areas may seem naive today to those of us who have lived to see the misuse of power and resources by giant bureaucracies, both public and private, which we still have not discovered how to control.

But if we are alert we will see in this realization itself one key to understanding both Makiguchi and the book. By comparing views which Makiguchi held at the beginning of the century with views which we held at its end is to commit an error of hindsight in which we expect Makiguchi to see the world through our eyes, rather than the other way around. We must recognize the time in which Makiguchi lived and worked, the stage of development of his own country, and conditions then existing in the world. For example, Makiguchi described in vivid detail what he saw happening to militarily weak nations and native peoples, how the "great powers," as he called them, had systematically conquered or annihilated these weaker cultures until almost the entire world had been divided among them. It would have been natural for Makiguchi to hope that his own country could avoid that fate, and this hope certainly must have influenced his thinking.

A further aid to our understanding of *A Geography of Human Life* is a realization of the need to consider the work in its entirety. Failure to do so may result in the reader's missing or misinterpreting Makiguchi's meaning. For example, at one point Makiguchi seems to accept imperialism and rule of the most powerful as a natural and normal dimension of international relations. But the fact is that Makiguchi's position, we find upon further reading, is the exact opposite. The discrepancy is explained when we discover that Makiguchi perceived imperialistic behavior upon the part of states as part of a process of human spiritual development in which imperialism represented a less advanced stage. He concluded that if

> the peoples of European nations continue to devote themselves solely to expanding their national power, by building arms and conducting armed aggression, disregarding the extent to which their conduct not only disturbs the peace and stability of other nations, but also creates crises in their own, ultimately they may end up witnessing the disintegration and destruction of their own nation. (Chapter 26, p.243)

The most serious criticism of *A Geography of Human Life*, however, is the charge, made most persuasively by Mori, that Makiguchi's concerns for individual growth and well-being blinded him to social realities and led him to dismiss them as unimportant. Upon first reading some of Makiguchi's views one may almost be inclined to agree with Mori. Deeper study of the issues involved suggests, however, that Mori failed to grasp the full implications of Makiguchi's ideas and world view. Mori's criticism loses some of its force when it is recognized that it stems from a basic difference between his understanding of individuality, society, and the relationship between the individual and the society, and that of Makiguchi.

Mori, sharing a view of morality which has its roots in modern (Western) philosophy—with its origins in Newtonian physics and the political philosophies of Thomas Hobbes and Niccolo Machiavelli—assumed a natural antagonism between the individual and society: individual gain is at the expense of society and that which benefits society represents loss for the individual. Mori reveals his basic philosophical orientation when he writes of "the confrontation of gains between individuals and society" and "the ability to analyze society scientifically."

Modern philosophy and the ethics which it spawned, with its assumption of an inherent antagonism between the individual and society, view history as a process of rhythmical movement from society to the individual and back again to the society, a pendulum-swing of excess to contrary excess. Within this conception, society prospers at the expense of its individual members and personal freedom of individuals can be achieved only by wrenching it from the collective. Given this general modern philosophical orientation, Mori cannot help but be critical of Makiguchi on this point.

Makiguchi, in contrast, shared the orientation of the classical philosophy[5] of the West—reinforced and complemented by strands of oriental philosophy in his Japanese heritage—in which the bifurcation of the individual and society is not made. In the view of classical philosophy, modern philosophy's assumption of an inherent individual-society antagonism is a false assumption.[6] From the viewpoint of classical philosophy, the pendulum-swing from excess to contrary excess to which the assumption of individual-society antagonism gives rise is unproductive and should be wrenched into a development. As David Norton, one of classical philosophy's most articulate contemporary spokespersons, observes:

The corrective constituting development is the refinement of crude individuation toward a profound individuation that discovers the inherent sociality of true individuals. This sociality is a whole that is to be won, not by suppression of its parts, but by their fulfillment as parts. (Norton, 1976, p. 63)

The sharp contrast in outlook between persons whose world view has been shaped by modern philosophy and those who have been nurtured within classical and Eastern philosophical traditions should now be clear. The former perceives human relationships as a trade-off, or tug-of-war, between the individual and society, whereas for the latter a good society is to be achieved through the fulfillment of its individual members rather than by their suppression. Within this context, Mori's difficulty in grasping the deeper meanings and implications of Makiguchi's thought is understandable.

We can concur with Mori in recognizing that Makiguchi largely limited his concerns to the development of persons of good character by means of a particular kind and quality of education. Makiguchi, as noted earlier, had a passionate conviction that the development of persons of good moral character depended on whether those persons develop a realization of their interdependence and interconnectedness with the natural and social phenomena in their environment. This could be accomplished, he believed, only through direct personal contact upon the part of each person with that phenomena, as noted above. For Makiguchi, the development of a society which would be good for human beings was out of the question without the development of persons of character through direct, first hand, experience with their immediate environment. What is needed, therefore, are educational structures and teacher guides capable of enabling every child and youth to have this kind and quality of learning experience. Communicating this conviction and demonstrating its practical application to the society of his day became his lifelong work and commitment.

Rather than dismissing Makiguchi's concern with the development of moral character as subjective naiveté, as Mori does, we are now discovering that the intractable problems which are threatening the future of human life on the planet can, in large measure, be traced to modern philosophy and the policies and practices of the industrial, natural science- dominated cultures which have arisen from its premises. Increasingly, we are becoming aware that our present dilemma is, at bottom, a moral and spiritual dilemma. Norton has pointed to the consequences of the moral vacuum at the heart of American society, and it will be appropriate here to quote from his argument:

> A primary precondition for peace, justice, and the well being of persons in a human society is the presence in the lives of at least a significant minority of its citizens of the moral virtue of integrity. I propose to show that integrity rarely occurs as a personal characteristic in American society, due to the pervasive influence of modern ethics, and that a direct consequence of this lack of integrity is rampant corruption and moral decay and the breakdown of our schools about which Americans are presently so concerned.
>
> Modern ethics discards the virtue of integrity as being inconsequential in human affairs. Since integrity, and the other moral virtues which integrity produces, as I will show, constitute the core of a truly human life, its absence in our society has far-reaching consequences. (Norton, 1990, p. 1)

In other writings, Norton expresses his intention to undertake

> a treatise in political theory, yet it cannot be inattentive to ethics, for it is a treatise in political theory in the classical mode, not the modern mode, and in the classical mode ethics and politics are inseparable. An answer to the primary political question, What is good government?, is dependent upon an answer to the primary moral question, What is a good life for a human being?, which is in turn dependent upon an understanding of what a human being is. (Norton, 1991, p. ix)

Norton here goes to the heart of the proposition, made also by Makiguchi, that true education is education for moral integrity.[7]

Further clarification of the kind of issues with which Makiguchi grappled and the significance of his conclusions can be found in the writings of Aldo Leopold, an American philosopher-scientist. The following passages of Leopold's, for example, reveal the same consciousness of a relationship between human moral development and the natural world about which Makiguchi wrote so passionately:

> There are some who can live without wild things, and some who cannot. These essays are the delights and dilemmas of one who cannot.
>
> Like winds and sunsets, wild things were taken for granted until progress began to do away with them. Now we face the question whether a still higher "standard of living" is worth its cost in things natural, wild, and free. For us of the minority, the opportunity to see geese is more important than television, and the chance to find a pasque-flower is a right as inalienable as free speech.
>
> These wild things, I admit, had little human value until mechanization assured us of a good breakfast, and until science disclosed the

drama of where they come from and how they live. The whole conflict thus boils down to a question of degree. We of the minority see a law of diminishing returns in progress; our opponents do not.

...An ethic, ecologically, is a limitation on freedom of action in the struggle for existence. An ethic philosophically, is a differentiation of social from anti- social conduct. These are two definitions of one thing. The thing has its origin in the tendency of interdependent individuals or groups to evolve modes of cooperation. The ecologist calls these symbioses. Politics and economics are advanced symbioses in which free-for-all competition has been replaced, in part, by co-operative mechanisms with an ethical content. (Leopold, 1949, pp.vii, 202)

A half century earlier—these observations were written by Leopold in 1948—Makiguchi envisioned a "humanitarian competition" which he believed could evolve in human experience as peoples and societies come to recognize the value of and need for *voluntary limitations on freedom of action* in their struggle for existence (Chapter 29, pp. 285-286).

The charge that Makiguchi was unscientific also requires a response. The issue is confused because what critics such as Mori mean by science and what Makiguchi meant by science are very different, as the following observation by Leopold makes clear:

We are not scientists. We disqualify ourselves at the outset by professing loyalty to and affection for a thing: wildlife. A scientist in the old sense may have no loyalties except to abstractions, no affections except for his own kind... The definitions of science written by, let us say, the National Academy, deal almost exclusively with the creation and exercise of power. But what about the creation and exercise of wonder or respect for workmanship in nature? (Orr, 1993, p. 30)

Makiguchi was a scientist in Leopold's image, but not in Mori's. His loyalty and affection for the earth and all that is of the earth is apparent throughout all his writings, and this is especially the case in *A Geography of Human Life*.[8]

Contemporary Significance

It will be clear from what has been said above that Makiguchi's work does not add significantly to current educational insights or to our understandings as to what good education entails. The educational ideas and proposals expressed by Makiguchi are, for the most part, being expressed and operationalized by increasing numbers of contemporary educators. The emphasis on holism in education which has emerged in Japan and the United States within the past decade is one example. At the same time, few contemporary educators have gone as far as Makiguchi in emphasizing the importance for education of direct learning within the learner's natural and social environments. Moreover, his proposal for organizing all levels of education as a journey into the natural systems of the learner's community, within the context of the discipline of a "new" geography, affords potentially useful insights and ideas and may, perhaps, be a useful and usable model for some learners and educators.

To emphasize Makiguchi's central concern again, direct learning of natural systems within the learner's community is crucial because growth of moral character, attitudes of appreciation and wonder toward the natural and social systems which sustain one's life, and a sense of responsibility toward those systems, are indispensable for individual happiness and social health and these outcomes can be nurtured in no other way.[9] He charged that the indirect, second-hand learning system that had developed in his country was the height of folly. Primarily a product of implantation from Western cultures, that system of education confined learners to classrooms and forced them to go through a meaningless routine of, as noted earlier, "memorizing and forgetting, memorizing, forgetting, and on and on." Furthermore, it severed the learners' ties with the natural systems making up their environment. Makiguchi contended that long continuation of such a superficial system of learning would lead to unhappiness for individuals, serious problems for society, and destruction of the environment.[10] The sense of urgency which he felt and which led him to publish *A Geography of Human Life* in spite of its shortcomings stemmed from his convictions about the dangers of this then predominant form of education in his country.

As noted briefly above, beyond its implications for geography and education, Makiguchi's work raises intriguing questions about the beginnings and development of contemporary societies. Was the type of industrialism which originated in the West, and which in ensuing years has come to dominate all the cultures of the earth, inevitable? Or could there have developed industrial societies with a different face? There has been a general tendency upon the part of the world's people, at least within the industrially advanced countries, to view the rise of industrial societies as an inevitable outcome of impersonal social, economic, technological, and political forces. Christopher Evans has written, for example, that "once the process of the Revolution was fully under way, its dynamic growth was remorseless, and no power, no man or combination of men, could set it back against its course" (1979, p. ix). Makiguchi's works suggest the possibility, however, that industrialism in Japan could have taken other forms and developed in other directions.

A Geography of Human Life was Makiguchi's attempt to respond to realities in Japan as he saw them. While he admired and approved many aspects of Western industrial culture, he counseled against wholesale adoption of the Western model and offered to his countrymen a vision of a uniquely Japanese industrial society which would draw on the strengths and assets of Japan's geographical situation and cultural heritage. Morris Berman's contrast between enchanted and disenchanted worlds is relevant here (1981, p. 16). While Makiguchi probably did not foresee the full extent of our modern dilemma or comprehend the potential for moral and spiritual bankruptcy to which our Western, scientific industrialism has led, I suggest that he sensed its dangers intuitively and committed himself to work for industrial development in his own society which would not sacrifice the "enchanted world" which he loved.[11]

How different the world might be today *if* the Japanese had, in fact, developed such a brand of industrial society, based on Makiguchi's perception of the environment and of education, and *if* that Japanese model had spread over the earth instead of the American-fashioned Western model! As we look back over the history of the 20th century from our vantage point, we recognize and accept the fact that the people of Japan during the 20th century's early decades rejected Makiguchi's vision as well as most of his admonitions. Just as Americans during the early years in the development of their industrial system in the United States rejected alternative models of industrial development which were available to them, the Japanese rejected the alternative proposed by Makiguchi.[12] Japanese society followed, with only slight variation, the American model of industrialism, based on unrestricted exploitation of the natural environment as well as of less technologically advanced human populations. We are now being forced to recognize the many negative consequences of the choices that were made during the formative stages of these two industrial giants.[13]

This recognition, and the clearer historical understanding which it fosters, can also bring to our awareness the realization that we, too, are living in the formative stages of a new cultural epoch. Persons who seek now to lay the ground work for a better and more humane 21st century, in education, in business, in all of society's social institutions, will find in *A Geography of Human Life* insights worthy of consideration and a wealth of ideas and practical methods to aid them in their efforts.

Spring 2002

—Dayle M. Bethel
Honolulu, Hawaii

Notes

[1] It is instructive to compare the view of nature held by Makiguchi with that of Western peoples prior to the Scientific Revolution. Note, for example, the following observation by Morris Berman:

> The view of nature which predominated in the West down to the eve of the Scientific Revolution was that of an enchanted world. Rocks, trees, rivers, and clouds were all seen as wondrous, alive, and human beings felt at home in this environment. The cosmos, in short, was a place of *belonging*. A member of this cosmos was not an alienated observer of it but a direct participant in its life. His personal destiny was bound up with its destiny, and this relationship gave meaning to his life. (Berman, p. 16)

According to Berman, this intimate view of nature and of the cosmos as a place of belonging were sacrificed as Western peoples came under the domination of the modern ethics and the exploitive view of nature spawned by the Scientific Revolution of the 16th and 17th centuries. Makiguchi sought to forestall this development in his own culture.

[2] We may better understand the depth of Makiguchi's conviction and his obsession with the need to share his ideas by noting Berman's conclusions as to the significance of Modern Western culture's world view:

> The logical end point of this world view is a feeling of total reification: everything is an object, alien, not-me; and I am ultimately an object too, an alienated "thing" in a world of other, equally meaningless things. This world is not of my own making; the cosmos cares nothing for me, and I do not really feel a sense of belonging to it. What I feel, in fact, is a sickness in the soul.
>
> Translated into every day life, what does this disenchantment mean? It means that the modern landscape has become a scenario of "mass administration and blatant violence" . . . Jobs are stupefying, relationships vapid and transient, the arena of politics absurd. In the collapse of traditional values, we have hysterical evangelical revivals, mass conversions to the Church of the Reverend Moon, and

a general retreat into oblivion provided by drugs, television, and tranquilizers. (Berman, p. 17)

While Makiguchi certainly could not have perceived the full extent of the disastrous consequences of the path Western societies had chosen to follow, what he did understand was enough to create within him a burning desire to help his own country avoid the dangers and pitfalls of the Western model.

[3]Makiguchi's views on the role of educators and other adults in the teaching-learning process, implicit in *The Geography of Human Life*, are more explicitly expressed and developed in his later writings.

[4]This is an example of seeming contradiction in Makiguchi's work. While he tells us that as far as he can see state intervention poses no threat to human freedom and well-being, he observes, on the other hand, that the nature of government bureaus is to constantly attempt to expand their territory. In fact, Makiguchi himself came to recognize the dangers of state intervention before he died in prison four decades after writing *The Geography of Human Life*, placed there by a powerful military bureaucracy.

[5]Classical philosophy refers here to the philosophical tradition in Western culture which has its roots in the eudaimonistic thought of Socrates, Plato, and Aristotle.

[6]However, while "egoism" and "altruism" are not concrete phenomena originally, once these conceptual distinctions between self and other have been made in human consciousness, it becomes entirely possible for individuals to behave as if they were.

[7]For further discussion of the role of modern ethics in the development of contemporary social problems and the importance of education for moral integrity, see Norton's *Personal Destinies: A Philosophy of Ethical Individualism* (1976) and, particularly, his later book, *Democracy and Moral Development* (1991).

[8]In this connection, see Kathleen Raine, "Towards a Living Universe," in Douglas Sloan, (Ed.), *Toward the Recovery of Wholeness: Knowledge, Education, and Human Values*, New York: Teachers College Press, Columbia University, 1984, pp. 86-102.

[9]This should be kept in mind while reading Makiguchi's discussion of industrial societies. He writes hopefully and optimistically of the possibilities of an industrial society in which the needs and well-being of all the society's members would be provided for. But this could only happen, in Makiguchi's understanding, through the development within the society of leaders of high moral virtue.

[10]In this connection, see David Korten's contention that the social and ecological crises we faced at the close of the 20th century can be traced to the long historical processes by which the human species has become increasingly alienated from community and nature. The prevailing "economics of alienation," he writes, must be replaced with an "economics of community." *In Context*, No. 36, Fall 1993, pp. 19-20. See also Alfred North Whitehead's observation (*The Aims of Education*, New York, 1967, p. 51) that "First-hand

knowledge is the ultimate basis of intellectual life. To a large extent booklearning conveys second-hand information."

[11]See Berman, particularly pp. 23 and 46.

[12]See Ron Miller, *What are Schools For?*, Brandon, Vermont: Holistic Education Press, 1997, p. 28 and Douglas D. Noble, "The Regime of Technology in Education," *Holistic Education Review*, Vol. 6, No. 2, Summer 1993, pp. 4-13.

[13]With regard to the Japanese case, see Koji Nakano, *Seihin no Shiso*, (The Concept of Honest Poverty), Tokyo: Soshisha, 1992.

References

Berman, Morris, (1981). *The Reenchantment of the World*. Ithaca, NY: Cornell University Press.
Burton, Catherine, "New Options: Governance in the Planetary Age." In *In Context*, No 7, Fall, 1984, p. 37.
Evans, Christopher, (1979). *The Micro Millennium*. New York: The Washington Square Press.
Makiguchi, Tsunesaburo (1903). *Jinsei Chirigaku*. Tokyo: Bunkaido Publishing Company.
Miller, Ron, (1990). *What Are Schools For?* Brandon, VT: Holistic Education Press.
Miller, Ron, (1993). *Great Ideas in Education*. Brandon, VT: Holistic Education Press.
Mori, Koichi, (1977). *Study of Makiguchi Tsunesaburo: The Founder of Soka Gakkai*. Ann Arbor, MI: University Microfilms International.
Norton, David L., (1976). *Personal Destinies: A Philosophy of Ethical Individualism*. Princeton, NJ: Princeton University Press.
Norton, David L., (1990). "Education for Moral Integrity," a paper delivered at a conference in Kyoto, Japan, July 20, 1990 on Alternatives in Education.
Norton, David L., (1991). *Democracy and Moral Development*. Berkeley, CA: University of California Press.
Orr, David W., (1992). *Ecological Literacy: Education and the Transition to a Postmodern World*. New York: State University of New York Press.
Orr, David W., (1993). "The Dangers of Education," in Ron Miller (Ed.), *The Renewal of Meaning in Education*. Brandon, VT: Holistic Education Press.
Sloan, Douglas, (Ed.),(1984). *Toward the Recovery of Wholeness: Knowledge, Education, and Human Values*. New York: Teachers College Press, Columbia University.
Toffler, Alvin, (1980). *The Third Wave*. New York: William Morrow.

Foreword

The twenty-first century—what kind of a century will we make it? How will we open up the horizon of this new millennium? This is the most important question confronting us, one transcending boundaries of race and nationality, one that all the citizens of the world must ponder, that all humankind must act upon.

The United Nations has wisely chosen to designate the year 2001 "The Year of Dialogue Among Civilizations." For only when bridges of dialogue have been built linking one civilization to another can we begin to advance step by step toward a single globe, the fulfillment of humankind's prayers for peace.

No matter how our positions may differ, how far apart our ideas may be, we are all human beings. And if we can come together to speak with one another on the basis of this common humanity, then however our civilizations may differ, we cannot help deepening our mutual understanding and appreciation of each others' cultures. This is my sincere belief, one based on the discussions I have had with world leaders and intellectual figures.

In the early years of the twentieth century, when imperialism dominated the age, a young educator and geographer, Tsunesaburo Makiguchi, who later became the first president of the Soka Gakkai, wrote a book entitled *A Geography of Human Life*. In it he described an ideal which he called "humanistic competition," whereby civilizations and cultures, by engaging in dialogue with one another, could carry out a kind of friendly and humanistic competition among themselves. In this way, he believed, they could open up a brighter future for the human race, one that promoted mutual harmony and prosperity for all. He was wise enough to foresee that the only proper course for human history to follow was to advance in a steady progression from military strife and competition to political competition, and from political competition to economic and then purely humanistic competition.

Now, having witnessed and endured the many tragedies of what has been dubbed "the century of war and violence," the twentieth century, we stand at a point where humanity is at last able to appreciate and share in Mr. Makiguchi's longing for "the century of humanism and peace." We must not turn aside from that goal now!

The understanding and expectation of Makiguchi's thought is now being expressed in the form of a new university dedicated to the education of the people of the world, Soka University of America, which opened its doors in Orange County, California, in 2001. Soka University of America has four missions:

To foster leaders of culture in the community;

To foster leaders of humanism in society;

To foster leaders of pacifism in the world;

To foster leaders for the creative coexistence of nature and humanity.

These aims represent the present day expression of the thought and ideals embodied in Makiguchi's *A Geography of Human Life*. In the title of Makiguchi's work, the words "Human Life" refer to the life span of human beings and to their lifetime activities. When human beings are separated from one another or separated from their place of activity, they cannot live as true human beings. Therefore, Makiguchi set out to explain in detail the relationship between people and their geographical setting. In other words, *A Geography of Human Life* is a study devoted to discovering how, while strengthening relationships between people and their environment, the culture of their society and their international situation, one can build finer human character, create new values, and enrich society and the natural environment.

Makiguchi fully foresaw the need for human beings to live in harmony with their environment. He predicted that none of the human sentiments such as compassion, goodwill, friendship, kindness, sincerity or simplicity could be realized to any appreciable degree without proper consideration for the natural environment, nor could human character be fully developed. To put it in somewhat different terms, one of the causes of the desolation of the human spirit that so troubles our world today is the fact that we have clearly forgotten how to keep in touch with the world of nature.

Not only have we failed to maintain a dialogue with nature, but we have sought to conquer and dominate nature, becoming a civilization whose greed drives it madly onward until it confronts a crisis of environmental destruction that threatens the survival of the globe itself.

Makiguchi's *A Geography of Human Life*, adopting a farsighted ecological approach, proposes that humankind carry out a dialogue with nature, offering ideas that if anything are even fresher and more pertinent today than when they were first set forth. The year 2003 marks the hundredth anniversary of the publication of *A Geography of Human Life*, a most appropriate moment for the publication of this English edition of the work by Caddo Gap Press of San Francisco.

The translation was supervised and edited by Dr. Dayle M. Bethel, a leading authority on Makiguchi's theories of education for whom I have the highest respect. I first met Dr. Bethel in November, 1974. At that time he had already devoted some ten years to the study of Makiguchi's work. His approach was that of a true scholar quietly but firmly dedicated to his research, a man motivated by strong convictions and intense engagement with his subject. Even now I recall being deeply impressed as he spoke of how Makiguchi's ideas on value creation contained important suggestions for the attainment of genuine human rights and world peace. Dr. Bethel, too, has sought to express Makiguchi's educational ideals and holistic ecological insights in a new kind of educational institution, The International University Asia Pacific. Established in 1975 in Osaka, Japan, TIU Asia Pacific is now a part of a worldwide movement committed to the transformation of education and society.

An English translation of another work of Makiguchi was edited and supervised by Dr. Bethel and published in 1989 by Iowa State University Press under the title *Education for Creative Living*. It was subsequently translated into French, Vietnamese, Spanish, Italian, Hindi, Assamese and Gujarati and published in these various languages, thus contributing to a worldwide understanding of Makiguchi's theories of value creative humanistic education.

It is my hope that this English translation of *A Geography of Human Life* will serve in similar fashion, or to an even greater degree, to provide a basis for dialogue between people and people, people and the community, people and the world, and people and nature. If it can act as a source of energy to waken the citizens of the world to the ways in which they as individuals are related to the life force and thus usher in a century dedicated to the dignity of life, I will be most gratified.

Makiguchi battled head-on with the forces of Japanese militarism and died a hero's death in prison. My fervent prayer is that the light of his undying ideals will infuse the hearts and minds of the youthful leaders of our twenty-first century world, and that they may help to make this globe of ours a single living entity of peace and symbiosis.

In conclusion, I would like to extend my sincere thanks to Dr. Bethel and the others who labored to produce this translation, and to Dr. Alan H. Jones, director of Caddo Gap Press, who made possible its publication.

Spring, 2002

Daisaku Ikeda
President
Soka Gakkai International
Founder of Soka University of America

A Geography
of Human Life

Author Makiguchi at the time his *Human Geography* was published. "My interest in geography and the ideas I had been developing grew deeper until they occupied my whole being. I could not think of anything else."

Foreword
to the First Edition

This massive volume, entitled *A Geography of Human Life*, was written by Tsunesaburo Makiguchi. At his request, I revised the manuscript and in the process included some additional information and comments of my own. I would like, therefore, to explain briefly my relationship to the book and to its author.

In the summer of 1902, Makiguchi, a man who was then unknown to me, came to see me. He told me of his long time ambition to write a book about the relationship between human beings and the earth, and he showed me a huge manuscript. He told me that he had quit a teaching position at Hokkaido Normal School in 1901, and had written the manuscript since that time. I encouraged him to continue his project and expressed my best wishes for its successful completion.

This spring, he came to me again and asked me to revise his manuscript. I was hesitant to attempt the revision of such a monumental undertaking, but because of the intensity of his commitment to his project and my own interest in the field of geography, I agreed to assist him. I spent six months in revising the manuscript and it has now been accepted for publication, bringing great joy to both him and me.

The original manuscript contained some 2,000 pages, but in the process of revision it has been reduced to approximately half that volume in order to make publication feasible. The manuscript was refused by many publishers, both because of its length and because Makiguchi was not a famous author. Finally, however, Bunkaido, a small but courageous publisher, accepted it for publication.

Today, most authors write only small books, and publishers tend to be afraid to risk publishing large books. Thus, it is encouraging to discover an author like Tsunesaburo Makiguchi and a publisher like Bunkaido. I look forward to seeing more work from this author and from this publisher in the future.

October, 1903

Shigetaka Shiga

Preface to the First Edition

It may appear audacious for a person of my experience and ability to attempt such a monumental undertaking as the publication of *A Geography of Human Life*. I would like, therefore, to explain some of the reasons which led me to write the book. I had taught geography for several years and found that the discipline generally was viewed as an unimportant and peripheral part of the school curriculum, even though the insights and principles with which it deals are vitally important to the life and growth of children and young people. I came to feel strongly that geography ought to be accorded a prominent position within the curriculum of our schools. This, in turn, led me to a conviction that if more meaningful and effective methods of teaching geography could be devised, many of the difficult educational problems facing our society could be solved.

With this general philosophical framework in mind, I began to gather material from various sources. Each time I made a lesson plan, each time I read a book, a magazine, or a newspaper, each time I listened to a person of experience and expertise, whenever I observed my natural or human surroundings, I would write down what I felt and what I thought, or I would copy down excerpts from books or papers. After several years, I had accumulated a massive amount of these notes and fragments.

Although I had no thought of publishing the material in the beginning, as the issues and principles involved became clearer to me I began to feel strongly that I should share my ideas. When I looked through the material I had gathered, however, I felt overwhelmed by the thought of trying to prepare it for publication, so I put it back in my desk, thinking that perhaps some use might be made of it in the future. In spite of this, the idea of publishing my material continued to haunt me. My interest in geography and the ideas I had been developing grew deeper until they occupied my whole being. I could not think of anything else. I could not even work to make a living. I finally concluded that I would have to do something to free myself from this obsession with geography. Thus it was that I decided to discontinue teaching and concentrate my time and effort on writing and refining the material I had accumulated.

Once I had taken these steps and contracted with a publisher who was willing to publish it, I had to complete the book. I worked early and late for many months in editing the material and proofreading, but I know there are still many defects and inadequacies in it. For these I apologize, and I will greatly welcome criticisms, corrections, and suggestions for improving the book from readers.

The choice of a title for the book has presented a special problem. I considered "Political Geography," but the various connotations of the term "political" make it unsuitable as a title for my work. "Cultural Geography" does not quite fit the content, either. "Anthropological Geography" would perhaps make a good title for this book, but the special use of the term "anthropology" to denote a particular discipline might lead to confusion. Thus, *A Geography of Human Life* is the most suitable title I have been able to come up with, and I will use it until a better title is forthcoming.

Because I am not a professional geographer, I felt it was essential that I ask a specialist in geography to criticize my work and assist in revising the material. It was extremely difficult to find such a specialist who would be willing to assume the responsibility of examining and assisting with the revision of such a long and wide-ranging volume. But, finally, my search led me to Dr. Shigetaka Shiga, a geographer of some renown, whose work had in the past greatly influenced my thinking and understanding of geography, although I had not previously met him. After learning of the nature of my work, he willingly accepted my request for his assistance. Though he was extremely busy with his own professional obligations, he spent more than six months revising my manuscript and offered many valuable suggestions which I have included in the final draft.

I could not begin to express my gratitude to Professor Shiga for the help he has given me. Thanks to him, the publication of the book proceeded much more quickly than it otherwise would have. I have been deeply moved and encouraged by his enthusiasm and his deep concern for improving the education of young people.

I wish also to express special thanks to Dr. Kumazo Tsuboi. I visited him three years ago and talked with him at length about many questions and problematic points which I had been unable to grasp clearly from my own studies. I have continued to rely on him for help and advice pertaining to academic matters and for this I will always be grateful.

Finally, I am indebted to many other friends and colleagues who helped directly or indirectly with this project. Some offered to assist with my living expenses while I worked on the book, some loaned or gave me useful books or other materials, some assisted with proofreading, others advised me in regard to language expressions and meanings. Without the help and encouragement of these good friends, the book could not have been published.

October, 1903

Tsunesaburo Makiguchi

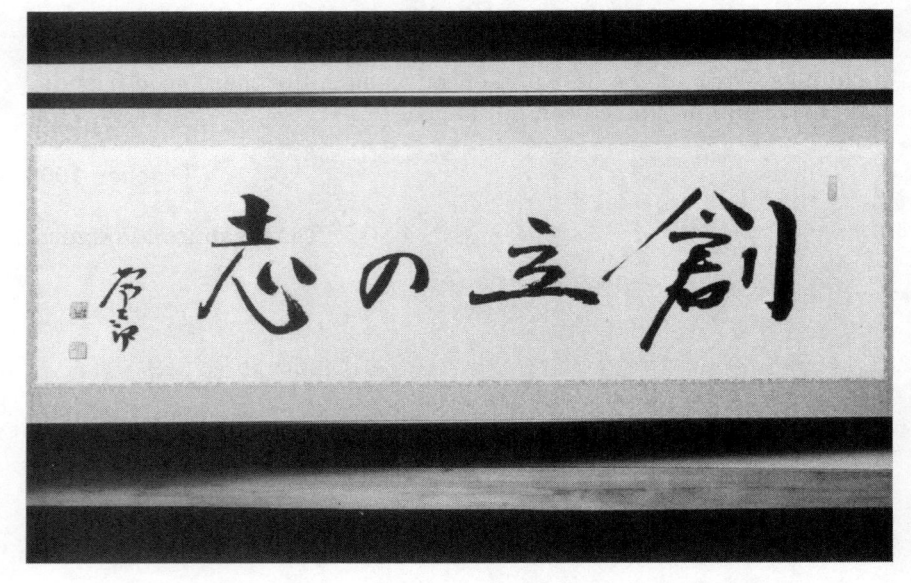

"Create,"a word much loved by Makuguchi, written in his own dynamic calligraphy. Pronouced "so," it is a part of the slogan "so-ritsu-no-shi," or "the creative will."

Introduction

Makiguchi's own writing implements.

Chapter 1

Earth and Human Life

The Problem

The relationship between human beings and the earth is very complex, but it is not something remote from our daily lives. Rather, the people/earth relationship is involved in everything we do, and it affects every aspect of our experience. In modern times, major problems have arisen in human affairs because we are inattentive to this relationship. While admitting its complexity, we can still seek to understand our relationship to the earth and bring it more clearly into our conscious awareness. Following reasonable methods of scientific inquiry, I propose that we start with observations of the most immediate facts of mutual existence.

Human Life and the World

I am from a poor village in Arahama in northern Japan, an ordinary man who has spent half of his life pursuing daily necessities, making little contribution to the world outside. However, when I consider the things surrounding me, I am astonished at the broad origins of the objects that affect my life. For example, a piece of wool cloth wrapped around my body was originally produced in South America or Australia and processed in England by the labor of British people and with coal and iron mined there. My shoes have soles made from leather produced in the United States, and the rest of the shoe is made from leather produced in India. On my desk is a kerosene lamp; it is silent, though the oil inside it might well be saying, "I sprang from the foot of the Caucasus Mountains along the coast of the Caspian Sea and arrived here after traveling thousands of miles." My glasses have lenses produced with skill and precision by people in Germany.

I began this chapter by describing such trivial things because it will be easier for us to perceive the extent of our interrelations with the larger world around us if we recognize the presence of such relationships in even the smallest aspects of an ordinary person's life. Imagine a person, a man of luxury, who rides an Arabian horse, wears a leather jacket made in Lyons; who warms himself in a fur coat from the Bearing Sea Coast or shades his head from the sun with a Panama hat. He refreshes himself with spices from the South Sea Islands, possesses gold from the Transvaal in Africa, and grooms himself with jewels from the Amazon Valley. Indeed, such a person would be depending on three different climates (tropical, sub-tropical, and frigid) to maintain his body temperature, on the soils of five different continents to feed himself, and on five different races to enrich himself.

A story is told about Katsutoshi Doi (1573-1644), a feudal lord of a vast domain in Japan. One day, he picked up a 30-centimeter piece of string from China that was lying on the living-room table in his home and ordered one of his retainers, Jimbe Ohno, to keep it for him. Several persons heard this command and scoffed, "What is the use of keeping such a short string? This isn't behavior suitable for a great lord."

Several years later, Doi called Ohno and asked him for the string. Ohno took it out of his purse. Doi took it, and used it to tie his sword to his belt. He said to his secretary, "When I ordered Ohno to keep this piece of Chinese string other people called me a miser. But he has kept it as I ordered. Let him have 54,000 liters of rice every year."

Then Doi explained why that piece of string was so precious. "Chinese people grew mulberry plants, fed the leaves to silkworms, took silk from them, and made that string. It was bought by a Chinese merchant, exported to Japan, bought by a merchant of Kyoto or Osaka through people in Nagasaki, and finally came here to Tokyo. How many people have worked to make that string and bring it to me? Heaven will punish us if we waste something made with so much effort just because it is short. Now I have tied my sword with this string and made use of it. That 30-centimeter string was worth 54,000 liters of rice to me."

This story may be apocryphal, but it helps us recognize that we depend on the world; it helps us realize how precious are the things which the world provides for us. We also recognize that this interdependence is an inevitable and a desirable course for all of us at the beginning of the 20th Century. It would be foolish to narrow our vision to our own small portion of the world, to worry uselessly about bygone troubles or busy ourselves in disputes and arguments over trivial matters. At the same time, we should avoid blindly following those who would have us neglect our immediate environment and community in the name of a misguided cosmopolitanism.

Human Life and Country

Though we owe the wider world a great deal, there is a small, specific part of the world which we are especially closely associated with and which we benefit from. I have mentioned the many benefits the world provides as a means of reminding us of the even greater and more profound contribution to our lives made by our own land and culture and people. These gifts are so close to us and so pervasive in our daily lives that we often fail to appreciate them and to recognize how precious they are to us. Because of this tendency to take our own country and its contribution to our lives for granted, we in Japan are sometimes confused and misled by persons and groups who have vested interests in organizations or countries abroad to an erroneous worship of foreign countries and cultures. This we must guard against.

While I do not support dreamy cosmopolitanism, it should be clear that neither do I support chauvinism. It is true that the present nation-state does protect its people from foreign invasion, grants them liberties, and safeguards their lives and wealth. But modern civilization has expanded the theater of human competition to all parts of the world. Steam engines and motors have reduced the distance and transportation time which used to separate one part of the world from another. Small-scale competition such as used to occur among villages has now grown into large-scale international competition. For this reason, everywhere in the world, whether the competitors be nations, states or races, each party watches thirstily for a chance to attack another.

It would be foolish to narrow our vision to our own small portion of the world, to worry uselessly about bygone troubles or busy ourselves in disputes and arguments over trivial matters. At the same time, we should avoid blindly following those who would have us neglect our immediate environment and community in the name of a misguided cosmopolitanism.

Today, the various nations are ever on the alert for opportunities to overpower and gain control over neighbors. In seeking to satisfy their ambitions, they do not hesitate to exercise aggression and commit atrocities. They even contend that this imperialistic model is natural and appropriate. Ironically, this is a time when a man who steals from an individual will be arrested and punished as a thief, but a man who robs people of their state and their culture is hailed as a hero.

> *Ironically, this is a time when a man who steals from an individual will be arrested and punished as a thief, but a man who robs people of their state and their culture is hailed as a hero.*

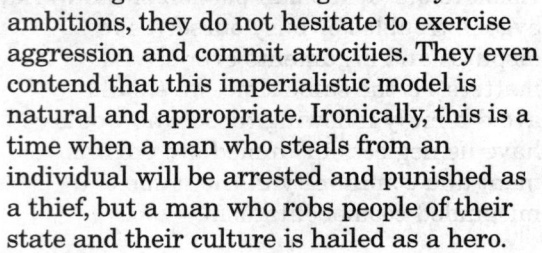

Human Life and Homelands

In attempting to sort all these matters out in my own mind, I arrived at a conviction that the natural beginning point for understanding the world we live in and our relationship to it is that community of persons, land, and culture which gave us birth; that community, in fact, which gave us our very lives and started us on the path toward becoming the persons we are. In other words, we must start from that community which has given us our rootedness as human, cultural beings. The importance of this sense of rootedness and personal identity which are given to us by our native cultural communities, our homelands, can scarcely be overemphasized. This insight is a first basic step toward the understanding we seek. I will return to this later.

Geography:
A Path to Understanding the Earth and Ourselves

We live on a planet which consists of 528 million square kilometers of land; in a country, Japan, which covers 370,000 square kilometers; and each of us lives in an even smaller part of our planet consisting of some one hundred or so square kilometers. Thought of in another way, I am one of some one hundred villagers in my native Arahama; I am one of 50 million Japanese, and I am a part of a world population of one and one-half billion persons.

This perspective arises from the study of geography. Geography emerged among the fields of human knowledge precisely because of the importance of understanding our relationship to the earth which sustains us. But the traditional discipline of geography has become so fragmented and over-specialized that today it is useless for that purpose.

I propose a new approach to the study of geography which both recognizes the dynamic nature of the earth and takes human beings and their richly varied cultures into account. For purposes of definition, I propose that we think of geography as a study of the relationships between the natural phenomena of the earth and human beings. But since definition is such a critical and controversial issue in the scientific world, I will simply use this as a working hypothesis in the following chapters. When it comes to practical studies of the earth and human life, let the study of geography begin with that small parcel of the earth where we live and have our roots, our homeland.

> *I propose that we think of geography as a study of the relationships between the natural phenomena of the earth and human beings.*

Chapter 2

Our Homeland as a Base for Observing the World

The Importance of Place In Human Experience

I have often pondered the mysterious power of our native land. A person traveling abroad yearns for his homeland more than anything else, while one who has never been away from his home seldom realizes his attachment to it. We take it all for granted until some specific foreign influence or experience awakens us to the attachment. Tomonao Hayashi expresses this longing in verse:

Each night of a journey,
I sleep in a different room,
but in every dream
my hometown appears.

This is a natural human feeling. Again, Abe no Nakamaro, who traveled in China, expressed his deep longing for home as follows:

Looking up into the skies
I see a faraway moon,
the same moon I saw at home
coming up over Mt. Mikasa.

This man was a favorite of three Emperors of the Tang Dynasty who held important official positions which provided him with a very comfortable living. Still, he remembered his hometown with deep yearning.

It is not only the rich and the noble who in their homelands rolled in luxury, but also human beings who in their homelands suffered great hardship who long for the land of their birth. An example of this can be seen in the case of Aogashima, a small volcanic island of about one hectare in the Pacific Ocean barely able to sustain life, which is introduced by Shigetaka Shiga in his book *On the Japanese Landscape*. At one time the volcano on the island erupted, discharging fire and raining down deadly lava and ash. Most of the people and animals on the island were killed. Only a few people were able to escape by boat to Hachijo Island. When the eruption stopped after thirteen years, they returned to their barren home island with great joy.

Similarly, Shumushu, the northernmost island of the Kuriles, is a desolate land layered in ice and snow. In order to try to improve the lives of the island's inhabitants, officials of the Land Development Bureau moved the natives of Shumushu to Shikotan, a southern island of the Kuriles. Shikotan was covered with flourishing beech and larch trees. Foxes frisked among the trees; brooks flowed gently here and there. Rewards were even granted to those who would industriously cultivated the rich fields on the island. However, the immigrants were not happy in this new "paradise"; in time every one of them drifted back to their barren island.

We can find other examples around us. In places where people from different parts of the country have emigrated, such as Tokyo or Hokkaido, one can often see social gatherings of people from this village or that prefecture. In these gatherings people from the same home town enjoy chatting together and for a while relieve their feelings of homesickness and nostalgia. They might explain their attachment as being because their parents, relatives, or friends still live there. This makes sense, but it does not explain the feelings and behavior of the Aogashima islanders or of the people from Shumushu who left nothing and no one behind. Some might say it is because "my homeland is rich in scenic beauty." Still, these answers do not bring all the aspects of the phenomenon into focus. Think about the case of the Shumushu islanders. In spite of the mild weather and lush natural features of Shikotan, they longed for their barren, desolate home island. We can only conclude that our homeland, the land of our birth, has a mysterious influence upon us.

This mysterious power may also function as a driving force. I have known people who had left their homes to study in a far off land who exclaimed, "I must succeed, or I can never return home, even though I die." The feeling that they could not go home except with honor and success can motivate a person to be active nationally and internationally.

Each of us, then, is deeply indebted to that homeland which gave us our life and nourished us in our helpless infancy. How can we repay this indebtedness? I suggest that we begin by recognizing its mysterious power.

The Sphere of One's Homeland

Let us now consider in more specific terms just what a homeland is. The answer is that one's homeland varies depending on one's vantage point. An infant living under the parental roof perceives all except his family and those with whom he interacts every day as threatening aliens. At this infantile stage, his homeland is limited to the living room and the garden.

To an elementary school child, the sphere of his homeland will be different. Children from various village communities come to study in the same district school. It is not uncommon to witness a situation in which a student from, for instance, "A" village, is insulted by a student from "B" village. The lines of sympathy by which the children take sides mark the "homelands" with which they identify.

I have already mentioned the social gatherings of people from the same prefectures which are held each year in Hokkaido and in Tokyo. Most of the people in these gatherings had neither met nor heard of each other at home. They are drawn together by the native dialect which they share and which is imprinted in each person's memory. Here, "homeland" is a prefecture, a district, or the old fief of which a person was once a part.

When a Japanese person walks down the street in London, she may see people of different colors. None of the languages, manners, religions, customs, and feelings she encounters is familiar to her. Who wouldn't feel a tug of unease upon thus being surrounded on all sides by aliens? If she then meets a Japanese and speaks in her native language about Japan, is it any wonder that she is filled with joy? It does not matter that the person she is talking to is, in fact, a perfect stranger whose name she does not even know. In such a case, one's homeland is a country or a nation.

If we carry this line of reasoning further, we come to realize that from a cosmic perspective, we can think of the earth itself as our homeland. Some religions encourage us to consider our true home as being beyond this present life and to think of the earth as but a temporary home. But, this is not the approach our study of geography is meant to take.

The point I wish to emphasize is that, even if our goal is to understand the whole world or the entire cosmos, the logical and natural starting point in our quest is our homeland. This idea has been criticized by some as being too narrow and provincial. While there is much to be gained by studying about distant cultures and countries, and we should be engaged in collecting new information from around the world, arguments about parochialism miss the point.

If we think seriously about it, we can see that every aspect of this universe can be observed in the small area of our homeland. Furthermore, because our homeland is the place where we live, where we walk, where we see and hear and gain impressions, where we perform, it is possible for us to observe everything directly. Thus, it is possible to explain the general nature of highly complex phenomena anywhere in the world through use of examples found in abundance even in the most remote village or hamlet.

In view of this wealth of examples and information all around us, it is astounding that so many people, and teachers in particular, neglect this kind of basic and profound observation and just stick to books, using all their energy in memorizing. They read, forget what they have read, so start to read again, forgetting, reading, forgetting, reading... and on and on. Finally they get tired of this round of reading and memorizing and forgetting—or perhaps begin to realize what a waste of time and energy it is—and put the blame on geography itself.

It may help in our understanding of the principle I am considering here to think about the great and famous people whom we look up to and who have made lasting contributions to human understanding and culture. Jean Louis Agassiz, for example, one of the great zoologists of modern times, made one of his important discoveries while fishing in a lake in his native Switzerland as a child. It is said of Dante, the father of poets in the middle ages, that he never took a step outside of his hometown, yet he knew every single detail of his surroundings. Similarly, Peter the Great is believed to have developed the qualities which made him a hero as he played in the lakes and mountains in his homeland.

When we consider persons of genius, we tend to believe that their accomplishments were possible because of their innate natural talents. We think, "I can't be like that. It's beyond me; it's impossible" We tend to perceive a wide difference between these great people of history and "ordinary people like us."

I am convinced, however, that in the beginning of life there is very little difference between people. Every person has inborn talents and potential. Then why do these differences come about? I believe it hinges upon whether or not a person learns to see and grasp the true nature of phenomena with penetrating insight and understanding. The "geniuses" I cited above honed their vision to a high degree simply through direct observation of the marvels of nature and the world around them.

Most of us only look at the surface of things. We abandon direct and intimate communication with natural phenomena and end up in slavery to books. Even after reading thousands of books, we remain ignorant of the insights and understandings we need for living fully and creatively.

The lofty insights, understandings, and principles of the universe are revealed in every tiny village or hamlet. The natural world can inspire us, foster our wisdom, and family, friends, neighbors, and community groups can nurture us in so many ways. This immediate, direct experience available to us through the natural and social environments of our homelands can foster compassion, goodwill, friendship, kindness, sincerity, and humble hearts.

If we truly understand and cherish our homelands, we can learn valuable lessons from them. Having done that, we are prepared to learn from travel. For example, Yoshida Shoin spent half of his life on the road. During the last days of the Tokugawa Shogunate, when intrigue and bitter inter-clan rivalry were rampant throughout Japan, he travelled to all parts of the country seeking to understand the needs, the problems, the hopes and desires, of the people in each place. We revere him today for his wisdom, his unbiased appreciation for different points of view, and his sympathetic concern for the welfare of the people he met. We can find another example in Sir Helmuth Moltke, a German general who also was renowned for his studies in

> *I am convinced, however, that in the beginning of life there is very little difference between people. Every person has inborn talents and potential. Then, why do these differences come about? I believe it hinges upon whether or not a person learns to see and grasp the true nature of phenomena with penetrating insight and understanding.*

> *The lofty insights, understandings, and principles of the universe are revealed in every tiny village or hamlet. The natural world can inspire us, foster our wisdom, and family, friends, neighbors, and community groups can nurture us in so many ways.*

geography. Both his work in geography and the brilliant plan for German federation of which he was the chief architect, can be traced to his experiences and observations as a youth travelling throughout Europe.

In spite of these kinds of examples, some people still hold that direct, intimate observation of one's homeland such as I am proposing is too shallow and provincial an approach to learning and a method of seeking understanding about the world in which we live. Therefore, let me stress my basic position again: every aspect of the entire universe can be found in the small, limited area of one's home community. But we have to be sensitive to these untold riches all around us, and we must learn how to be effective observers.

The Nurturing of Genius

I have suggested above that the difference between the great geniuses of history and other "ordinary people" is not a matter of heredity, that geniuses are not born geniuses. At birth, every person possesses potential for greatness. It is one of the tragic realities of contemporary life that in most people this inborn potential remains dormant and undeveloped.

> ... the difference between the great geniuses of history and other "ordinary people" is not a matter of heredity, that geniuses are not born geniuses. At birth, every person possesses potential for greatness.

My search for the reasons for this deplorable state of affairs has led me to realize that the people we think of as geniuses had developed a way of "seeing" which enabled them to grasp with penetrating insight and understanding the true nature of the world around them. Most people, on the other hand, "see" only on a surface level. They satisfy themselves with second hand information and never develop the capacity for direct and intimate communication with natural phenomena. Thus, their lives become stunted and their potential greatness lies unchallenged and unrealized. This is a great loss both for them and for the world.

Can anything be more important, then, than to discover how to plan educational experiences which will enable every person to develop this deeper understanding of life and nature which is so essential for living a fulfilling and rewarding life? This realization led me to see the field of geography as a central focus for planning educational experiences for children which can foster this natural, deeper way of seeing and learning about the world. While I do not deny the importance and the place of books and other kinds of second-hand learning materials, I maintain that children can achieve the full potential of their humanness only through direct, active, personal communication with natural phenomena. This is a basic principle which we must never lose sight of in our educational planning. This is a key to enabling each child to discover and nurture the potential greatness within.

This suggests that each child's immediate geographic community, consisting of the natural environment, family, and village or neighborhood, should constitute both the setting and the curricula for learning. Every aspect of the entire world and the cosmos itself can be found in that small world of the child, wherever it may be. The chapters which follow are designed to provide a broad outline or overview of the various kinds of phenomena which can be observed in this microcosm. It is my hope that teachers and others who assume responsibility for guiding the learning experiences of children will find these ideas and suggestions helpful. I offer this work as a map for those who would assist children and young people in their exploration of the world around them.

Chapter 3

Interacting with the Earth

Interaction with the Earth In the Process Of Becoming Human

We are born of the earth; we live on the earth; we are inspired by the earth; we die on the earth. The earth is our home. Confronting the earth will be an important first step in our preparation to learn about the world which has given us birth, the earth which nurtures us each day that we live. How then can we observe, and make contact with, our surroundings?

We can say, first, that there are two general ways in which we interact with the earth. One is physical, the other is spiritual. Our initial, direct contact with the earth is physical, as it is with other animals and with plants. In other words, every connection we make with the earth is made through our body, without which we could not directly experience the earth.

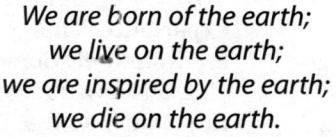

But it is through our spiritual interaction with the earth that the characteristics which we think of as truly human are ignited and nurtured within us. Our spiritual interactions with our surroundings are almost endless in variety and diversity. It is difficult to classify them into separate categories, but for my own studies, I have found it helpful to identify eight different kinds of spiritual interaction we

We are born of the earth;
we live on the earth;
we are inspired by the earth;
we die on the earth.
The earth is our home.

have with the earth, dividing them in two general types, objective interactions and subjective interactions, which I have designated as experience and encounter respectively as shown in Chart 1.

Chart 1: Kinds of Spiritual Interaction

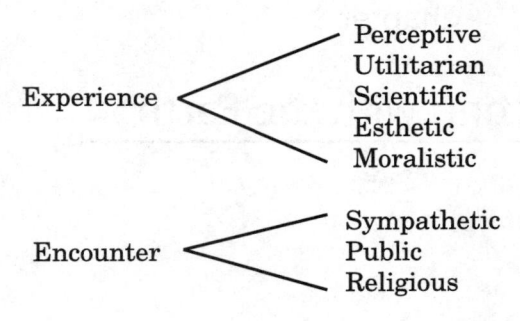

Experience
- Perceptive
- Utilitarian
- Scientific
- Esthetic
- Moralistic

Encounter
- Sympathetic
- Public
- Religious

Experience

Perceptive Interaction

Imagine yourself in a quiet environment surrounded by green fields and clear water, majestic mountains towering above, streams and rivers winding toward the sea, the wind lightly brushing your face as the sun streams down through the clouds. Your heart and soul are overwhelmed by the beauty, the freshness, the wonder of the experience. This is what I mean by perceptive interaction with our environment. Some would make light of such simple, perhaps superficial, observations of nature. However, this kind of experience is important as the foundation for more spiritual and intellectual activities and, thus, will initiate deeper interactions.

It is as if the mind and heart that had been asleep are suddenly awakened and stimulated to seek intellectual communion with the environment. Our natural curiosity is quickened and we begin to appreciate the marvelous diversity of nature, perhaps becoming curious about the human culture and customs of the place as well. This inquisitive state of mind is the starting point for deeper interaction with our environment and true learning.

Utilitarian Interaction

The farmer who is concerned about his crops and the merchant who worries about price fluctuations are examples of what I mean by utilitarian interaction. Both use the environment for their own survival. This type of interaction might thus be thought of as interaction in our own interest.

Not all things provided by the environment are beneficial to human beings. Alerted to what may be harmful and cause suffering or even death by warnings from the environment itself, or based on their own experience as well as counsel and principles of survival handed down from their ancestors, human beings seek to encourage the beneficial and discourage the harmful. This is the basis for utilitarian interaction with the environment.

Scientific Interaction

Awakened, by perceptive interaction or utilitarian interaction, the human heart and mind are not content to merely passively observe and experience the surrounding environment. We are led to marvel at the deep and mysterious interrelationships which seem to link the various aspects of our environment, and we are motivated to explore and analyze the cause and effect relationships underlying them. This leads to identifying, comparing, contrasting, and analyzing natural phenomena in order to form a comprehensive structure of concepts and to discover the principles that govern their interrelationships.

This type of interaction forms the foundations of the various sciences. Whatever the field, a scholar's interest is first awakened by some question or some puzzling phenomena; then he is led to speculate and form hypotheses concerning the principles governing the inter-relationships among various factors and, finally, to integrate them into the body of well-organized knowledge that constitutes an academic discipline. It is not uncommon to find scholars who are so stimulated and guided by such intellectual curiosity that they become absorbed in their research to the extent that they forget to eat and sleep. The scientific development we have achieved is an outcome of this kind of hard work. It is not only for scholars. The results of this kind of interaction accrue also to businessmen and talented people in many fields when they experience new situations in their own work.

Aesthetic and Moralistic Interaction

The impact of the environment on the human heart and spirit is not limited to the aforementioned practical and scientific interactions. The various phenomena in our environment, with all their amazing complexity and diversity, exist in harmony, maintaining consistency and balance. The relations of part to whole and among the parts fit together, serving the purpose of the whole. Observing and experiencing this beauty and harmony in nature stimulates and excites our senses and our emotions. We are moved and our spirits become purified and cleansed. As a result those whose natural talents are artistic in nature are inspired to express their experience in music, poetry and literature, painting and sculpture.

The emotions which this beauty and harmony in nature invoke in us also work their influence in our moral lives as well. The same psychology is at work when we recognize and appreciate goodness and virtue in the human world as when we appreciate the natural beauty of nature. However, in the case of moral beauty (goodness), the ideal image is not expressed in pictures, or carvings, or great literature, as in the fine arts, but in human character and human actions.

Encounter

The spiritual interactions described above have been categorized according to their nature and characteristics. However, all of these types of interaction have one thing in common: to regard all phenomena external to oneself as material for experience and objects of study, clearly distinguishing the self from objects external to the self. Thus, they share an objective approach to nature through contact, observation, and speculation as a basis for making objective judgments about phenomena. This characteristic distinguishes the type of human activities I call "experience" from another major type of human spiritual interaction with the environment. In contrast to this objective cognition, our spirit also regards external objects and ourselves as entities which share one and the same world, each being a part of it. In this sphere, human beings interact with the environment on more intimate terms. We can call such reciprocal interactions "encounter" to distinguish them from "experience."

Experience in this cognitive sense means primarily intellectual interactions, whereas encounter implies emotional interactions. We accumulate knowledge through experience, but we nurture emotions through encounter. Within this general framework, the remaining three types of interaction, sympathetic interaction, public interaction, and religious interaction, should be considered in the realm of encounter. The objects of the interactions are different among the three: other individuals whom one regards as partners and friends in sympathetic interaction, one's community and the society to which one belongs and is a beneficiary of in public interaction, and the God or Buddha or spiritual reality that one reveres in religious interaction. With this further explanation, we can now consider interactions involving encounter.

Sympathetic Interaction

When we enter into intimate relationships with parents, brothers and sisters, friends, or neighbors, we are moved and affected by their words and their facial expressions. We share their pain and their grief, their joy and their happiness. And if we are alert and observant, we will notice that this is true not only of our relationships with people, but also of our relationships with animals, plants, and even inanimate objects such as rocks or stones. For example, we feel sympathy and pity if we see an animal or a bird suffering. And we sometimes feel sadness at the sight of inanimate objects being destroyed or mutilated.

Again, persons who have been away from their homelands for extended periods not only miss the persons who were important to them in their earlier life, but they often recall also with deep love and affection the mountains and the fields and the rivers that they once knew as if they were old friends. We even feel attached to and close to inanimate things which we have used and loved for a long time. These are examples of sympathetic interaction with inanimate things in our environment.

Thus, I conclude that in our sympathetic interaction with our environment we should regard people, animals, trees, rivers, rocks or stones in the same light as ourselves and realize that we have much in common with them all. Such interaction causes us to wonder, if not consciously think, "If I were in their (or its) place, what would I feel. . . or do?" Sympathetic interactions occur, therefore, when you encounter that person or object at a deep emotional level and are able to place yourself in the position of that person or object, perhaps regarding the other as one of your own kind, a part of yourself.

Public Interaction

It is our nature as human beings to form societies. No one can live totally alone. It is through association in society that we can provide not only for our basic needs and security, but for everything that makes our lives fulfilling and rewarding. This realization leads to the universalization of sympathetic feelings initially directed toward a specific individual or object. Growing awareness of our indebtedness to our society gives rise to feelings of appreciation and a sense of social responsibility within us. It is this realization of our indebtedness to the society we call our homeland and our appreciation for its rich contribution to our lives which produces feelings of patriotism and love of country. Beginning in our very personal relationships in our homeland, our sympathetic concern and appreciation expands to include the larger society and, ultimately, the whole world.

Religious Interaction

Through my various interactions with the environment, I observe that in the midst of the complex and awe-inspiring diversity of nature there is harmony, symmetry, and evidence of universal law. And, in this ever-changing world, as I explore human history and seek to comprehend human destiny, I become conscious of an order underlying everything. I begin to realize that there is something beyond our control. I am just one of the things in the universe which is created and sustained by something higher. Realizing the presence of this something higher, this something incomprehensible, this something beyond our understanding or imagination, I feel so very small and limited. Unconsciously, my heart fills with awe and reverence. This is how we are drawn into communication with the infinite. This is the spiritual interaction we describe as religious.

Spiritual Interaction and Personal Growth

As we have just seen, there are many different ways in which human beings interact spiritually with the external world. It may be helpful to think about this in personal terms. At first, your interaction with your environment may be on a very shallow basis. You observe mountains or rivers, for instance, only on a very superficial level, as something "out there." But as you develop your own life and your personal interests, you will not be satisfied with such superficiality. You will want to go further and enter into deeper kinds of association. The particular kind or kinds of interaction which you have with the world around you at any one point in your life will depend, first of all, on who and what you are, and secondly on when and how the interaction occurs.

Let me try to give some examples. Some persons, as they become better acquainted with their environment, may be curious to learn more about rocks, trees, water quality, hydraulic power, etc., and begin thinking about how to make use of them. They may wonder about and want to know about heights, lengths, shapes, origins, and the ways in which these various environmental features have influenced their surroundings. Or they may see these same things in the environment with artistic eyes and be inspired to express their experience in poetry, literature, painting, or music. Again, they might perceive the mountain or river or cliff before them as a training ground for their physical endurance and prowess. Or they might receive inspiration and insight into the unity of nature and the cosmos from the same mountain or river.

There are, therefore, many different levels or depths at which persons can interact with the environment, depending on who the person is and who or what the interaction is with. The level or depth of interaction depends on each person's spiritual growth and development.

It is through interaction with this outside world that we can make healthy, balanced, personality growth. Therefore, I say that this outside world, especially the natural environment, can truly be our educator, our enlightener, our leader, our consoler. Our happiness in life is very much connected with nature; it depends on the closeness or depth of our relationship with nature.

Shall we try to look at our interactions with the outside world through nature's viewpoint? Nothing is more generous or more fair than nature. Nature never, ever closes its door to anyone. Nature never judges us by our social status, never discriminates between rich and poor. Those who are lost or discouraged can find sympathy and compassion in nature, but nature is incapable of flattery. Nature will remain silent unless we come seeking a relationship sincerely and earnestly.

So what should we do to keep company with nature? We need only to come to nature, without fear, without flinching; come to nature with sincerity, honesty, and sympathy; come seeking a close relationship with her. Then she will not only welcome you, but come to meet you, take you by the hand, and kiss you. She will love you tenderly, encourage and uphold you, and at last, open the essence of her spirit to you. You will begin a friendship which will last forever.

History abounds with examples of this intimate relationship between nature and human beings. There is Newton, who forgot to sleep or eat and, according to some accounts, even forgot his own bride, in the intensity of his relationship with nature. There is Tyndall, who failed to realize the extent of his frostbite, absorbed as

> *Nothing is more generous or more fair than nature. Nature never, ever closes its door to anyone. Nature never judges us by our social status, never discriminates between rich and poor.*

he was in discovering the secrets of Alpine glaciers. There are so many explorers, artists, religionists and others who followed their hearts and forgot themselves as they came to know and appreciate the wonders of the world around them.

Individual interactions with the outside world in many different fields form the foundation of our society. I will consider the social dimensions of our life in the world in later chapters. The following categorization of social life will provide a framework in preparation for this later discussion.

Chart 2: The Dimensions of Social Life

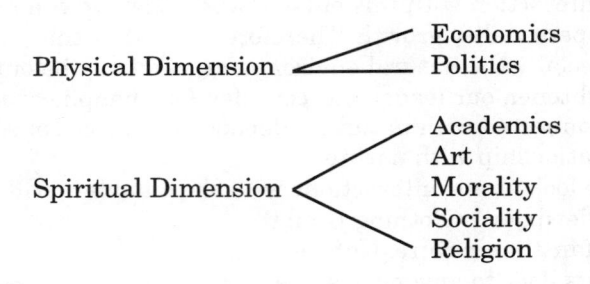

Physical Dimension
- Economics
- Politics

Spiritual Dimension
- Academics
- Art
- Morality
- Sociality
- Religion

The various human-environment interactions in which we engage contribute to individual development and social development at the same time. When individuals whose characters have become balanced and morally mature through deep interactions with the natural environment gather together, the society they create will provide a healthy, open, social environment capable of nurturing individual growth.

Criteria For Selecting Elements For Study

We have considered the reasons for focusing our study of the world in which we live in our homelands, but which elements of our homelands should we single out for study? When we begin to observe our surroundings, many things rush into our awareness and call to us at the same time, overwhelming and confusing us. Each homeland is a complex cultural whole consisting of innumerable distinct elements and aspects. How can we choose from this profusion those elements we should study or those elements we should study first?

Fortunately, some general guidelines which can assist us in making these choices have been suggested by pioneers who have preceded us. The more helpful of these are listed in Chart 3.

Chart 3: Guidelines for Our Quest

- ◆ from nearby to far away
- ◆ from singular to plural
- ◆ from known to unknown
- ◆ from whole to part
- ◆ from general to specific
- ◆ from cause to effect
- ◆ from visible to invisible
- ◆ from the individual to the whole
- ◆ from simple to complex
- ◆ from concrete to abstract

With these guidelines to help us, and beginning in our own homelands, let us set out on our quest for understanding of the world around us.

Part One:
The Earth as the Base for Human Life

36   A Geography of Human Life

Makiguchi (left) with his seminal *Kyodoka* (local studies) group, including the man who influenced America's conservation president Theodore Roosevelt, Inazo Nitobe (upper left insert).

Chapter 4

The Firmament

The Sun and Human Life

Though the sun is a distant body separated from the earth by some 148 million kilometers of space, it is, in a very real sense, a powerful influence and the source of all phenomena on the earth. The sun is so pervasive in our lives that we tend to take it for granted. It radiates the light and heat we need, two variations of the same physical function in the universe. Though light and heat are closely related as far as their impact on our lives are concerned, there are some differences in the ways they function.

Human beings need and long for sunlight. Evidence of this is the great investment which we have made in inventing means of improving light and replacing the sun in the dark. In Japanese myth, there is an episode indicative of the special regard we Japanese have for the sun in which myriad gods plead with the sun goddess, who had hidden herself in a cave, to come out so that the world could once again know light. A nightless city is analogous with great pleasure and well-being, whereas a land of eternal darkness is perceived as the most terrible of fates.

The fact that a certain amount of sunlight is indispensable for human survival is evident from comparison of the health of those who work outdoors and those who are confined indoors. Oxidization is indispensable for the survival of organisms, and light is a necessary element involved in this process. Since light affects the growth of all organisms it also indirectly influences human life. For example, sunlight affects bacteria, a source of various contagious diseases which are harmful to humans, in ways which favor human beings. Discoveries made with the use of modern microscopes and recent developments in medical science reveal that those microbes, however small they are, are formidable enemies of humankind and higher animals because of their astonishing propagative power. Fortunately, however, when exposed to bright sunlight even the most prolific bacteria are destroyed.

Moreover, such factors as the direction from which sunlight radiates on the earth (forming the basis of the seasons), the daily management of time (that is, the sun's creation of the three divisions of morning, afternoon, and evening), our custom of eating three meals a day, and the standards for designating direction such as North-South, East-West, and the meridian, while not impinging on human survival, are nevertheless important. The awe and majesty which fills our hearts when we see a sunrise or the brilliant red of a sunset on a summer evening suggests how much the sun has influenced the aesthetic and religious realms of our lives.

Since the light and heat of the sun both directly and indirectly affect all aspects of human life, being the single most important source of myriad earthly phenomena, it seems only natural that feelings of gratitude and reverence directed toward the sun have emerged in some cultures. In ancient times the sun was worshipped as the creator and revered as a spiritual entity with immense power.

The Japanese and the Sun

In naming their country our ancestors chose a name based on the belief that a special relationship existed between their people and the sun. Though reverence for the sun was nearly universal, adopting the word "sun" to name our land and people was a choice unique to Japan. In recent years, as scientific knowledge has become widespread, the tendency to see mysterious spirituality in the sun has declined and the sun has come to be regarded as a large flaming body radiating great heat and light. However, since science is but one means of observing and knowing the world, both our culture and our lives will be the poorer if we dismiss reverence and appreciation for the sun as merely a mistaken idea or idol worship. As Ruskin noted, a cloud is just a wet fog in science, but it can be a golden altar in the fine arts.

The early Japanese named their country "Nippon" (the place from which the sun rises), designed the rising-sun symbol for their national flag, and worshipped the sun goddess as the ancestor of the emperor's family and the founder of the nation. These historical facts reflect the unique kinds of interaction which the Japanese sought to build between themselves and the sun. Nichiren is said to have experienced a spiritual awakening under the stimulus of the morning sun, and Munetada Kurozumi, the founder of the Kurozumi sect of the Shinto religion, is also said to have felt a calling by the mysterious light of the sun when he prepared to bid the sun a last farewell before unbearable misery led him to take his own life. There are many similar examples. Whether these episodes were products of traditional belief or not cannot be easily determined, but the large number of such episodes tells us that special interactions and a strong affiliation with the sun have long existed among Japanese people.

> ... the tendency to see mysterious spirituality in the sun has declined and the sun has come to be regarded as a large flaming body radiating great heat and light. However, since science is but one means of observing and knowing the world, both our culture and our lives will be the poorer if we dismiss reverence and appreciation for the sun as merely a mistaken idea or idol worship.

These special feelings toward the sun upon the part of the Japanese are closely related to the location of the nation. The vast Pacific Ocean extends to its east, and the continent of Asia extends to its west, with the Japanese archipelago at Asia's eastern-most tip. As an independent state, never successfully invaded by any foreign power, the Japanese expressed their idealized image of their country with the name "Nippon," a national flag featuring a rising sun, and reference to their position on the globe as the "far east," implying that their country is located at the world's eastern extremity, from which the sun rises. It is probably for this reason that most religious or spiritual edifices in our country, such as Hyuuga and Ise, face east and are directly lighted by the morning sun.

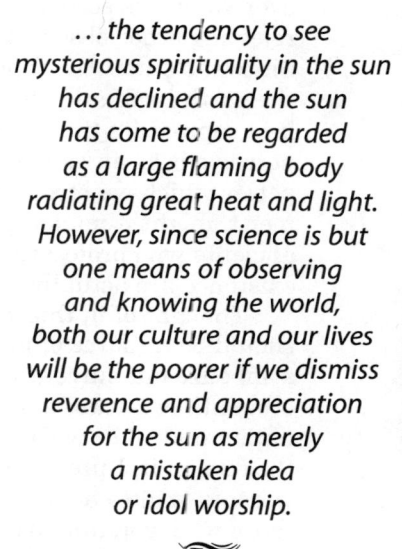

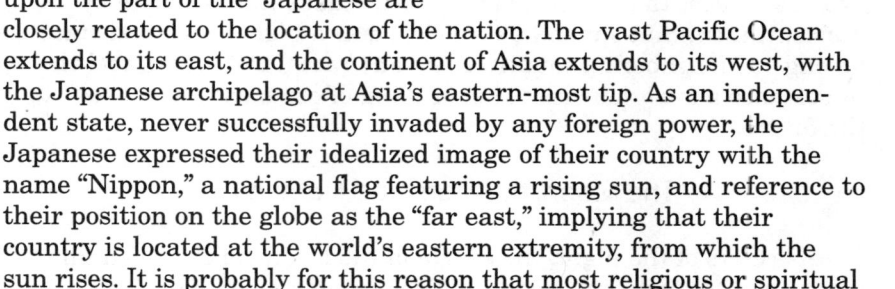

Today, as people living in the modern world, we Japanese are faced with the problem of how these ancient traditions and attitudes toward the sun should be interpreted. Some historians and philosophers are critical of this traditional thought of Japan and dismiss it as primitive. We must admit that these traditional views and myths are somewhat ethnocentric and close to boasting of our own nation. Presenting ourselves as the only beloved child of the sun is, of course, a rather childish thing to do. But at the same time, totally denying our traditional reverence for the sun as primitive and misleading will be a great loss. Scientific observations have led to the view that the sun is nothing more than a flaming mass of physical material. However valid this scientific observation may be, are we justified in rejecting other observations made from differing points of view? Since the sun is the fundamental source of all light and energy which the earth itself and all phenomena of earth depend on, and since it best represents the great power of creation, is it unreasonable to perceive it as an existence most symbolic of that essence or absolute power which we recognize in our religious experience? If this view has merit, might it not suggest that various animistic beliefs of these ancients who professed faith in the most fundamental source of their existence are actually quite advanced?

Thought of in this way, I believe that our Japanese view of the sun should be a source of pride. The rising sun flag seems to me to well symbolize our current national ideal. If you compare our flag with others that feature a ferocious animal or bird as its symbol and its national ideal or with a flag with an imaginary dragon trying to eat the sun on it, I prefer ours. Carlisle has observed that those who worship snakes or cows become like snakes or cows themselves, while those who worship foxes or badgers become like foxes or badgers. The moral and intellectual character of a nation cannot rise above the expressed ideal that its people respect. Perhaps it may not be by accident, then, that Japan has developed as a highly regarded state among our neighboring countries. At any rate, I cannot but feel the importance and seriousness of the calling of our nation as we look to the future.

The Moon, the Stars, and Human Life

As rulers of the night, the source of the lovely lights which fill the night sky, the stars and the moon also have far-reaching effect on human life. Indeed, a variety of interactions are constantly taking place between the moon, the stars, and life on the earth both materially and spiritually. Because their appearance differs from one geographical area to another, the way that they exercise their influence differs accordingly. I cannot here consider all of these different ways in which our lives are affected by these celestial bodies; a few simple observations will suffice.

Our first thoughts when we think of the moon and the stars are of the matchless beauty, romance, and inspiration which they add to our human experience. The moon especially has long been a favorite theme of poets and lovers, as well as a consoler of discouraged and lonely hearts. It has seemed at times to some a symbol of the ever changing destiny of human life. But the feelings which one experiences at the sight of the moon are influenced by the cultural and historical context of any given society. More will be said of this in later chapters. The important phenomenon of the moon's influence over the movement of ocean water and the tides will be discussed in the chapter about the ocean.

Among the thousands of stars in the firmament, the one most influential for our life is the north star. It has served as the standard coordinate in defining location and position on the earth because it does not change its position and there is a unique configuration of "Big Dipper" stars around it which provide constant directional clues. For this reason it has been especially valuable for ocean navigation. The north star has also been perceived as a model of moral courage and integrity, prompting the saying that a man of virtue who governs his people effectively is just like the polar star which does not move but is followed by other stars.

Chapter 5

The Earth

The Earth and Human Life

In a tiny corner of the world, I shelter myself from rain and dew in a humble thatched house and cultivate a very small patch of land to feed myself. However, being aware of the rich variety of phenomena that influence my life, I cannot help thinking of the way the whole earth operates. I look around and, although my eyes can see only a few kilometers in any direction, my heart and mind fill with excitement and wonder and curiosity about the earth and about the relationship between the earth and my life on it. I begin to realize that if we would seek deeper understanding of this relationship, we must prepare ourselves to make observations and inquiries into several different aspects of the planet, such as its topography, dimensions, movements, and structure.

When you stand in a field and look around all you can see is flat land. You will not notice any signs that suggest curvature. Thus, in earlier eras people believed that the earth was a flat, immobile mass, with the sun, the moon, and stars rising from one end and setting in the other. It is understandable that even today, some people believe this. However, more than two thousand years ago Greek philosophers already argued that the earth was a spherical body based on a number of pieces of evidence. Pythagoras said that since the earth had to have a perfect shape it had to be a sphere. Other philosophers reasoned that the earth must be a sphere based on such evidence as the shadow projected on the moon at the time of lunar eclipse, from the way the mast of a navigating ship disappears and reappears from the horizon, the way that stars appear and disappear when one advances toward the north or the south, and the fact that the rising and setting of the sun and the moon differ depending on the locations of observation. However, at that time people in general were set in their belief of a flat earth. Even at the time of Columbus' discovery of the new continent, his observation that the earth may be spherical in shape was laughed at in the Spanish court. It was only after Magellan's round-the-world navigation (1519-1522) that the theory at last became generally accepted.

The most important consequence of the earth's being spherical is that it causes differences in temperature between north and south. Because of the curved surface, angles of sunlight differ from place to place. Since the heat received from sunlight depends on its angle, differences in angle cause variation in the temperature and the surface area that receives sunlight. However, since zoning based on temperature also depends on the movement of the earth, I will come back to this issue later.

Another important aspect of this reality is that we can divide the earth with hypothetical lines both vertically and horizontally in order to specify a specific location or to make various observations in regard to the earth. Various technical terms have been invented to facilitate these observations and measurements such as axis, poles, equator, latitude, and longitude.

The Impact of Human Beings on the Earth

The total area of the surface of the earth is roughly 500,000,000 square kilometers. The present human population is 1.5 billion. Though the human species is slower in breeding compared with other animal species, the human population of the world is expected to double in the next 25 years. If the population continues to grow at this rate, its size will be enormous in 1,000 years. Thus, unless some artificial reduction in the human population occurs, the earth will soon be filled beyond capacity. This, in fact, is what a man named Thomas Malthus has predicted. He theorized that the growth of the human population would exceed the growth of food production and that unless such growth is abated by some means, food shortages and famines will lead to a human catastrophe.

Fortunately, at least part of the Malthusian theory has been proven wrong by the fact that real population growth occurs in proportion to the growth of means to support life. However, to a certain extent, population growth of the human species cannot be abated and thus a struggle for existence is inevitable. This reality leads to problems of colonization, emigration, and their related evils. The aggressive attitudes of the great powers in the modern era and their lust to invade other countries whenever possible are some of the contemporary results of this struggle.

As a result of the untiring efforts of explorers and expeditions, human beings have left their footsteps in every corner of the world, making almost the entire area of the earth into their habitat. It is possible today to go around the world, a distance of 39,000 kilometers, in as little as 66 days. When we think of Magellan's expedition that took more than three years, we cannot but be impressed by the progress which has been made since that time. Recently the Russian Minister of Communication made an even more surprising prediction. He foresees that in the near future humans will be able to go around the world in 33 days, only half the time now required.

The figures quoted above assume a speed of 48 kilometers per hour on the Siberian Railway. If that transportation system develops further, thereby reducing the amount of travel time in the Orient, the time to travel around the world could be reduced to 30 days. When we consider the fact that in the days before the Meiji Restoration, it used to take 20 days to travel from Edo (Tokyo) to Mutsu (in Aomori Prefecture) we realize that traveling this vast world has become similar to traveling in our own small country just a few years ago. And to add further to our consternation, today, as a result of the invention of the telegraph, we can read here in Japan news about happenings in London, about 17,500 kilometers from Japan, the next day.

Thus, although human beings are not capable of reducing the size of the earth, by developing transportation systems they have succeeded in reducing the vast separations between them. Therefore, we Japanese should remember that despite the great physical distance existing between our isolated nation in the Far East and the center of Europe, Europe is now closer to us than some of the remote rural areas of our own country.

The Parts of the Earth and Human Life

Each part of the earth's surface affects human life in its own way. But before beginning discussion of these respective parts of the earth and their specific significance and influence, we must consider the two major categories which constitute the earth's surface, land and water.

Land and water each influence human life in a special manner based on their own characteristics. Solid land gives a stable habitat to human beings. It provides human beings with immobile assets which serve as a firm foundation for their life and contributes to the evolving of a specific culture in a given land. In contrast, the fluid nature of water provides human beings with means of transportation.

When a person moves and settles in a new place there are great difficulties which must be overcome because of the fixed nature of land. However, once one transfers to a boat, it is possible to drift from place to place with relative ease. The point is that land is durable and difficult to control while water is flexible and easy to manage. Land is an immobile element in life while water is a mobile element. Land can be thought of as symbolizing the independent existence of human beings whereas water symbolizes unity or integrity. Land separates human beings while water unites them. Thus, the two elements confront each other, having opposite properties and influencing human life in opposite ways.

> Land separates human beings while water unites them. Thus, the two elements confront each other, having opposite properties and influencing human life in opposite ways.

Everywhere on the earth, these two properties of the earth, land and water, compete with each other, each seeking to further its own influence. Indeed, it has been precisely those places where these two forces have dynamically met and interacted that human beings have inhabited and propagated themselves. It was also those places where early civilizations evolved and developed. The fact that industrial development can be seen primarily along coastal areas and in river valleys also provides evidence of the critical importance of the two elements.

From this perspective, we can regard the earth as a theater of war between these two major forces, each trying to overwhelm the other. Peninsulas represent land's aggressive action into water, whereas gulfs, lagoons, and inland seas represent water's invasion into land. This impression will be further strengthened as we proceed to investigate specific areas of the world.

Land has its base in the northern hemisphere. With the North Pole as its center, land extends radially in three directions. Each of the three segments has a wedge shape with its tip protruding into water. On the other hand, water has its base in the southern hemisphere. With the South Pole as its center, water also exhibits three major segments protruding from three directions into the northern hemisphere toward the North Pole. Water becomes increasingly limited in area as it proceeds northward, just as land area does in relationship to the South Pole.

This confrontation and competition between land and water accounts for the earth's contour with each force configured in three major segments. The Indian Ocean seems to have been somewhat overpowered by the land mass of the Asian continent, while the other two oceans have proceeded deep into the Arctic Circle, meeting each other to form the Arctic ocean, thus breaking up a major land segment. So we can see how liquid, flexible water has tended to overwhelm firm, inflexible, rocky land, nearly breaking three continents into halves. As a result of this process, although one continent remained unbroken, there are now five continents.

Interestingly, human beings have participated in this competitive struggle between land and water and brought considerable influence to bear upon the struggle itself. Since water is much easier to control than land, human beings have assisted water and through united action with it they have divided Europe and Africa. They will divide the last continent into North and South America in the near future. (Note that Asia and Australia had already been broken apart by water alone).

When we recognize this human differential in attitude toward land and water, we cannot help being impressed by the exquisiteness of Creation which has constituted an earth with nearly three parts of water and one part of land. If we split the earth into halves, with London and New Zealand serving as poles, we can see a similar division into hemispheres in terms of the ratio between water and land. However, land actually occupies only one-seventh of the southern hemisphere, with the rest of the land area in the northern hemisphere. It is noteworthy that land concentration is especially marked between the latitudes of 45 and 72 in the northern hemisphere.

Land constitutes the dry surface of the earth, providing the foundations both for individuals and states or societies. Unless a person aquires a patch of land as a foundation for life, that person will be reduced to a homeless vagrant. And in the case of ethnic groups as well, if a group does not possess an area of land which it can claim for its own, it will be belittled and abused, and treated as bands of wanderers or refugees, as is seen in the troubled Middle East.

Because of this need for a stable home on land, tenants yearn to become landlords and landlords seek to expand their properties. In the same way, people of small nations aspire to grow to be larger nations, while the people of large nations aspire to grow into great nations. Thus, from single individuals to the great civilized nations, human aspirations, in essence, involve occupying larger areas of land and water. Thus, we witness the seemingly endless conflict between nations over national borders.

But relations between land, water, and human life extend even further. The influences of land and water on our lives vary depending on their specific forms. When you look over the terrain you can observe various shapes: flat, protruding, indented, steep, winding. Diversity in earth forms is beyond description. For the sake of simplicity, however, several general terms have been formulated to classify them. Those forms which soar into the sky are called mountains; flat areas are called plains. Among plains, plateaus and lower plains are distinguished according to their altitudes. Places of marked indentation are valleys. An innumerable variety of earth forms are encompassed by these general terms.

Now let us look at the borders between land and water. Here again, a wide variety is found. Land areas which face water on three sides and connect to a major land area on one side are called peninsulas. The tips of protruding land are referred to as capes or promontories. Narrow strips of land which connect two major land areas are called isthmuses.

Another type of classification is made between continents and islands. Islands are lands surrounded by oceans on all sides. This definition appears to be clear at first glance. However, if one observes a little further, it becomes ambiguous. If we consider the globe as a whole, continents are also surrounded by water. The size of the land area involved can be seen as a relative matter. Therefore, the distinction between continents and islands proves to be less clear-cut than it at first seems. In an attempt to solve this problem, geographers have proposed additional definitions. Wagner defines an island as a land area surrounded by water in which oceanic influences reach inland as far as the center of the area, thus affecting the climate. By this definition, Australia, for example, cannot be regarded as an island. Land areas which have, within themselves, all the resources required for the development of human civilization, having no need of importing resources from outside, are generally classified as continents. The types of land area classification may be summarized as follows:

Classification based on the oceanic influences that derive from land-water relations:

- ◆ continents
- ◆ islands

Classification based on the forms resulting from land- water relations:

- ◆ peninsulas
- ◆ isthmuses
- ◆ coasts
- ◆ capes

Classification based on land forms and altitude:

- ◆ plains—plateaus, lower plains
- ◆ mountains—ridges, valleys

The major part of the earth's surface, as we have seen, is water and not dry land. Although water on the surface appears to be even and similar everywhere, it actually is not. As in the case of land, water can also be classified into different categories according to its location and form. And as with land, everywhere on the earth, human beings have given different names to different types and forms of bodies of water to distinguish them.

Water surrounded by land and water surrounding land are distinguished and referred to as land water and sea water, respectively. Among bodies of water classified as land water, those which flow are called rivers while static ones are called lakes. The largest bodies of sea water are called oceans and have been divided for classification purposes into three major oceans. Each major ocean diverges on its periphery and flows into the curved or indented portions of land. Among these, those which are nearly surrounded by land are called seas, inland seas, bays, gulfs, and ports. Narrow bodies of water which connect two oceans are called straits. The areas close to coasts are referred to as coastal waters.

The classifications stated above may seem clear at first but, again, upon more careful scrutiny, they are found to be ambiguous. For purposes of scientific study, water is divided into two major categories based on the state of its surface. Under this classification, sea water is regarded as static like that of lakes and is distinguished from the constantly flowing water of rivers. Waves and currents of sea water are interpreted as movements limited within a given range and not regarded as dynamic.

This classification gives a somewhat structured picture of water. However, for our purposes, other types of classification that can better reflect the actual state of water will be useful. Thus, we will employ the following three criteria for distinguishing types of water:

Distinctions based on the dynamic/static nature of the water surface:

- ◆ mobile water: water that flows constantly in a specific direction—rivers
- ◆ immobile water: water that is static as a whole, despite limited movements—seas, lakes

Distinctions based on forms of relations with land:

- ◆ land water: isolated or nearly isolated waters on land—lakes, rivers.
- ◆ sea water: water that surrounds continents—oceans

Distinctions based on distance from land—definition of territorial waters:

- ◆ inshore
- ◆ deep sea

Chapter 6

Islands

Characteristics of Islands

Islands and Climate

The major factor affecting the lives of the inhabitants of islands is their peculiar climate. Some islands are distant from any of the continents, others are close to one. In either case the influence of the sea reaches all areas of the land, resulting in changeable climates, but not extreme ones. Changes in climate and temperatures are moderate compared with continental land areas. In general, the topography of islands is complicated and there is a greater variety of life forms than on a continent.

Benefits of Islands

There are special benefits of islands and island countries with regard to human habitation. Most islands which are big enough to form countries are well suited for humans to live in. This can be seen if we compare our own island country with our neighboring continental countries. The seasonal changes in climate and moderate temperatures in Japan permit a comfortable life style and are conducive to good health. The large variety of animal and plant life enables us to live well without over-dependence for resources on foreign countries.

The Mentality of Islanders

For the above reasons, Japan and Britain have developed dense populations. Land areas such as these island countries are not only well-suited to material development but to mental development as well. Changeable, moderate climates stimulate people and foster mental development. The British people, for example, received cultural influences from the European continent, but as a people they soon surpassed the source of that influence. The same thing can be seen in Japan, which learned and accepted many things from the continental cultures of both Europe and Asia. Continental countries, on the other hand, seem to accept external cultural influences much less readily.

Again, island people tend to be characterized by strong patriotism and work together to fight against encroaching enemies. We are proud of this mentality and continental nations respect it. Diplomatic relations in the history of our empire are based on this lofty patriotism. Islands in general have fewer internal differences and divisions to deal with than continental peoples, and unity comes easier. This is perhaps understandable because unless islanders succeed in driving away their enemies they are doomed because there is no possibility of escape to other land areas as there is on continents. Such realities as these influence the mental development of island people.

At the same time, these very strengths which are associated with island living contribute to the weakness of insularism, which is also a pronounced characteristic of islanders. Island people tend to be narrow-minded, arrogant, content with small successes, not overly generous, and with tendencies to act in isolation. Patriotism is in evidence at times when there is threat of an enemy, but once the danger is gone, people fall into quarreling with each other and are slow to unite in the interests of achieving long-range goals. This can be seen in our daily lives, particularly on some of the smaller, isolated islands.

Then again, seas act as barriers for underdeveloped peoples, so it is not surprising that islands are often backward and underdeveloped. Their ideas and thoughts are narrow because their range of experience is narrow. But since island living is conducive to human material and mental development, although islanders are slow to be stimulated at first, they will develop quickly once they awake, as the cases of Japan and Britain illustrate. So these negative characteristics should not be considered as inevitable or permanent.

Fortunately, the seas have now become a vital means of transportation for developed peoples. Thus, once island inhabitants reach a level of development at which they can utilize these means and interact with more developed peoples, their range of experience will become wider, the passive patriotism will become progressive, and the country will become a world-power, such as Britain has. Britain surpasses other civilized countries thanks to being an island.

Kinds of Islands

Classification by Origin

Islands can be classified into two main divisions: continental islands and oceanic islands. Continental islands were once a part of a continent before becoming separated by erosion or volcanic upheaval or depression. Britain, Japan, and most East Asian Islands are good examples of continental islands. These islands are separated from their adjacent continental land masses by shallow seas and steep sloping shores facing the ocean.

Oceanic islands, on the other hand, are not related to continents in any way. These island have their origins in ocean bottom volcanic eruptions, residue of old continents, or deposits of dead sea coral. There are many examples of oceanic islands in the South Pacific.

For purposes of classification, Borneo, Celebes, and New Guinea seem to be continental islands, but they are actually formed by residues of an old continent from the standpoint of the structure of mountains and seas around them. Coral islands have been formed in many peculiar shapes and rise just above sea level. There are more than 670 coral islands in the Pacific Ocean. Volcanic islands, such as those which make up the Kuriles, usually form a chain of islands in the form of an arc.

Classification by Location

Here again it is useful to divide islands into two types which are roughly parallel to the continental-oceanic classification; that is, isolated islands and continent-related islands. Our interest in this case, however, is with the extent of influence of continental land masses on an island. Darwin wrote, for example, that on islands more than 480 kilometers from a continent, there are no mammals which walk on land. The Falkland Islands, which are 450 kilometers from South America, do have mammals because icebergs floated to the Falklands in ancient times.

Life forms on isolated islands tend to be unique and their climate is not affected by continental land masses. The human inhabitants of isolated islands were cut off from the cultural and political life which developed on the continents until the late 15th century, when ocean navigation developed. The Kingdom of Hawaii and some of the other Pacific islands are good examples. Now, however, only traces of these original island cultures remain and this kind of cultural uniqueness of isolated islands is no longer useful for purposes of classification. The climatic difference between isolated and continent-related islands, on the other hand, is a permanent difference.

The role of isolated islands as places of refuge, rest, storage for water and coal, etc., has become important as world trade has developed. For this reason most of the Pacific islands have now (1900 A.D.) been occupied by European countries. The value of these islands will greatly increase after the Panama or Nicaragua Canal is built. We Japanese must be very careful in this regard.

Continent-related islands, as has been suggested earlier, have close relationships with adjacent continents both with respect to climate and culture, as can be seen in the cases of Japan and Britain. In Japan, for example, the temperature fluctuation between day and night and between summer and winter is much greater than in isolated islands of the same latitude because of the influence of the Asian Continent. And since the climate is more closely related, it is natural to find similar ties in plant and animal life also.

When we study a map of the world carefully, what seem to be some general rules or regularities concerning distribution of islands become apparent. First, note that there is a big island close to the east coast of each continent: Japan to Asia, New Zealand to Australia, Madagascar to Africa, Newfoundland to North America, the Falkland Islands to South America. Second, there are island chains to the east of the seas separating large continents: the East Indies (Indonesia) between Asia and Australia, the West Indies (Caribbean) between North and South America. And, though less clearly an example of islands in this category, Crete and the other smaller islands of the Aegean Sea between Eurasia and Africa.

We can observe, further, that small islands near a large island tend to have the same relationship to the large island as continental islands have to continents. The influence on the climate of the small island is not as great, but the small island tends to be subject to the main island in matters of politics, and sometimes it is very important in national defense.

Islands in Lakes and Rivers

Islands in lakes create picturesque scenery by adding variety to otherwise placid stretches of water. Islands in rivers, in contrast, are in most cases built up from silt and sand carried by river currents and are not very scenic in most cases. On the other hand, islands at the lower ends of major rivers usually have large cities spring up on them because water transportation is convenient and the soil is very rich. A further observation which can be made in regard to these island cities at the lower end of large rivers is that surrounding water serves as a natural defense against enemies, thus they are often chosen as locations for castles or fortresses. In time some of these island cities become capitals or district centers. Deltas are good examples of this.

The Role of Islands In Trade and Military Campaigns

Islands have played an important role in the development of trade and as military installations for extending national influence. St. Lawrence Island in the Bering Strait has been an important trading point for the natives of North America and North Asia. Hawaii is still an important relay station between America and Asia. And it is natural that some islands in strategic locations have become battlefields. Sicily, for example, between Europe and Africa, has repeatedly been at the center of armed conflict between contending powers. Strategically located islands have served one or both of these purposes. Singapore is another example of the former and Malta the latter. The British undoubtedly expected that Hong Kong could serve as both, but it is probably a little too far south to serve an effective military function.

At any rate, the location of certain islands makes them convenient staging areas from which a foreign power can invade nearby political entities. Boko Island, in the Ponfu Archipelago, provided a convenient point from which Japan was able to invade Taiwan[1] and South China. If there had been a good port big enough for thousands of ships to anchor in North Kyushu in 1281, 100,000 Mongolian invaders probably would not have drowned in the typhoon which saved Japan from invasion in that year. In short, to the extent that small continental islands or small islands adjacent to larger islands provide good footing for foreign invaders, they have a special value and play a special role in military affairs.

A list of the world's important islands would include Hawaii, Hong Kong, Singapore, Ceylon, and Malta in the Mediterranean Sea. All of these, it should be noted, with the exception of Hawaii, are British territories. In the near future, when the Panama Canal is opened, the Galapagos Islands will increase greatly in importance. British politicians are already eyeing them greedily.

Another interesting point in regard to the historical role of some islands is the part they have played in providing refuge or places of exile for failed political or military heroes. Teiseiko[2] fled to Taiwan, Napoleon was exiled to St. Helena, and several Japanese Emperors were exiled to Oki island. Thus, islands can serve as refuges or jails. Sakhalin and Siberia, for example, still serve as places of exile for unfortunates in Russia. These historical experiences of certain islands can often be seen reflected in the characters and customs of the inhabitants.

Islands and Islanders In the Modern Age

The features and characteristics of islands which we have been discussing stem from the fact of their separation from other countries. In our time, however, with the development of water transportation, the former barriers of space have been removed, greatly diminishing the protection formerly provided by space and separation, often at the expense of the well-being of the island's native inhabitants. Now most island countries have lost their independence. For example, Hawaii lost its independence earlier than smaller continental countries. Japan was also in danger of exploitation when it was opened to the world in the middle of the 19th century.

But perhaps this observation is too pessimistic. When we try to look at this matter in a more optimistic framework, the dangers to small island populations may turn out to be blessings. Once islanders are awakened, the stimulus will make them active and then the water around them will become a very convenient medium for transportation. Then, too, some island countries have been able to grasp the command of the sea and become natural leaders. So whether their natural locations become a source of their success or the cause of their decline depends to a very great extent on the peoples' consciousness.

Notes

[1] Taiwan was renamed "Formosa" by the Portuguese in 1590. After World War II, it reverted to the old name under the Kuomintang Chinese who dominated the island following their flight from Communist Chinese forces on the Chinese mainland.

[2] Teiseiko (1624-1662 A.D.) was a surviving retainer of the Ming Dynasty in China. He fought unsuccessfully against the Ching Dynasty in an effort to restore the Ming to power.

Chapter 7

Peninsulas and Capes

The Character and Origin of Peninsulas

The importance of peninsulas in human affairs is illustrated by the fact that modern European civilization had its origin in the peninsulas of Greece and Italy. For this reason, scholars have been particularly interested in the role of peninsulas throughout history.

Peninsulas face seas on three sides and they are connected to a continental mainland by narrow strips of land on the fourth. Peninsulas are formed in various ways. Some are formed by the uprising of land areas between islands and mainlands such as the Shantung Peninsula in China. Others are formed by the accumulation of soil between an island and a nearby continental land mass. Still others are formed by the erupting of volcanoes.

It often happens that the peninsula has very little relationship with its mainland and develops characteristics very similar to those of islands. For example, there is the Corinth Peninsula, which is attached to Greece by a very narrow strip of land, and the Arabian Peninsula, which is isolated by a desert. There are many others which are isolated by rivers, lakes, or swamps. The Korean Peninsula is separated from the mainland by a range of mountains, giving it time to develop an independent culture.

These peninsulas had opportunities to develop independently, but their aloofness usually did not last as long as for islands isolated by seas. As mainland civilization developed, peninsular barriers became negligible, and the peninsulas gradually lost their unique characteristics and separate cultural identities. This quasi island nature is reflected in the Japanese term for peninsulas which means "half island."

Penninsulas and Civilizations

There are numerous examples throughout history in which a peninsula has been a factor in the rise of a particular civilization. I have previously noted the rise of the Greek and Roman civilizations. Other examples which could be cited are the rise of Christianity in the Arabian Peninsula, Buddhism in the Indian Peninsula, and Confucianism in the Shantung Peninsula in China. Perhaps these are merely coincidences, but there may be some common principles at work here.

One thing that is well documented is the role of the Korean Peninsula in the transmission of Chinese culture to surrounding areas. Similarly, Greece and Italy have served as transmitters of civilizations from Asia and Africa and then provided the stage in which they could develop into new forms. Asian civilizations went through a peninsula, Asia Minor, to Greece, and European civilization spread to the Western Hemisphere as a result of the voyages of Columbus, who was supported by Spain on the Iberian Peninsula. This cultural transmission role of peninsulas can be seen to have been involved in all of these cases.

In the days before water transportation had developed, different civilizations arose in different land areas which were separated from each other by seas. Later, as they came into contact and began to form new civilizations, it was natural for them to gravitate toward peninsulas as they sought sea access and the shortest possible sea routes. Moreover, peninsulas that jut into oceans are close to ocean currents which has resulted in accidental immigrants landing on their shores from time to time, thus creating serendipitous intercultural contact. To the extent that the peninsula remained aloof from the mainland culture, it offered the opportunity for the traits and characteristics of the new culture to take root.

In summary, then, continents can be perceived in a general way as birthplaces of cultures and civilizations, peninsulas as transmitters of culture, and islands as arenas in which cultures meet and intermix. This is borne out by

> ...continents can be perceived in a general way as birthplaces of cultures and civilizations, peninusulas as transmitters of culture, and islands as arenas in which cultures meet and intermix.... Japanese history has changed as a result of the role of peninsulas as transmitters of culture.

Shiga's observation that Latin culture came to us from the Iberian Peninsula and North European culture came from Flanders to the west coast of Kyushu, which has the most peninsulas in Japan. Later, in the 19th century, Anglo-Saxon culture came to the Miura Peninsula and the Izu Peninsula. Japanese history was changed as a result of the role of these peninsulas as transmitters of culture.

The Destiny of Peninsulas

The Asian and European continents each have three peninsulas on their southern coasts. Indochina, India, Arabia in Asia, and the Balkans, Italy and the Iberian Peninsula in Europe. In general, most peninsulas are located toward the south of their attached mainlands. This tendency may have something to do with the fact that civilizations have arisen in lower latitudes and then spread into higher latitude areas.

Now, what can be said about the fate of peninsular countries such as Greece and Rome, where civilization flourished 2,000 years ago? Likewise, India and Arabia are names of great civilizations, but only in history. Are there any laws which govern the destinies of peninsular countries? They seem to have prospered early in their history and declined as soon as they had transmitted their civilizations to other areas, whereas island countries are progressing steadily toward the future.

A major difference between islands and peninsulas stems from the fact that the mountains, lakes, or deserts that separate mainland and peninsula are the kind of topographical features that are effective initially in keeping primitive mainland groups out while the peninsular culture is growing stronger. But when the peninsular countries become rich, the motivation of neighboring tribes and nations to invade them increases. It is perhaps an irony of history that peninsular peoples, who for long periods were provided protection from invasion by topographical barriers, should be destroyed because they had become too lax in matters related to self-defense.

At any rate, we can observe this general pattern in the history of peninsulas: as centers of culture arose on continental mainlands, the mission of their peninsulas was over and they soon declined. Island countries must be careful not to fall into the same destiny, for the sea, once a protective barrier, is now a very convenient passage.

Capes

Capes have been of historical significance as landmarks for ship navigation. The names given capes often reflect their historical connection with specific explorers or voyages. Capes also serve as dividing points between seas and oceans. But aside from these characteristics, capes have been of only minor importance in human affairs, although they do influence the directions of currents and the distribution of fish.

Chapter 8

Land Features:
Isthmuses, Mountains and Valleys, Plains

Isthmuses

Isthmuses as Land Bridges

Narrow strips of land connecting two larger land masses and bringing two bodies of water into close proximity with each other are called isthmuses. The waters involved can be oceans, lakes, or rivers. Water transportation being more convenient than by land, isthmuses tend to serve as bridges between two bodies of water. This often leads to the development of large cities on isthmuses.

More precisely, cities will rise at the extremities of these land bridges, at the ends where land is closest to land. For example, the isthmus between the Adriatic Sea and the Danube River is narrowest at Vienna. The one between the Seine and the Loire is narrowest at Paris and Orleans. Nuremberg is between the uppermost points of the Danube and the Main. Leipzig is between the Main and Elbe, Innsbruck the Danube and the Adige, and Aleppo the Euphrates and the Mediterranean Sea.

Modern Uses of Isthmuses

With up to date earth moving equipment it is now possible to construct canals or boat-carrying railways at isthmuses. The development of quick, cheap means of transporting goods across isthmuses is important for modern travel and trade, not only for shortening water shipping distances but also for saving the cost and the trouble of loading and unloading cargo. The construction of canals is the best way to accomplish this, but it is difficult and costly, especially when there are hard rocks or other obstacles to contend with. The problems and cost of building canals has led to the development of railways to carry boats filled with cargo across isthmuses, such as the Tijuana-Tepek railway in Mexico and the one built across the narrow neck of Nova Scotia. But these tend to be makeshift arrangements and there are now further efforts being made to construct canals in such cases.

The convenience and advantages of canals which have been built in recent years have been clearly demonstrated. The Suez Canal, the largest canal built up to the present time, reduces the distance between London and Japan by 3000 sea miles. Plans have been considered for a canal through Nicaragua for some time, but more recently there have been reports that a decision has been made by the United States to make a second attempt to construct a canal across the Isthmus of Panama. A Panama Canal would be approximately one-third the length of a canal through Nicaragua.

It is reported that the United States will lease a strip of land six miles wide along the canal and will have police power in the canal territory. The United States' first attempt to build the canal twenty years ago failed because of inadequate budgeting, but this time it will likely succeed in constructing the canal. When it is finished, the Panama Canal will shorten the distance between New York and Japan by about 6000 sea miles, and relations between the East Coast of America and Eastern Asia will become closer.

Mountains and Valleys

Mountains and Culture
   It has been said that the length of coastline is a measure of the level of development of civilizations; the more irregular, the better. The same can be said in regard to the complexity of the topography of an area. By forming valleys and adding to the complexity of terrain, mountains greatly affect the development of culture.

Since in Japan much of the country consists of rugged mountains and hills, it is natural that mountains have an especially close relationship to our lives. Whenever we look up, the mountains are there: an integral part of our world, friends. As children we grow up in the shadows of the mountains and come to love them almost as we love our parents. Their presence grows within our minds and deeply affects our lives and personalities, unconsciously. So we can say that the mountains educate us and contribute to the kinds of persons we become.

Let us take Switzerland, another mountainous country, as an example of the influence of mountains on human life. Switzerland was the birth place of European liberalism and of many great people. Some of the world's foremost educational reformers, such as Pestalozzi, Agassiz, and Herbart, were born and grew up in Switzerland in the shadow of the Swiss Alps.

First among the many things which contribute to our lives and enrich us is the indescribable beauty of the mountains, and we Japanese find special beauty in their shapes. We can find mountain summits, for example, in the shape of domes, cones, tables, or bowls which reveal much about their origins. Some summits were formed by volcanic rock. These usually have a round crater at the top but often the wall of the crater will be found to have collapsed, giving rise to some bizarre or unusual formations. In some cases, there is another small cone rising from the summit of the mountain. Japanese people often name mountains after their shapes. Thus, we have a Mt. Sword, a Mt. Fine Sword, a Mt. Spear, and a Mt. Horse. Snow adds beauty to mountains so it should come as no surprise that we also have a Mt. White. It is understandable that artists and poets and writers find so much inspiration for their work among the mountains.

At the same time, the same tendencies toward insular and provincial outlook which are often found in island countries can be found in mountainous districts as well. Mountainous areas tend to be isolated, slow to develop, and to tenaciously hold on to old ways. Mountain people can be jealous, exclusive, and quick to quarrel with one another.

We must admit that this tendency toward insularism still remains in Japan. Japan is an island country and a mountainous one, both characteristics which encourage a narrow kind of patriotism. We Japanese need to consider how we can become a more generous and open-minded people.

The Height of Mountains

The influence of mountains on human life varies depending on their height, so their naming often include some reference to altitude. In general, mountains below 500 meters are called "hills," those between 500 meters and 2,500 meters are "middle mountains," and those above 2,500 meters are "high mountains." The higher a mountain is, the more difficult it is for people to travel. Subject to gravity, we must exert greater effort in going upward than in going horizontally, and most of us prefer taking a longer way around than climbing upward.

As mentioned previously, mountains have served throughout most of human history as one of the natural barriers which separated and isolated cultural groups and societies from each other. In Asia, the Himalayas separating the Indian and Chinese peoples permitted each to develop independently. Obstacles to travel posed by mountainous terrain have often provided the opportunity for smaller groups to develop their own civilization without being suppressed by larger and more powerful groups. In modern times, advances in travel and the exploits of mountain climbers and explorers have served to lessen the isolating effect of mountains, yet they are still important as we see from the fact that most of the borders between countries are formed by mountains.

Mountains enrich the variety of plants and animal life in a country. High mountains can literally be regarded as botanical gardens because their plant life ranges from plants which require a tropical climate to those which thrive in frigid zones. This same wide variation in types of animal life can be found on mountains as well. Japan, for example, thanks to its mountains, has many kinds of trees, such as cedar, Japanese cypress, and various needle leaf trees which grow at high altitudes. In some mountainous districts of Japan, one can sometimes see the incongruous sight of monkeys huddling together under bamboo trees bent low by the weight of the snow. Bamboo and monkeys, both of which originated in the tropics, living together with snow! Such a sight could not be imagined in a mountainless country of plains and prairies.

The height of mountains also has a great influence on the rivers of a country. We can think of mountains as giving birth to rivers. When humid air containing vapor from the seas strikes against mountains, it rises along their sides. The higher up it goes, the cooler it becomes. As the air cools, its saturation point goes down with the result that the vapor turns into clouds, fog, rain, or snow and, falling to the ground, becomes the source of a river. So the higher mountains are, the richer will be the sources which feed the rivers. Most of the big, rich rivers have their sources in high mountains.

Mountains cause vapor to condense and their ridges divide the precipitation when it falls, just like a peaked roof. So the ridges are called watersheds. Water erodes the sides of mountains, carries soil to the plains, and transforms the land. Mountains provide the framework for the land and its topography depends on them. Unfortunately, most books on geography explain general topography first, then try to relate mountains and rivers to that concept. This is contrary to the natural phenomena and the explanation tends to be arbitrary and dogmatic. If we really desire to understand the geography of a region, we should first study its topography on a map and notice the directions of mountains and rivers. Then we can create the features of the land as an image in our minds.

Plains

Plains and Human Life
    Most of us live out our lives on plains; it is on plains that villages and cities arise, and where the struggle for existence is most severe. Plains, offering greater certainty in matters of productivity than any other type of topography, are the most important places on earth for humans; mountains may be left for trees and animals and snakes. Plains are for growing of grains, vegetables, and domesticated animals. So in general the mountains are left as forests and plains are used for agricultural enterprises.
    Some mountains and seas are, as we know, highly productive mining and fishing grounds. But as important as these are, they are usually too unstable to provide a secure basis for our lives. Farmers, on the other hand, barring natural disaster, can produce crops with much more certainty, so agriculture is much more reliable than mining or fishing as a means of living.
    In contrast to mountains, plains are relatively convenient for travel. Thus, there is more movement of people and goods in plains areas. In contrast to the exclusivity of mountain people, plains people tend to live in cooperation and rely on one another. Plains throw people together in the hustle and bustle of the world, making some degree of limitation and restriction of individual freedom inevitable.
    Plains can be classified into three main types: valleys, coastal plains, and dry heights. In the following discussions, I will use "plains" to refer to valleys and coastal plains and "heights" to designate plains which are located on dry heights.
    Plains encourage the pursuit of knowledge and openness to new ideas. Shiga once observed that people who live in plains are smart, generous, and practical and will become the pioneers of civilization. But "smartness" can sometimes be frivolous and effeminate. The easier life which plains make possible can result in people's becoming greedy and accustomed to luxurious living. Thus, the strengths and weaknesses of plains people are the opposite of those of mountain people.
    Again, in plains there are few natural barriers to race, thought, and culture. This is conducive to a high degree of social unity. This

same tendency can be seen in the fact that plains encourage the rise of ownership of large tracts of land and large countries. China, for example, has maintained its unity in race, thought, and culture primarily because of its plains topography. Germany and the United States have grown into federations encompassing vast territories. Russia is a massive empire, and Brazil occupies so much land area in unstable South America for the same reason. On the other hand, plains are conducive to the collapse of empire as well. Once the unity that a strong leader has built up on a plain begins to crumble, we can see the cultural equivalent of a massive river flood. The history of China's twenty-two dynasties clearly illustrates this.

Due to their relationship to low-land plains, mountains, and prevailing winds, heights have very limited precipitation. In some heights areas there is sufficient rainfall to enable dry-land grasses and shrubs to grow, providing temporary grazing for such livestock as cattle, sheep, goats, horses, and camels. But when the grass and plants have been nibbled away, the people must move their livestock on to new grazing areas. Thus, nomadism is the most common style of life on heights.

Heights and Social Organization
The tenuous relationship between lands and people in nomadic lands makes it impossible for stable societies to form. The only basis upon which a society can develop in such situations is lineage. The result is a society divided into many families or clans which are continuously struggling with each other. This is perhaps why the people who live on these high, dry plains are quick to resort to violence rather than depend on intellect. Shiga characterizes people on heights as cruel and ferocious, who will plunder indiscriminately because they are poor, while plains people tend to be gentle, intelligent, and practical. Though people on heights welcome guests in peacetime, they often invade low-land plains countries which are rich and filled with natural benefits. Then they will plunder or massacre without hesitation, like a flood overrunning the land.

The Persians, Afghans, Huns, Turks, and Mongols originally lived on heights in Central Asia. In time each overran richer lowland plains cultures, leading to the establishment of Persia, Afghanistan, Hungary, Turkey, and some of the Chinese dynasties. The Mongols in the 13th century and the tribes led by Timur in the 14th century are good examples of the latter.

Deserts

High plains where there is little or no rainfall and few plants become deserts. Deserts tend to form in continental heartlands. Some of the largest are up to one hundred miles across and are generally considered to be not only useless but also obstacles to land transportation. On the other hand, nature has given us camels, equipped with the ability to go for as long as thirteen days without water or food. So perhaps we do not need to abandon deserts as totally useless.

At any rate, there is one rather remarkable point we can note about deserts, possibly a coincidence: three out of five of the birthplaces of the major ancient civilizations are on rivers running between deserts. The Nile, between the Sahara and the Arabian Deserts, the Tigris and Euphrates, between the Arabian and Persian Deserts, and the Amudarya running through the Turkestan Desert.

One of the interesting aspects of deserts is the desert caravan which uses camels, "ships of the desert," for travel and transportation of goods. Though camels can endure thirst, carry loads weighing from 150 to 200 kilograms, and walk 25 to 30 kilometers a day, they are inconvenient when compared with real ships. It takes more then 3 months to cross the Sahara from Central Sudan to the Mediterranean, even by the shortest possible route.

There are other problems with caravan travel, also. Gangs of robbers, similar to the pirates which attack ships at sea, are a constant threat, forcing the merchants and others who make up the caravan to carry rifles, pistols, or swords to protect themselves. And then there are sandstorms which bury caravans just as ships sink into the sea. The markers they depend on for direction can become covered with sand or even buried completely, causing caravans to lose their way in the vast desert.

In the Sahara and Arabian Deserts, there are oases which are fed by underground sources of water. In these oases, plants, particularly dates, can grow and people can live. In some cases the underground water supply is abundant enough for irrigation wells to be constructed, making possible a larger area of cultivated land.

In the future, if we can develop the ability to make rain fall or find some other means of irrigating desert areas, people will be able to live in former deserts. For example, in Algeria, French technologists have dug many wells since the French occupation of the country. This has enabled the native peoples to get water and cultivate what once was desert. The people there call it "water of God". Since the French

68 A Geography of Human Life

have made possible these great achievements, perhaps such ideas as bringing water from the ocean, creating vapor to make it rain, and turning deserts into rich, inhabitable lands may be more than illusions. In short, we can look forward to greater utilization of deserts in the future.

Chapter 9

Rivers

The Role of Rivers in Human Life

A populated area is a watered area. Big rivers foster big cities, streams give birth to villages. Prosperity depends on how much water flows. We can learn these elementary insights while strolling along any of the streams that run through our communities.

A river is defined as water which takes a definite course across the land. Rivers are to the land what blood vessels are to the human body: thanks to its rivers, the land can function and come alive. Lack of water makes a desert of the land; unwatered land is comparable to a paralyzed human body. It is when land is vitalized by an abundant supply of water and an efficient water system that human beings can lead a normal, healthy, and happy social life.

Water systems consist of the various streams or branches which flow from mountains, hills, and underground springs. As we row along a river we can see how these many branches join, form larger streams and, finally, flow together to form a mighty river. Again, such a water system can be compared to a large tree which consists of leaves, branches of many different sizes and shapes, and a trunk.

Just as a water system consists of all of its streams and tributaries, a drainage system includes all of the land area irrigated and vitalized by the river and branches that compose the water system. Water systems can teach us a valuable lesson applicable to all of our human affairs: when the power of many small efforts are joined together in a unified system, great power becomes available.

Length, Width, and Depth of Rivers

Whether or not a particular river can be used as a means of transport depends upon the balance of three factors, that is, its length, width, and depth. While these factors are interwoven and interconnected with each other, I will deal with them separately here as a matter of convenience. The ultimate value of a river in terms of its suitability for navigation depends very largely on its length, whereas width is least important in regard to transport. There are few ships which would be unable to navigate a river if the river is deep enough.

Therefore, we can say that depth is the key element which determines a river's potential for ship navigation, but the depth of a river is in turn related to its length. Experience gained through use of the Suez Canal provides criterion as to the depth required for ocean-going ships. The canal is nine meters in depth, enough for any vessels presently in use. As progress in shipbuilding leads to the construction of larger vessels, the future usefulness of the canal may depend on more depth.

In Japan, most of the land area consists of mountain ranges, and rain falls along the steep slopes. Such geographical features cannot produce long rivers. Accordingly, Japan has no rivers which are deep enough for navigation by ocean liners. There are, however, some rivers in the world which can accommodate ocean liners. For example, the Yangtze in China is 5,900 km long. At Hankou, 1,300 km above the river's mouth, a ship drawing 20 feet of water can float. A 600 ton steamship drawing 5 feet of water can float up to 1,850 km above the mouth. Navigation is possible even further upstream, though the river has some rapids.

The Yangtze has eight harbors. The total length of the river, including all of its branches is 22,220 kilometers, which is equal to half the circumference of the earth. Its drainage area covers four and a half times as much land area as the whole of Japan, a vast expanse perhaps beyond Japanese people's imagination.

The most useful rivers have two characteristics: a large volume of water and a steady amount of water. An examination of the Minato River (in Kobe City) can help us to appreciate the significance and interrelationship of these two features. The Minato River usually has little water. Several times throughout the year, the riverbed is visible, with only a little water remaining in puddles among the gravel. When it rains, however, rushing torrents overflow and erode the river banks and damage cropland. Flood-prone rivers of this kind are especially common in cases of rivers whose headwaters are in areas which have been recklessly deforested. In such cases, quantity of water and variations in quantity are influenced by the state of the river's source, the number of its branches, the volume of rainfall, the nature of the soil, and the quantity of vapor heated by the air. All these features are important when we consider the relationship between river systems and human beings.

While length and depth contribute to a river's value for transportation, the width of rivers tends to be a risky and inconvenient impediment for people and animals who must cross the river. Thus, streams are bridged and ferries established. We have invented floating bridges and pontoon bridges and invested in gigantic iron bridges. Means of coping with the obstacles posed by the breadth of rivers have various social, economic, and other repercussions. For example, several roads may converge on a single bridge, detouring considerable distances in some cases. Similarly, cities often grow up around bridges.

Moreover, from ancient times, many decisive battles were won or lost at riversides, and castles were often built at riversides or in areas isolated by water. The advantage of the flow of water of a river and the disadvantage of width are opposed to each other and in inverse relation. A larger river is more convenient for water-borne traffic, but more inconvenient when it comes to crossing it. Facilities designed to overcome the disadvantage of width conflict with transport along the river. In other words, bridges impede river navigation. We can often see cases in Europe in which the use of steamships is hindered by the prevalence of bridges. At Antwerp, in Belgium, a plan to overcome this problem was devised by building a bridge which enables passage across the river but also provides for ship navigation as well. This is accomplished by building a set of girders into the bridge which spring up to permit a ship to pass below.

The Rate of Flow of Rivers

Rivers can also be classified according to how fast the water flows. They can range from rushing torrents to slow, gentle currents flowing sluggishly to the sea. The value and utility of rivers in human terms vary according to their speed and rate of flow. Some rivers have rapids at their head but are slow and sluggish at the end. In Japan, the Tenryu, the Imizu and the Kuma, known as the "Three Rapids," represent this kind of river. The Yodo, the Tone, and the Kitakami are also relatively slow. Small steamships can travel on these rivers.

Several factors affect the speed of river currents:

The Degree of Incline
It goes without saying that speed increases in proportion to the steepness of the slope. As the incline becomes steeper, the river becomes a rapid stream, a torrent, or a waterfall when the degree becomes a right angle.

The Degree of Bending and Twisting
When going down a sharp incline, one spirals down to counteract the steepness of the slope. Similarly, the bending and twisting of a river serve to increase its length, decrease the degree of inclination, and reduce the crest. As a result, the speed of the river is decreased.

The Condition of the River Bed
In most rivers, the speed of the current in the middle of the river is different from that near the bank. Even an unskilled swimmer can swim against the current near the bank, but in the center of the river one can only swim with the current. The reason it is easy to swim against the current near the bank can be explained by the friction of the water and the land. Friction is also the explanation for another phenomenon, the fact that rate of flow is much slower at the bottom of a river near the riverbed than at the surface. Because friction with the riverbed decreases the rate of flow, the condition of the riverbed, that is, whether it is hard or soft, even or uneven, influences the speed of river currents.

The Volume of Water and the Width of the River
The volume of water influences speed as well. As the amount increases, the center of the stream is farther from the riverbed and subject to less friction. Increase in volume also causes increase in pressure. And the greater the volume, the greater will be the rate of flow, other things being equal. Moreover, as we would expect, a narrow river flows faster than a wide one which has the same volume of water.

Among all these factors, inclination is the most important. The inclination determines whether or not a river can be utilized as a means of transportation. According to some studies, an inclination which has a vertical/horizontal ratio of more than one to two hundred makes transportation impossible.

The Thames River in England is one of the most valuable rivers as far as human beings are concerned. Its total length is 346 km, which is shorter than the length of the Shinano or the Ishikari rivers in Japan. The Thames, however, has produced big cities, and can accommodate the passage of many ships and cargo. This is because of the quantity of water and the rate of flow. The inclination of the Thames is 30 meters over its total length and it flows at the rate of 83 km per hour.

The Direction of Rivers

The utilization of rivers for human purposes varies according to the direction of the flow. In this connection, rivers may be described as vertical or parallel. The difference between a vertical river and a parallel river is that a vertical river traverses a mountain or mountain range while a parallel river flows parallel to mountains. Vertical rivers are more valuable for our purposes than parallel rivers. Whereas the parallel river runs through one climatic zone, the vertical river runs through plural climatic zones. In one climatic zone, the distribution of plants and animals is limited. Thus, in the case of a parallel river, few products can be exchanged. A vertical river, on the other hand, because it runs through multiple climatic zones, has potential for distribution of many kinds of plants and animals. Examples of a vertical river are the Nile in Africa and the big rivers in North and South America. The Yangtze and the Yellow Rivers in Asia are examples of a parallel river.

The Parts of a River

Let me comment briefly on rivers as a process, in terms of the movement of water. Rivers may be divided roughly into three parts: the upper river or its headwaters, the lower river or mouth, and the river itself, the middle river. In viewing a river as a process, the totality of the river must be taken into account, each part playing its own unique role in the life of the river. Setsudo Saito gives a vivid description of river process in his book, *A Record of Moving Down the Kiso River*. He traveled from Fushimi to Kuwana, a distance of some 78 km, departing in the morning and arriving at Kuwana before dark. Following are notes which he made during the trip:

> The current is strong and the boat is gliding rapidly downstream. The ridges of the mountains seem to tremble as we pass them, one after another. The scene before me immediately flits by and is left behind. I have the sensation that the shore is racing and the mountains are

rushing by. I feel as though I am not moving at all, and it is my surroundings which are moving. When the boat goes near the rocks, waves arise, the boat swirls around, and the spray wets our clothes.

Here Saito describes his experience at the upper reaches of the Kiso River. He makes only one reference to the middle portion of the river: "I have left the gorge, and the Inuyama Castle is emerging on the mountain in the distance." In regard to the view of the lower river, he writes:

> The river here widens, and the speed of the current slows. I have left the mountain slopes far behind and there are no scenes here to attract the eye. I lie with my head on a straw mat, and I can feel the boat moving slowly against the wind. The boatman is rowing with all his strength, and the constant grating and squeaking of the oars against the boat are irritating.

Here, in the short span of only 78 kilometers, Saito could observe all of these vastly different expressions of this marvelous river.

The Upper River

All of the characteristics and the individuality of the upper reaches of a river come from its steep slope. The shape of a stream is determined by the topography of the land area which it traverses. Freely flowing water takes the shape of ford or waterfall when it courses over steep terrain. As the water gains momentum, it hits rocks in its path with great speed, forcing its way into crevices and literally attacking the rocks. This erosive action wears away the face of the mountain, and chunks of loosened and dislodged gravel are transported to the lower parts of the stream. It is this erosive process which creates the breath-taking sights and scenes and streams which delight us and draw us back to the mountains.

In the past, the primary function served by these upper reaches of our rivers was that of inspiring artists. Recently, however, another potentially important function has become recognized. That is the utilization of water power. We have used this form of power, hydro-power, derived from the rapid flow of water over steep mountain terrain, in limited amounts since ancient times. When we go upstream in mountainous areas, we can hear the sound of waterwheels and see them grinding rice and other grains on every steep slope. Advancing more deeply into the mountains, we can still find the more primitive, original form of water power, a hydro-powered millstone.

The hydro-powered plants which have developed from these simple types of water-driven apparatuses are becoming a driving force of material civilization in the 20th century, outstripping steam power. Thus, the upper reaches of our rivers now provide human beings not only with beautiful scenery, but with seemingly unlimited power as well. Hydro-power, moreover, is potentially a far more significant and valuable source of power than coal because it is free of charge and nearly inexhaustible. It would be the height of folly to waste this precious natural resource.

Electric power generated hydraulically at the upper reaches of a river can be utilized by various industries around that area. This means a saving of human and animal power, which in turn saves costs and increases net income. Indirect as well as direct profit can be enormous. For example, the industry generated by a hydro-power plant leads to increases in land prices, wages, commodity prices, and so on. In addition, it provides new jobs for local people. There are many other benefits of hydro-electric power as well.

Our own land extends over a distance of 3,900 km from the northern tip of Hokkaido to southern Kyushu, but it is a mere 39 km to 195 km in width, east to west. Mountain ranges run along the center of this narrow archipelago for nearly its entire length, like a backbone. Immense quantities of vapor condense on both sides of the mountains and fall as rain and snow, flowing into the Pacific Ocean and the Japan Sea.

This small archipelago has 111 rivers from 20 km to 35 km in length, and 210 of 39 km or more. Since these rivers flow over very narrow, steep terrain, they become rapids or fast flowing streams. This means that the longest part of these rivers consist of their upper reaches. In fact, some have no middle or lower reaches at all. Thus, most of these rivers have great potential for hydro-electric generation.

There are other benefits which the upper reaches of rivers can provide. One is rich deposits of minerals and ore which often crop out due to erosion. In many cases, the normal geological processes of folding and upheaval involved in mountain formation push mineral deposits to the surface. However, the weathering of mountains and the action of plant cover over long periods of time makes it difficult to find these mineral and ore deposits. It is running water which uncovers these deposits and brings them to the surface. That is the reason for the prevalence of mines located at the upper reaches of large rivers.

The Middle River

When the steep terrain of the mountain is left behind and the fall of the river becomes a gentle slope, the river is much more closely related to our lives. At the upper reaches, the inclination was steep and the downward momentum of the stream was rapid enough so that the current could carry gravel along with it. Now, the slope of the river is becoming more gentle and the speed is slowed drastically. The stream can no longer carry the gravel along in suspension and it is scattered out, fan-shaped, as the river becomes wider on the flatter terrain it now passes over. The gravel, carried along under high pressure, served as a tool with which the river attacked and eroded the rocks at the upper reaches of the river. Now, however, the stream

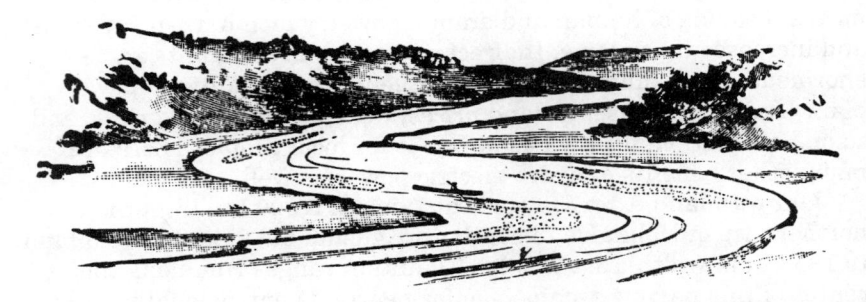

has to abandon the gravel. In other words, the river no longer has its powerful tool and is no longer able to erode the rocks in its path.

Thus, at the middle reaches, we do not find the kind of majestic scenery which the struggle between water and rocks creates at the upper reaches. As if in compensation for this loss of beauty, the action of the decelerating stream in scattering sand and gravel over a wide area of the valley increases the value of the soil for cultivation. In this way the slowing stream contributes greatly to our lives. But when the middle river is viewed from a broader perspective, it can be seen that this function of carrying and depositing sand and gravel alternates with flushing them away during periods of flooding. In other words, the stream is both constructive and destructive: the people who cultivate the land both suffer and are benefited by the action of the river. The accumulated organic soil increases the productivity of the land, but on the other hand, occasional floods damage their crops. One deluge can change the land from rich cropland to a stony riverbed.

The Lower River

After traveling through the hillsides of its middle reaches, the river flows in more gently sloping terrain as it continues its journey to the sea. The current no longer has sufficient speed or strength to erode rocks in its path or to transport gravel. Now it can carry only powdered sand and organic matter, and as it approaches the mouth of the river the current slows and this sedimentation in turn is deposited.

The Mouth of the River

In one sense, we can think of the mouth of a river as the death of the river. For at its mouth, the river flows into other bodies of water or in other ways loses its identity. There are five ways for a river to end:

(1) by flowing into other streams
(2) by emptying into a lake or marsh
(3) by being swallowed up by the land
(4) by emptying into an inland sea
(5) by flowing directly to the sea.

The value and usefulness of a river for humans is determined largely by which of these deaths applies in the case of a particular river. It goes without saying that rivers belonging to (3) are of little value. A number of inland rivers on the Asian Continent are of this type. Rivers belonging to (1) and (2) transfer their energies to the other rivers, lakes or marshes into which they flow and contribute to the usefulness of and value of those bodies of water. Rivers of type (5) are of the greatest value. For example, the great value of the Yangtze, the Rhine, the Ganges, and the Indus rivers is due to a large extent to the seas which they flow into. Rivers belonging to type (4) — the Nile, the Danube, and some of the large rivers in the eastern Eurasian Continent — have less value for transportation than the rivers of type (5) because they flow into smaller bodies of water. However, not all rivers included in type (5) are of equal value. Rivers which flow into frozen areas or tropical seas emit methane, reducing their value.

The influence of rivers on our lives varies according to shape as well as location. Rivers can be one of several different shapes at their mouths:

◆ **The Funnel-Shaped Mouth:**

The river opens out toward the sea, and forms a kind of harbor.

◆ **The Mouth with a Lagoon:**

A lagoon is formed because sand accumulation blocks the mouth. Then the stream breaks through the block and flows into the sea.

◆ **The Delta Mouth**

A delta is created at the mouth, and the mouth branches out into two or more streams across the delta.

◆ **The Ordinary Mouth**

The river flows into the sea directly. This is a common type of mouth. In many cases, the end of the river empties into the sea parallel to the shore line because of gravel and sand accumulation at the mouth.

The most useful and beneficial rivers are those which have funnel-shaped or delta mouths. Deltas tend to form at the mouths of rivers which flow into calm inland seas. As the speed of the current slows, more and more sand accumulates, forming sandbars which divide the stream into several different branches which pour into the sea. Every time a flood occurs, the sandbars become larger and larger, while the streams become narrower. A delta built up through this process contains much fertile soil consisting of the sediment which has been transported by the current from the upper reaches of the river. Moreover, the delta mouth often develops into convenient gathering points for ships from both the sea and the river. These beneficial features attract more and more people and a large city springs up. Many important cities of the world fit into this classification. Examples are Osaka, at the mouth of the Yodo River, Hiroshima, at the mouth of the Ota River, and Cairo, in Egypt, at the mouth of the Nile.

In contrast to the delta mouth, a funnel-shaped mouth tends to develop along ocean shores where the fluctuation of the tides is great and waves are high. The Rhine, the Thames, and the Amazon are examples of this kind of mouth. In these rivers the force of the tide flushes away sedimentation and erodes the soil, with the result that the mouth of the river becomes deeper and broader and is able to accommodate large ships. This is the reason why the funnel-shaped mouth makes a good port.

The Influence of Rivers on Human Life

I have considered the influence of rivers on our lives in terms of several individual factors. In actuality, however, it is all of these factors interacting together which influence human life in so many ways. Rivers provide plants with fertile soil as well as water. They provide animals with drinking water. They contribute to the transmission and dispersion of plants and animals. Salmon and trout, special products of Hokkaido, swim upstream and spawn in the headwaters of rivers. And the erosive actions of rivers uncover veins of minerals and precious metals, flush away harmful substances, and deposit layer after layer of rich top soil on the land in its watershed. These are but a few of the physical influences of rivers upon our lives.

Rivers also influence our spiritual life. Rivers are the birthplaces of ancient civilizations. Ancient Egyptian civilization, for example, grew up along the Nile. The civilization of Mesopotamia developed around the waters of the Tigris and the Euphrates. Indian civilization emerged from the Indus, ancient Chinese civilization from the Yellow River and the Yangtze, Roman civilization from the Tiber, and modern European civilization from the Rhine and the Thames.

Since ancient times, poets, painters, and other artists have found inspiration for innumerable works of art in the beauty of hills and rivers. This testifies to the strong influence of rivers in the development of our human sense of beauty. How could one live without the experience of feeling appreciation for the beautiful world around us! A drop of water hitting a stone, making an exquisite sound like the music of a koto; a stream in which the water is so clear that we can count the fish swimming in it; the reflection of a bright moon in the eastern sky shining in a lake, making the water look like rippling, melted gold; water cascading over a steep cliff, creating a breathtaking waterfall and inspiring Rai San'yo to write:

> The torrent flows like lightning, and leaves fertile soil in its wake.
> The mountain's reflection in the water is now imperfect, now perfect,
> as though the water disturbed the reflected mountains out of
> jealousy.

Just as mountains deeply influence our minds and spirits, so, too, do our rivers. But while the mountains give us impressions of height and strength and grandeur, rivers speak to us in images of patience,

> Just as mountains deeply influence our minds and spirits, so, too, do our rivers. But while the mountains give us impressions of height and strength and grandeur, rivers speak to us in images of patience, constant effort, and magnanimity. Throughout the ages poets have attempted to express the images and feelings prompted by rivers.

constant effort, and magnanimity. Throughout the ages poets have attempted to express the images and feelings prompted by rivers:

> A drop of water soon to be a part of the ocean; now it passes under a leaf.
> —Tokugawa Ieyasu

> The Ishi River; the current is so clear that the moon flows along the stream.
> —Chomei

Our spiritual life is deeply influenced by rivers. But I want to stress again how much rivers can also contribute to human purpose. Water is very pliable. Even a baby can play with it. If we dig a small ditch, water can run along the ditch as we will it to. By this principle water in a canal flows along under human control. In Japan, we have only the Tone Canal and the canal between Lake Biwa and Kyoto. But in China, Yangdi, the Sui Emperor, ordered the building of a canal 1,268 km in length. Today, that canal, including all its branches which connect the Yangtze, the Yellow River, and the Huai, is one of the longest canals in the world.

Consequences of Our Failure To Appreciate the Wonder of Rivers

There seemingly is no end to the blessings and benefits of rivers for our lives: fishing, punting on a stream, living by the side of a river, traveling leisurely down a stream, eating marine products, enjoying the beauty of the landscape formed by the rivers and the mountains. We cannot find words to express appreciation and gratitude for the wonders of rivers. I once talked with a soldier who went on an expedition to the north of China. I have never forgotten one of his comments about that experience:

> I grew up by a river. And many times as a Yamato-bushi (a samurai or Japanese soldier) I was in maneuvers in fields and mountains which were full of running water. But when we entered the vast Asian Continent, lack of water was the thing that was hardest for me to adjust to. There we found only one stream about 20 or 30 km in length. And once, after a long march, we saw an oasis, but when we

got to it, we found it was nothing but mud and sludge. This is the actual nature of North China and Manchuria. It was not until I had lived in a land with little water that I realized the worth of water.

How great should be our appreciation for the wondrous gift of rivers![1]

We should not be surprised then if, because of our failure to appreciate rivers, and our defying nature in their use, a generous Providence and the god of water are forced to teach us a lesson and wake us up. In recent years, we have experienced increasingly serious floods in our country which have taken a terrible toll in human and animal life, wasted crop land, houses and property destroyed, and people dead of hunger. Thus, while the benefits of rivers are great, the damage is also enormous. But rivers work without any intention of giving pain. If we understand the nature of rivers, we can control the power of rivers without suffering the results of their wrath. Government officials and experts are taking many measures in an effort to control flooding: river improvements, emergency plans, flood warnings, regulations, erosion control, and so on. But all of these are but temporary measures. The radical measure which we should be taking is forest conservation and preservation of trees at the heads of rivers.

In order to prevent flooding, we have to get to the root of the problem. This requires that we take into account four different origins of rivers:

Rivers Supplied by Rainfall

This type of river looks much of the time like little more than a graveled path with perhaps traces of a few pools in the riverbed. But once a heavy rain falls, a rapidly flowing stream suddenly appears which can soon become a raging torrent, overflowing its banks and destroying everything in its path. Such is a river which has its source in rainfall. The Minato River in the west part of Osaka Prefecture is this type of river. This type of river is prone to flooding and causes great damage.

Rivers Flowing from Lakes or Marshes

Examples of this type of river are the Yodo from Lake Biwa, the Tenryu from Lake Suwa, the Agano from Lake Inawashiro, and the Kushiro from Lake Kussharo. All of these rivers have their sources in lakes. Their water is generally clear, the quantity of water is relatively stable. In contrast to rivers whose source is rain water runoff, rivers of this type rarely flood.

Rivers Flowing from Snow-covered Mountain Summits

Some mountains in continental interiors are eternally capped with snow, and the snow-cap becomes a source of rivers. The Ganges and the Indus from the Himalayas, the Rhine and the Rhone from the Alps are examples.

Rivers Flowing from Springs

There is, finally, a type of river which flows constantly without depending directly on rainfall, or on being fed by lakes or marshes. These rivers have their sources in water which falls on forests and mountains in the form of rain, dew, frost, or snow. It trickles down through leaves and branches and is protected by fallen leaves, moss, and the shade of the trees. It penetrates into the soil, into crevices in rocks, and under moss and leaves. Then the water seeps out, joins with other water and becomes the source of a river.

Except for a few rivers in Toyama Prefecture which flow from snow-covered summits or lakes, most of the 300 or more rivers in Japan are of this latter type. Some of the better known examples are the Tone River in the Kanto district, the Chikugo in the Kyushu district, and the Yoshino in the Shikoku district. What is especially striking is the realization that rivers of this kind cause few floods, even under conditions of heavy rainfall. (The Minato River which I mentioned above as an example of a river having its source in rainfall, used to be of this type).

When I observe the heads of these rivers, I marvel at the work of nature. Here is the wisdom of nature visible and apparent for any sensitive and alert person to see. But what is the basis of this splendid natural phenomenon? The answer, of course, is the forest. Whether a river is a source of blessing for us or a source of suffering and disaster depends to a very great extent on the condition of the forest at its headwaters. While the wise elder statesmen of former years valued the forest, took measures to preserve it, and enabled us to receive the river's blessings, our recent, short-sighted politicians neglect it, and permit deforesting without thought. Thus do we experience the wrath of the river and suffer its revenge.

The reality which must be recognized is that deforestation changes the source of a river from springs and seepage to that of rainfall. And as noted above, when the source of a river is rainfall, a few days of dry weather invite a drought and a ten-day rain causes a flood. Moreover, when a mountain is denuded by over-logging, even one heavy rain flushes out earth and sand, levels hills, carries away fertile soil from the middle reaches to the lower reaches of the river, raising the riverbed and making embankments useless. Under these conditions, it is natural that floods occur.

Rivers and the Earth

Thus far, I have considered the relationships between rivers and people. I have shown that we can discern the state of human life in a given district from the distribution of rivers there. I reviewed and compared the distribution of rivers in Japan, and suggested the reasons why some areas have many rivers and others have few. I then extended this analysis of rivers to the world at large. From these studies, I have drawn the following general conclusions:

◆ The most influential factor in regard to river distribution is the existence of forests. The number of rivers in a given area is directly related to the forests in the area. This suggests the following observations: First, rivers originate in thick forests, and, second, deforestation destroys the woodland streams where rivers originate. A glance at a world map lends support for this theory. For example, the barren land in North China lacks water, and Spain, likewise, has few rivers. On the other hand, the dense forests in the tropics are full of rivers, marshes, swamps, and wetlands.

◆ Another influential factor in river distribution is the geographical nature of the land. Very hilly, rough land has more water than level land. The rougher the land is, the more rivers the land has.

When I observe the heads of these rivers, I marvel at the work of nature. Here is the wisdom of nature visible and apparent for any sensitive and alert person to see. But what is the basis of this splendid natural phenomenon? The answer, of course, is the forest. Whether a river is a source of blessing for us or a source of suffering and disaster depends to a very great extent on the condition of the forest at its headwaters. While the wise elder statesmen of former years valued the forest, took measures to preserve it, and enabled us to receive the river's blessings, our recent, short-sighted politicians neglect it, and permit deforesting without thought. Thus do we experience the wrath of the river and suffer its revenge.

◆ The altitude of mountains and river heads influences the volume of water. The higher the river head is, the more water flows. On the other hand, the lower the source, the less the volume of water. Thus, the inclination of the land is directly proportional to the amount of water and the number of rivers in the area.

Note

[1] Shiga has written at great length about the miracles performed by rivers and their actual and potential benefits for human life. The smallest stream, for example, can power a "hanatsurube," a kind of hydro-powered pump, capable of pounding one or two bales of rice a day, while the largest rivers can potentially generate millions of horsepower of hydro-electric power by harnessing their waterfalls. North of Tokyo, several villages around the head waters of the Tama River harness the remainder after drawing off water for irrigation. One village in particular, Haijimamura, has only a small ditch running through it with a width of less than 2 meters, yet that has proved sufficient to accommodate many small waterwheels with a diameter of 2 to 3 meters. This effective utilization of hydro-power has spurred the development of the village. As a result, Haijimamura is one of the wealthiest villages in the Kanto region.

Rivers also flush away gravel resulting from erosion. And rivers hold rain water, waste water, and filthy water, and convey them to the lower reaches of the river. This means that rivers are, in a sense, sweepers for the earth. Rivers work with never a complaint about heavy duty, breaks for smoking, or being paid. We owe much to our rivers and they merit our appreciation.

Again, rivers convert useless soil into useful soil. What a miracle this is! Shiga refers to studies by Charles Davidson concerning the average rate of soil erosion of seven large rivers: the Mississippi, the Danube, the Ness, the Rhone, the Po, the Ganges, and the Yellow River. Davidson concluded that a river takes some 1,500 years to erode one-third meter of land. Thus, if we assume an average height for land on the earth of 678 meters, the earth will become level ground in 5,600,000 years. "What power resides in rivers," Shiga marvels, "which can convert hills and mountains into plains!"

Chapter 10

Lakes and Marshes

Characteristics of Lakes

Water that has ceased to flow forms a pond, a swamp, or a marsh. A large body of water of this kind is called a lake, and lakes can be classified into four types, according to the patterns of water circulation:

Lakes Which Have an Outflow to Rivers but No Inflow from Rivers
Lake Suwa is an example of this type of lake. It has only limited inflow from mountainous areas, and its outflow, the Tenryu River, is much greater than its inflow. It is assumed that spring water from the bottom of the lake supplies water to the lake. Lakes of this type supply rivers with clear water in adequate quantity. They function as both suppliers and adjusters for rivers.

Lakes Which Have Inflow from Rivers but No Outflow to Rivers
Lakes of this type are rare in Japan, but the Eurasian Continent has several, including the Caspian Sea, the Aral Sea, and the Dead Sea. Type 2 lakes receive river water but do not release water except through evaporation. This process produces salt. After millions of years of this process, the lake turns into a saltwater lake with water similar to sea water. That is presumably why the Caspian Sea is called a "sea" and not a "lake."

Lakes Which Have Both Inflow and Outflow
Lake Biwa is an example of this type. The Yokota, the Nibo, the Echi, the Ane, and the Ado flow into Lake Biwa and the Uji pours

from it. Another example is Lake Shikotsu, which has one river flowing into it and another flowing out.

Lakes Which Have Little Inflow and Little Outflow

An example is a crater at the top of a mountain. The crater stores rain and snowfall and does not release it. Pattern (4) lakes are usually in inaccessible locations for human beings. Consequently some scholars do not count them as lakes or classify them as pattern (2) lakes. However, unlike a pattern (2) lake, pattern (4) lakes have little inflow. Thus, I believe that a separate category for this type of lake is justified.

Origins and Locations of Lakes

Most lakes contain traces of their history and the process of their formation that can be detected through observation of a lake's shape and location. For example:

◆ Crater lakes are formed when rain and snowfall or spring water from the bottom of a crater is stored in the crater of a dormant volcano.

◆ Some lakes are formed by volcanic activity. That is, after a volcanic eruption, the accumulation of volcanic ashes and rocks obstructs the flow of streams, and the obstructed water becomes a lake. Most of these are located at the foot of volcanic mountains or in ravines between mountains.

◆ Depressions on the ocean floor become lakes following major shifting of continental land masses and the upheaval of the ocean floor. The Caspian Sea and the Aral Sea on the Eurasian continent and Lake Kasumigaura in Ibaraki Prefecture in Japan are examples of this type.

◆ Lakes form in depressions caused by movements of the earth's crust due to earthquakes and other seismic activity. Water is stored in the depressed areas and lakes are formed.

◆ Lakes are sometimes formed when a landslide blocks the flow of water of a river, flooding the area above the slide. The blocked water forms a lake.

◆ Lakes can be formed from rivers when the river develops too many bends and twists to handle the flow of water from higher elevations, or when a flood opens a new path for the river. Then the abandoned part of a river becomes a lake.

◆ Lakes form in the lower reaches of rivers when high winds form sand barriers at the mouth of the river, damming the water and creating a lake behind the barrier.

◆ Some lakes owe their origin to glaciation during the ice age. There are many examples of this type of lake in Western countries, especially in the Alps, but Japan has no lakes of this type.

◆ Lakes are formed when dams are built across a river for the purpose of flood control or irrigation.

◆ In some countries, though not in Japan, lakes are sometimes formed when beavers build nests of branches and driftwood, causing the damming up of a stream or river and creating a lake.

The location of each lake determines to a great extent its influence on human life. For example, among the types of lakes listed above, those caused by volcanic activity, by landslide, by glaciation and, in some cases, by movements of the earth's crust, are primarily located in the mountains. These lakes create scenes of almost indescribable beauty. Deep and full of clear water, they have high shores, and the mountains and forests are reflected in them. They provide, especially for urban people, opportunity to breathe clean refreshing air and experience renewal and reunification with nature. In addition, lakes in the mountains are potential sources of hydroelectric power.

Among the other types of lakes, those created as a result of the interruption of a stream are, for the most part, located in plains. They are of less value as scenic spots because they are shallow and monotonous in appearance, but they are more valuable for purposes of irrigation and as means of transportation than lakes in mountainous areas.

Material Relationships Between Lakes and Human Life

Lakes and marshes provide indirect as well as direct benefits for our lives. Beyond serving as sources of water supply, lakes allow sand and mud to settle, and they purify water; that is, they serve as filters. At the head of a river, lakes make water clear. At the middle reach of a river, lakes cause gravel to settle and the accumulation prevents floods. At the mouth of a river, lakes preserve harbors from sedimentation by sand and mud. For example, Osaka Bay is blessed because of its relationship to Lake Biwa. Lake Biwa filters the Yodo River; thus the Yodo does not carry a lot of gravel and sand to Osaka Bay, and there is no need to dredge Osaka Port, unlike the Yamato and other rivers without lakes.

Again, as I have previously observed, lakes work to regulate water volume. When a heavy rain continues for several days, rivers may flood, but lakes do not flood and the water level rises only a few centimeters because the lake can spread the increased volume over all of its broad surface. Lakes store water, saving the lower reaches of rivers from flooding even through prolonged rains, and, on the other hand, preventing them from drying up even during periods of protracted drought.

Lakes also serve to moderate the local climate. The surface of large bodies of water takes more time to both absorb and radiate heat than the surface of land. In the daytime and in summer, the land by a lake absorbs heat and the lake emits coolness to the land gradually, thus moderating the heat; on the other hand, at night and in winter, the land gives up heat while the lake emits warmth gradually, moderating the cold on the land. Moreover, lakes supply water vapor to inland and mountainous areas, preserving those areas from being parched.

This moderating function and the water vapor which is thereby produced foster the growth of plants, and the clear, cold water supplied by a lake provides an ideal environment for the propagation of both vegetable and animal life which thrives on the vegetation. Switzerland is a good example. That country has a number of lakes around which cattle are raised, and butter, a specialty of Switzerland, is produced. Another consideration is that lakes provide a natural aquatic environment. Thus, inhabitants around the lake and in mountainous areas can obtain fresh fish and other marine products.

Lakes and marshes ultimately fill up and vanish, leaving behind what geologists call a "basin" covered by rich soil. This process occurs over a period of many years as a result of successive layers of silt and sediment from the surrounding area accumulating on the bottom of the lake. As the bottom of the lake rises, so does the surface of the water, and one stream after another develops through which the water of the lake escapes. Eventually the head of the lake begins to dry up and the dry area continues to increase until the lake has disappeared completely. The fossil remains of fresh water plants and animals found in the sedimentary layers of ancient lake basins provide geologists with one of our best means of studying the past history of the earth. Many of the small plains in Japan were created by this process of lake sedimentation.

This same action that leaves behind rich soil, in some cases leaves a layer of rock salt. As we have observed previously, lakes having inflow from rivers but no outflow to rivers, such as the Caspian Sea and the Aral Sea, become saltwater lakes through many years of evaporation. When lakes of this type dry up they leave behind layers of rock salt. Two of the thickest layers of salt presently known are in Portugal and near Berlin in Germany. Certain areas in China also have immense salt deposits.

The Role of Lakes in Ancient Times

The moderating effects of lakes on climate provide optimum conditions for the survival of the human race as well as of other living creatures. For primitive people, constantly on the move looking for animals and plants, lakes may have provided the first stationary residences because they could supply pasture and clear water for animals. In line with this idea, some scholars have assumed that lakefronts were the earliest locations for human habitation.

There is some support for this assumption. For example, when a severe drought struck Europe in 1853, a lake in Zurich, Switzerland dried up and some old stakes were found protruding from the lake bottom. These stakes revealed much about the lives of the ancient people who had placed them there. According to anthropologists who studied them, they had been a part of what is referred to as "pile dwellings." This type of structure is built by driving long stakes into the lake bottom in the middle of a lake, constructing a log hut on top of them, then building a bridge to span the distance from the hut to the lake shore. From the viewpoint of contemporary people, this kind of home would probably be perceived as too damp to live in and very inconvenient because of the need to enter and leave it by only one bridge. But the reason these early humans lived in such an uncomfortable and inconvenient dwelling is that they could escape being attacked by flesh-eating animals, such as bears and wolves. Thus, the greater sense of security provided by these pile dwellings more than offset the inconvenience.

The highland plateau in central Turkey known as the Pamirs contains archeological remains which some scholars believe were the earliest human residences of which we have record. If this is accurate, it means that this cold highland plateau was once a large lake, and that it moderated the climate of the area in sufficient measure to make it a desirable location for people to live, providing further evidence that lakeside areas were the earliest sites of stationary human residence. Remains excavated in Central Asia in the vicinity of the Caspian Sea, the Aral Sea, and other locations also appear to support the theory that ancient sea beds became plateaus as a result of upheavals of the earth's crust.

Lakes as Means of Transport

Another important consideration is that lakes were one of the earliest means of human transportation. The surface of a lake is usually calm so that even the crude rafts and boats constructed by primitive people could float on it. In our attempts to reconstruct the prehistoric past, we can imagine that rivers are an older means of transportation than the ocean, and that lake transportation predates river transportation. Lakes in isthmian areas especially were important means of transportation.

It is almost certain that lakes will play a more and more important role in human affairs in the future. The Suez Canal, for example, which is 163 km long, was built through utilizing several lakes, Lake Manzala, Lake Timsah, Lake Great Bitter, and Lake Small Bitter. Undoubtedly, the existence of lakes will figure into the construction of canals in the years ahead, also.

Lakes and Spiritual Sensitivity

Lakes are sources not only of material benefits, but of spiritual enrichment as well. What person is not moved and uplifted by the sight of a lake surrounded by mountains and trees, the sky and the clouds reflected in the water. The spiritual essence of such scenic beauty forms the ground out of which has become some of our culture's most beautiful and inspiring art forms. The Japanese garden, in particular, is an expression of the beauty and loveliness of lake and mountain, indispensable factors in an authentic Japanese garden. Sitting quietly in a garden after the day's work, drinking a cup of tea, while the beauty of surrounding nature refreshes one's soul: such an experience helps us gain perspective and appreciation for the larger universe of which we are a part.

It is natural that beautiful lakes and mountains provide inspiration for the art of landscaping in Japan. It is not hard to imagine a superb view of Lake Biwa, Lake Suwa, Lake Ashino, or Lake Chuzenji as the source of Japanese garden design. Today, landscape gardeners make a garden by putting materials together in an attempt to replicate the beauty and serenity of natural mountains and lakes. Truly lakes have been an important cultivator of our aesthetic sensibilities.

Lakes are sources not only of material benefits, but of spiritual enrichment as well. What person is not moved and uplifted by the sight of a lake surrounded by mountains and trees, the sky and the clouds reflected in the water? The spiritual essence of such scenic beauty forms the ground out of which has become some of our culture's most beautiful and inspiring art forms.

Chapter 11

Seas and Oceans

The International Situation and the Ocean

Thanks to advancements in transportation in modern civilization that allow us to travel anywhere on the earth in a short time, no nation in the world can stand alone. The globe has become one tremendous market in which supply and demand are major forces which shape our lives. In today's world, it is no longer possible for a nation to be isolated economically, even though it can become politically independent. Within the context of the market, every nation must interact and team up with other nations for its people's livelihood. Each nation plays a role in selling what it has produced in the larger context of the world market.

One economist has described modern nation states as "commercial communities," instead of "nations". The differences between "developed nations" and "developing nations" are that the former sell high-quality articles, and the latter sell raw, unprocessed goods; the former trade with foreign nations, and the latter engage only in domestic trade. Thinking in terms of our own nation, if we were to compare Japan to a store in this great world market, we would have to acknowledge that it is but a shabby shop selling raw silk, tea, and various miscellaneous goods.

The ocean is the world's thoroughfare for the global market. However, this great market cannot function if the ocean is not open to traffic. Roads can transport us only within the boundaries of one nation. Travel abroad requires the acquisition of a passport, and we can travel in a foreign nation only in time of peace. In periods of hostility, interruption of passage is inevitable. Accordingly, only on the open ocean, which is beyond the range of land-based weapons and not covered by international conventions on coastal sovereignty is free passage possible at all times.

Developing Nations and the Ocean

The disadvantage of the ocean as a means of transportation is its vast expanse and the danger of storms and high waves. Due to these obstacles, we Japanese were confined to the Japanese Archipelago before the coming of the Black Ships at the end of the Edo Period (1600-1867). Likewise, European nations were confined to their own continent before the pioneering voyages of Vasco da Gama and Christopher Columbus. The obstacles to ocean travel appeared so awesome that people in nations which we think of today as "developing" nations were discouraged and prevented from utilizing the oceans for going abroad.

Now, the oceans have become a common and convenient means of transportation in the world because the human race has overcome these difficult obstacles by wisdom and courage: the invention of the mariner's compass, ships powered by steam engines, and the brave deeds of explorers and adventurers. Oceanic transportation has been greatly advantageous for developed nations, but for developing nations, it has been nothing short of a disaster. Many developing nations have been reduced to ruin because of the plundering and rapine of developed nations plying the sea. India, which is a large nation with a long history, has been colonized by England, a small nation. Burma, Vietnam, and many of the other nations in Southeast Asia are under the control of developed nations. China, Korea, and Thailand are on the verge of disintegration. These tragedies came from nations separated by seas, not from adjoining lands. In other words, the opening of marine transportation also opened the way for colonization. Given maritime realities, we must recognize that Japan is practically encircled by enemies.

It is a miracle that Japan has been saved from falling under the domination of European nations. Must we come to a final conclusion, then, that the ocean is advantageous only to developed nations, and disadvantageous to developing nations? I do not think so. Indeed, the ocean has historically protected developing nations from invasion, enabling them to nurture and strengthen their own society and culture within the geographical boundaries of their nation.

However, now is a time of great transformation; that is, the ocean which has long served as a barrier is now becoming the world's most convenient means of transportation. People in developing nations have failed to appreciate or understand the significance of this transformation. They have continued to perceive the ocean as a barrier, and to depend on the seas around them for protection. Such shortsightedness and weakness upon the part of developing nations is a primary factor in their domination by developed nations. Enterprising people, people who are alert and courageous, can utilize and benefit from the opportunities offered by the ocean and become more and more prosperous. On the other hand, people who fear the unknown and who avoid venturing forth on the oceans invite invasion and their own ruin.

Developed Nations and the Ocean

Developed nations have largely overcome obstacles to ocean travel; in a word, they have opened new frontiers. The whole earth, except for some worthless waste lands, has been divided up and is ruled by developed nations. The only remaining unclaimed area where there is room for development is the vast ocean. Therefore, the "Great Powers," that is, the leading developed nations, are fiercely competing for maritime power. The sea is the last stage of competition.

The wealth of the world has been concentrated along coastlines until now, and this may be even more true in the future. In the current world, whether a nation rises or falls depends on whether or not it can command the sea. This being the case, it is natural that the Great Powers of Europe place great emphasis on marine development. Francis Bacon (a British philosopher, (1561-1626) said in 1623,

> At the present time, having maritime power is a great advantage for European people, especially for the British. The first reason is that most European nations face the sea. The second is that a nation having maritime power can obtain more wealth from India.

The whole earth, except for some worthless waste lands, has been divided up and is ruled by developed nations. The only remaining unclaimed area where there is room for development is the vast ocean. Therefore, the "Great Powers," that is, the leading developed nations, are fiercely competing for maritime power. The sea is the last stage of competition.

In a similar vain, Sir Walter Raleigh, a distinguished British statesman, (1552-1618) asserted that

> Those who command the sea dominate world trade; those who dominate world trade possess the wealth of the world; and those who possess the wealth of the world conquer the world.

This philosophy has been deeply impressed upon the hearts and the minds of the British people. They consider Great Britain a nation which will not decline. It is often said in Britain that "Great Britain is the master of the sea, and the master of the sea is the master of the world." This is an important ingredient of British pride in their nation. Germany also has begun to advance into the ocean. Turmoil on the continent and a surplus of labor and capital forced Germany to launch forth into the ocean. Some insight into the German view of the world is afforded by the following comment by Friedrich List (1789-1846), a German economist and advocate of protectionism:

> The ocean is an open thoroughfare of the world. This is a vast field in which all people of the world can act. This is a stage on which we can demonstrate our ability, foster enterprise, nurture the people's rights, and develop the world economy. We have to understand these facts. That is our duty. Advancement into the ocean is a mission bestowed on us by Nature. A nation without vessels is the same as a bird without wings, a fish without fins, a lion without teeth, or a military person without weapons. A nation which does not possess ships invites enslavement by other nations.

The Pacific Ocean and the Great Powers

At the present time, the Great Powers are focusing on the Pacific Ocean; it is being watched with keen interest by the entire world. The following statement, a summary of a speech on "The United States and the Advance into the Pacific Ocean," delivered by Theodore Roosevelt (1858-1919), on May 13th in 1903 at San Francisco, demonstrates how intense that interest is:

> The Pacific Ocean is a great stage upon which to expand commercial rights in the 20th century. The rise of Australia and Japan, the colonization of the eastern coast of Asia by the European nations, testify to the importance of the Pacific Ocean. Nevertheless, China wished to keep its prosperity without national defense. Their failure provides us with an object lesson. Our nation is expanding along the coast of the Pacific Ocean. As a first-class power among Pacific rim nations, we are proud of our long coastline from California, Oregon, Washington, Alaska, Hawaii, and the Philippines. Our borders are stretching further and further.
>
> The United States occupies an advantageous location toward the Pacific Ocean. If we make full use of this geographical reality, we will be able to control the area of the Pacific rim in an amicable way in

the future. We are making quick progress in this area. We are now laying a submarine cable, a steamship route, and a canal to connect both sides of the Pacific and the Atlantic Oceans. These works greatly improve our commerce, and strengthen our navy and army. If we can keep our moral courage, we will be able to accomplish great things.

Maritime Nations and Island Nations

There is a remarkable difference between maritime nations and island nations. In recent centuries humankind, as we have seen, has been to the ocean and found that it is not fearful, but friendly. The ocean, moreover, provides opportunities for travel and transportation, free from obstacles and complications. The difference which I wish to describe, however, has to do with people's attitude toward the ocean and the behavior which accompanies it. After much thought and study, I have concluded that this difference, in turn, may be due in some measure to the great difference between oceanic temperaments and the continental temperaments.

Islanders have many marvelous traits. But at the same time they also have some very undesirable and detrimental traits, one of which is their tendency toward insularism. I suspect that a major source of this insular character of islanders is their experience of being encircled by a boundless expanse of ocean and being cut off from outside interaction and relationships. These isolated circumstances limit their imagination and the utilizing of their talents. In other words, they seek only for immediate profit and pleasure and tend to quarrel over trifles. Their outlook is restricted to the narrow confines of their island. Therefore, their attitude toward foreigners is one of arrogance and conceit, on the one hand, and fear and suspicion on the other. Their patriotism is passive and defensive.

The character of maritime people is very different. While islanders' outlook is limited to their land and inshore sea, maritime people look toward the sea and beyond it. Their goal is to gain maritime power and to command as much of the sea as possible. Seventeenth century Portugal, eighteenth century Netherlands, and present-day Britain have their eyes on the ocean. Thus Britain must be included among maritime nations.[1]

The attitudes and behavior of maritime people are the exact opposite of those of islanders. Whereas maritime people are enterprising and adventurous, islanders are conservative; one is open-hearted, the other is suspicious; one is broad-minded, the other is narrow-minded; one is friendly, the other is exclusive; one is justly proud of their own nation, the other worships foreign nations.

Let me give some concrete examples of what I have been describing. The disposition, that is, the attitudes and outlook of British people, differed greatly from those of Japanese people at the time of the Meiji Restoration. But how about comparisons between the British and the Japanese outlook today? Now, we must recognize that even among Japanese people, there are some differences in outlook, such as between navy men and army men; and there are even greater differences between military people and civilians. However, these differences among the Japanese are not in disposition or outlook, but are differences of degree. There are cases in history in which an island nation has become a maritime nation. Britain, which used to be an island nation and is now a maritime nation, testifies to this. The general view in this nation is that Japan's sphere of influence extends only to its own territorial soil and its nearby waters recognized by international law. This is a narrow-minded view. Although we definitely should not invade foreign nations, it is possible for us to extend our influence to the ocean where there is freedom to expand and to compete with the Great Powers on their own terms.

As we have already established, in our contemporary world whether a nation rises or falls depends on whether or not that nation can command a portion of the sea. The sights of the British people extend from their territorial soil and waters to the surrounding ocean, the Indian Ocean, and the Pacific Ocean. Thus, we can see, Francis Bacon's message has been taken seriously by them and has become their national goal. It is self-evident, I believe, that we Japanese had better expand our view.

Ocean Currents and Human Life

The ocean is navigable because it presents no barriers to objects which float on it. There is, however, something else: a unique water flow within oceans known as "ocean currents." This phenomenon, a flow of water in water, is exceedingly strange. Unlike currents in rivers, ocean currents are indistinguishable from the water surrounding them and they are much larger than the largest rivers.

We can learn about the nature of river currents with such simple tools as a desk top and ink. Ocean currents, however, cannot be investigated by such simple experiments. We can only conjecture about them after tens of kilometers of ocean navigation. The key is driftage. For example, in one experiment the Fisheries Agency threw tin buoys into the ocean and recorded the locations where they washed ashore. Debris from ship wrecks and other material which has been lost or has fallen into the ocean has also increased our knowledge of ocean currents.

There are two types of ocean currents; one is warm and the other is cold. One has a higher temperature than the sea around it, the other is lower in temperature than the sea around it. Both types have a direct influence on the climate of the land on nearby shores. The warm current heats the air above it, and the warm, damp air heats the shore. On the other hand, the cold current cools the air above it, and the cooled air cools the shore.

As a result of the effect of sea currents, Japan has a rainy season every May and June. The rain sometimes does some damage, but on the other hand, it is a great benefit to farmers and their crops. Thanks to our rainy season, Japan is a great rice producer. Again, due to the influence of a warm current in the Pacific Ocean off the shore of Japan, the Kii Peninsula has a mild climate that is favorable for the growth of citrus fruits. But one of the most important impacts of ocean currents on Japan is the marine products to which we have access because of them. Our cold currents influence the production of sea weed, kelp, and sea animals such as the sea otter, walrus, and seals; also fish, such as salmon, trout, codfish, and herring. Our warm currents yield sardine, sea bream, prawn, shrimp, crab, squid, octopus, and numerous other forms of sea life. A land surrounded by both warm and cold currents is a providential nation. In this regard, Japan is most blessed by ocean currents that deeply affect our lives, our land, and our culture.

The Ocean and Climate

Studies of the ocean and climate reveal a great difference between the climate of coastal areas and that of areas further inland, a difference that becomes apparent with but a little observation. Farmers and fishermen, directly affected by climate, become acutely aware of such differences. In addition to their kind of practical knowledge, we can obtain more precise data today by measuring instruments installed at many points throughout the world. The data accumulated by these measurements is recorded in isothermal charts and precipitation distribution maps.

Study of these maps for any particular region reveals that inland climates are generally dry and have wide temperature fluctuations between day and night and summer and winter. Coastal climates, on the other hand, are humid and temperatures are moderate throughout the day and the year. One of the causes of these differences can be traced to the effects of ocean currents. Even in our own narrow island of Japan[2] we can easily sense the reality of the climatic gap between coastal and inland areas. Our furthest inland district is a distance of only 160 km from the sea, but those inland areas are the hottest, coldest, and driest areas of the island.

The ocean is both the source of rainfall and a moderator of temperature, climatic conditions to which all plants and animals, as well as humans, are subject. The oceans exert a great influence on us. We who receive such enormous blessings from the ocean should seriously seek to understand its mysteries.

It should be mentioned that the ocean contributes in various ways to human health. Many resorts, for example, are built along the coast so as to take advantage of the clean ocean air. The shore is especially favorable for sufferers of respiratory diseases because the ocean moderates the climate. Rapid changes in temperature are one of the worst problems for persons with respiratory illnesses. Thus, they are naturally attracted to the ocean. There are numerous cases of patients recovering from lung diseases as a result of extended ocean voyages. In view of the fact that more and more people suffer from lung diseases due to the progress of civilization, the ocean is well worth utilizing for reasons of human health.

The Ocean and World View

Contact and experience with the ocean greatly influence the outlook of people. Those who have a constant view of the vast ocean and sky, and those whose view is restricted and narrow have very different dispositions. Fishermen, for example, in seeking schools of fish, can see a long distance and develop acute powers of observation. Such ability is precious today. The reason is that with the progress of civilization and living in an increasingly complicated society people are becoming nearsighted both in mind and body. Consider the contrast between the city-dweller and a person who is at home on the sea: the former is pale and weak, the latter tanned and robust. Is this not evidence of the effect of the ocean on our health? Rich urbanites understand this and devote much time and money to sea bathing and enjoying the benefits of the ocean.

The Ocean and Industry

For industry, the ocean is an endless source of blessing and potential profit. As previously noted, the ocean moderates the climate and provides abundant water. Beyond these basic benefits for industry there are many others. Aquatic creatures, which are carried by ocean currents, are the most important products presented by the ocean. The sea is to the fishing industry what the land is to agriculture and forestry. When the people of a land have cultivated as far up the mountains as they can go, they begin to look toward the ocean. Some parts of the ocean near the seashore have already been developed as marine ranches which yield various types of products from a given ocean area, just as fields on the land produce crops. For example, aquaculture businesses involving cultivation of oysters, clams, and cockles have recently developed in Hiroshima Bay. In Tokyo Bay, aqua farms cultivate sea weed. In Matsushima Bay, eel are being raised in breeding ponds. Moreover, the ocean has far greater room for development than the land. When we have command of the sea, the sea supplies us with inexhaustible natural resources.

On land, people have to spread fertilizer and cultivate the fields in order to assure continual harvests. In the ocean, however, people need neither to fertilize or to cultivate. They can obtain ocean resources to infinity, provided that they fish on the present scale. However, without command of the sea, we lose all of these resources. This is the reason why Japanese people have to turn a blind eye to poaching in the sea which is near Japan but beyond Japan's command of the sea.

The salt industry also benefits from the ocean. Sea water contains an average of 3.5 percent salt. Inland sea water contains even more salt. For example, the Mediterranean Sea has a salt content of 4 percent. We can obtain unlimited salt from sea water or inland sea water, if we can develop effective extraction methods.

The greatest gift of the ocean to us is the shipping business. As noted earlier, the ocean is the world's most convenient means of transport. Therefore, those who work in the shipping industry can make large profit, larger than in any other ocean industry.

Waves, Tides, and Human Life

Waves and tides are remarkable phenomena which greatly affect our experience with the ocean. Waves result from up-and-down motions of water caused by wind. Most waves are less than 10 meters, but some rise to a height of 13-15 meters or more. Waves may be useful as protection from invasion for island nations, but aside from that, there has been no way found to utilize the tremendous power of waves for human benefit up to the present time. Recently, however, experiments have been conducted in the United States and Germany which seek to utilize wave power to generate electricity. If these efforts to produce energy for human needs through wave power are successful, surging waves, which in the past have been viewed only as threats to navigation, may provide a new source of power for industry. This will certainly lead to a closer relationship between humans and the ocean.

A less direct contribution of waves to human life goes mostly unrecognized. That is the erosive action of waves on land. When salty waves clash against rocks, they attack, erode, and corrode the fragile parts of the rocks, carrying away broken pieces. Then they attack the rocks again with salty water containing the broken pieces. This continuous erosive action, over time, creates the breath-taking sights which add to the loveliness and beauty of the earth's shores, beaches, and precipices.

Another phenomenon associated with the ocean is its tides. Tides refer to the rhythmic, twice each day, ebb and flow of the surface of ocean water along coasts and beaches. The primary factor in the creation of tides is the gravitational attraction of the moon, which is the closest astral body to the earth; a secondary cause is solar gravitation. Working in tandem, sun and moon together cause the spring tide twice a month, at the period of the new moon and of the full moon, when the gravitation of the sun and moon attracts the earth from the same direction and from opposite directions respectively, allowing the tide to rise exceptionally high. But when the gravitational attraction of the sun and moon works from different angles, the effect is described as a neap tide, that is, a low tide. The range of the tides, from the highest tide to the lowest tide, is usually less than 2.5 meters, although narrow straits or harbors may have a greater range. In Japan, the highest tide, 5.5 meters, has been observed at Shimabara Bay in Kyushu, and the lowest, 27 cm, was at Futamiko on Sado Island in Niigata Prefecture.

The Ocean and Human Emotions

There is a short poem which expresses a little of the feeling which we Japanese have for the sea:

*Although there are no mountains,
white clouds rise above the sea
and froth blossoms like flowers floating on the waves.*

Something similar is expressed in the following passage from an article about the emotional relationship between the British people and the ocean written by John Rapock (1834-1913), a British banker, natural scientist, and member of parliament:

> We British people love our coastal scenery. We recognize the sea as our second home. We prize the clean, pure ocean air so highly that "sea air" has become almost a synonym for "refreshment." We need only to imagine the ocean and we can experience a thrill of ecstasy. We find much more of beauty and magnificence and sense of freedom in the sea than in the sky. It is said that if a poor woman from Manchester goes to the beach, she will be just as enthralled by the beauty and splendor of the sea as the richest of her countrymen.

Is this why the British are so lighthearted and full of enterprise? Although Britain occupies only a small corner of the world, its people recognize their homeland as a base of freedom from which they can rove and thrive around the world. I sometimes wonder why Japanese people do not find more enjoyment in the beauties of the sea. Despite the fact that Japan is encircled by the ocean and we have grown up hearing the sound of waves, Japanese people have been slow in expressing admiration for the sea or singing about the ocean. Is that because the ocean is beyond the bounds of Japanese poets' imagination? Or is it simply that Japanese people have not noticed or taken interest in the sea?

A study of Japanese surnames, for example, bears out this observation. Surnames generally express both the mental and the material relationship between a people and nature, and Japanese surnames clearly suggest a closer relationship with the land than with the sea. In Japan, the origins of many surnames can be traced to mountains, rivers, fields, plains and other words related to the land. However, there are few surnames which have their origin in the sea or the ocean.

The reason why the Japanese have not found more joy and delight in the sea may be a fear of the ocean. Some aspects of this fear may be instinctive, but some are artificial. An indication of the artificial fear is the fact that most parents would prefer their child to become a farmer rather than a sailor, join the army rather than the navy. The shadow of fear turns a world of beauty and wonder into a place of dread and horror. If only people could overcome the fear of the sea, they would feel a sense of closeness, love, admiration, and veneration. As for me, I will try to approach the sea with friendship.

Waves turn a monotonous ocean into an expressive one. A gust of soft wind brushes the surface of a calm sea, and the water ripples on and on, as though it were beaming with joy. Sea mews and cormorants sleep among the ripples by twos and threes, groups of children gather shellfish at a beach with their trousers rolled up. The soft breeze becomes stronger, and more waves ripple, turning vast stretches of the deep blue ocean into a splashed-pattern of blue and white. The sea beams like a shy maiden breaking into a pretty smile. But when the wind becomes still stronger, waves from afar surge higher and higher, approaching the shore with white foam on their crests and break against the rocks of the shore as though to scatter white flowers.

One cannot help but marvel at the wonders of the sea. But let us consider further the things which float upon the sea, adding to the beauty of the sea itself. How splendid, for example, is the sight of a pair of whales, half visible among horizontal waves, or a merchant ship dashing before the wind with its masts at full sail, a steam-ship trailed by smoke, or again, a group of warships moving in formation like wings of a crane.

And islands! Islands, too, are among the exquisite things of the ocean. Sakurajima looks like an incense burner placed on a fresh tatami mat; Matsushima with venerable old pine trees on its peak, their green heads reflected in the water; the charming islands of the Seto Inland Sea.

The sea expresses itself in ever so many ways. It changes with the sunrise, sunset, moonrise, and moonset; whether it is foggy, cloudy, or a clear blue sky. When the rising sun emerges over the surface of the water, beaming rays of golden light onto the waves, fishermen who are full of hope for a new day set out in their fishing boats, harmonizing a sea chant with the sound of their oars. In the deepening dusk, the same fishing boats return, emerging one after another out of the mists and clouds. In some areas, even after a veil of darkness has descended upon the water, fishermen can be found in their boats luring fish to their nets by torch light. The sea holds too many beautiful things to mention them all.

Still, the power of the ocean, the power of its waves and tides, can be awesome. In the words of a Japanese poem:

Waves surge roaring to the shore,
breaking themselves to pieces on the reef.

These words may have been inspired by a typhoon, for then the world becomes utterly dark and the turbulent waves rage as if to overturn the world. Is it any wonder that people become terrified at the great power of water? But sooner or later, we will overcome that fear and be inspired by a wider view of the ocean. At any rate, we cannot help but have enormous esteem for the essence of Nature displayed by the ocean. Once you enter into the infinite ocean, whether in a warship, a strong merchant ship, or a small boat, you become but a dust particle upon the blue sea. The ship is tossed about by the waves as if it were a leaf.

To venture into the vastness of the ocean is nourishing to the soul. There we can move along, the blue sky for an umbrella, dressed in sunshine, bathed by sea breezes, pillowed by the waves. We become liberated from the social pressures and the bondage of the land. On land we must face the realities of troublesome class systems and other kinds of social bondage. But once we escape from this artificial world and experience the greatness of Nature, we begin to think of rising above the ordinary. This must have been the experience of Yamada Nagamasa, a voyager who ventured to foreign lands during the Edo period (1600-1867) and was roused to action. So it must have been with Columbus also. Perhaps this explains why so many great people throughout history come from sea-going cultures.

It is natural, then, to find differences in the feelings and emotional life of maritime people and mountain people, of sea-oriented people and land-oriented people. In general, the ocean is a place where we can escape from the ever-present limits of time and space, and taste the infinite power of Nature. Even wild fishermen and brutal pirates cannot help praying for divine grace. A sense of entrusting the Ultimate with their lives comes into being spontaneously. This is why fishermen are pious, and most maritime people in Japan worship Konpira or Suiten-gu, the guardian deities of water and ocean.

> *To venture into the vastness of the ocean is nourishing to the soul. There we can move along, the blue sky for an umbrella, dressed in sunshine, bathed by sea breezes, pillowed by the waves. We become liberated from the social pressures and the bondage of the land. On land we must face the realities of troublesome class systems and other kinds of social bondage. But once we escape from this artificial world and experience the greatness of Nature, we begin to think of rising above the ordinary.*

I would like to conclude this section with a part of a chant composed by Tenkei-zenshi (1648-1735), a Zen priest during the middle of the Edo period. The chant expresses and reflects the close relationship between the ocean and human feelings of piety and awe. One understands piety only after experiencing the greatness of the ocean, and piety deepens the relationship between people and the ocean.

Where goes that ship?
Whose lives are tossed by the sea, led by the wind?
Four boards make the ship;
Will the nails hold?
One mast, for sailors one in heart and mind.
Six sails, call them sight and touch, taste and scent,
sound and one elusive sense.
It sails straight before the wind, but like his ship
the skilful steersman flexes, careful of the waves.
If he wavers, does he not know the goal?
Does he fear the open sea?
Attacked by waves, look to the hatches,
seal all portals!
A moment's delay, and all could be lost.
With faith in providence and presence of mind,
all shall come safely to port.

Trends in Japan and the World Concerning the Ocean

We in Japan must give serious thought to the relationship between population and our total land area. Several years ago, Japan's population was 35,000,000. Now, our population has increased to 47,000,000. It will be 50,000,000 in just a few years. The population in Japan is increasing by 500,000 per year, and if it increases geometrically, it will reach 100,000,000 within 70 years.

The total area of Japan, including the new territory of Taiwan and the P'eng-hu Islands, is 410,670 square km. It will be difficult for one hundred million people to live on these small islands. Moreover, the population will double or triple in 100 to 300 years. How should we deal with this population problem? After long struggle with this problem, some scholars are concluding that the only solution to the population problem is colonization. However, we have to face the reality that the Western nations have already colonized the greater part of the world. Only arid, sterile parts of the world have been left untouched by Western nations.

Some Japanese people have sought to find new opportunities by emigrating. When their numbers were small, they were welcomed, or left alone. But, as numbers increased, an anti-Japanese outcry arose.

The more we emigrate, the more severe the outcry will become. This has led in America and Australia to the development of movements and legal action to bar entry to Japanese. These movements will become stronger as more emigrants go to these nations. People who go in search of work will be destined to meet prejudice and ill will. This is deeply regrettable, but we cannot blame the people in those nations.

Is there any means whereby we can cope with the population problem without colonization? This is a crucial question we have to face. Before considering this question, let me turn to the European experience. At first, these European nations poured their excess population into North and South America. After drenching those areas, they turned to Australia in the southern hemisphere. Then, they went to Africa and divided it among themselves. The boundless expanse of Africa is now under the rule of the United Kingdom, Germany, France, Italy, Spain, Portugal, and Belgium. Even the Sahara Desert is dominated, by France. The sand, the birds, everything in Africa belongs to the Europeans. After this exercise in divide and rule in Africa, the only place left to colonize is China. Therefore, all of the European nations are focusing on China. They are now hesitating over how to divide it, while they work out diplomatic arrangements among themselves.

So, the European nations have colonized North and South America, Australia, and Africa. They are now poised to dominate China. What is next? Their next exploitation will be directed to the ocean, which occupies three quarters of the whole surface of the earth. Surplus population and capital will be directed toward the sea. The ocean will be the post-China colony.

The capacity of the land is limited, whereas population keeps on increasing. It is probably only natural that people begin to look toward the sea for solutions to the problem of excess population. In some parts of Japan, where population is growing to the extent that more and more people are emigrating, aqua farms are developing to harvest marine products in the same way as agricultural produce. In Okayama Prefecture clam farming has recently begun; Hiroshima has been famous for its oysters for 300 years, and seaweed is an important aqua farming product of Tokyo Bay. The increasing pressure of population is the stimulus which gives birth to initiatives of this kind. We have already cultivated almost all the cultivable soil on the land, so we are beginning to pioneer in the cultivation of the ocean.

Japan and the Marine Products Industry

On the basis of the realities I have discussed above, it is my conclusion that colonization is not an appropriate means of solving the population problem for Japan. The wisest course for us lies in cultivating the ocean. Just as the European nations are now turning to the ocean, developing the sea is the only way ahead for the Japanese. In fact, I would go so far as to say that advancement of a marine products industry in Japan is important for the future of both Japan and the world.

Western nations, having already begun development of the sea, are now exporting marine products to foreign nations. Japan exports no marine products whatever, even though there are over four hundred million people in China who desire marine products that Japan could supply. What is more, the European powers are laying a network of railways covering the whole of China, and are planning for ocean liners to penetrate rivers deep within the central regions of the nation. The development of this modern transportation network provides an unusual opportunity for Japan to move its own Japanese-produced marine products into the interior of China. The further shipping goes inland, the simpler it will be for our products to reach the interior.

The promotion of a marine products industry in Japan could be beneficial in two important ways. First, it would be a means for Japan to make a good profit through the selling of its products. Second, by meeting the Chinese desire and need for marine products, this kind of trade could strengthen our ties with China and encourage friendly relations between our two nations. I strongly believe that the solution to many of the problems facing the nations in the Far East depends on the development of a thriving Japanese marine products industry.

Notes

[1] The term, "maritime nation" is used here to designate any nation which has the maritime disposition as defined above, even though it is not encircled by the sea.

[2] The reference here is, presumably, to Honshu, the main and largest Japanese island.

Chapter 12

Inland Seas and Straits

Inland Seas

Historical studies indicate that over 3,500 years elapsed from the first navigation on the Nile, the Tigris, and the Euphrates to Columbus's sailing out on the Atlantic Ocean in 1492. During this long period, the Mediterranean Sea served as the main means of transportation for people living along its coasts. This suggests that it took the human race a great many years to develop navigational skills from those required for sailing on the calm waters of lakes and rivers to the skills needed for sailing on the stormy, unfriendly waters of seas and oceans.

Some ancient civilizations prospered along the coasts of inland seas. Inland seas such as the Mediterranean Sea were stepping-stones to the ocean. It almost seems as if Nature granted us inland seas as a place to practice the art of navigation. Historians give credit to peninsulas for the birth of civilizations such as Greece and Rome. I cannot help thinking, however, that the Mediterranean Sea was the central factor that made these two peninsulas the origin of European civilization.

If it had not been for the Mediterranean Sea, modern European civilization would probably not have spread beyond the seasides and plains of Greece and Rome. But, as we know today, those seasides and plains are only one tiny part of modern civilization. Thus, I conclude that if ancient civilizations did originate in peninsulas, inland seas must have supported the civilizations which thrived on those peninsulas.

In our examination of inland seas and civilization, we do not need to seek examples in far-off Europe. We can find a good example right here in Japan and the Seto Inland Sea. The Seto Inland Sea is surrounded by three large islands: Honshu, Shikoku, and Kyushu. This is roughly equivalent to the Mediterranean Sea and its three surrounding continents: Asia, Africa, and Europe. However, the Inland Sea is in many respects just like a large river. The largest part lies between the Chugoku District of Honshu and the island of Shikoku, and even there it only has a width of 40 km. Furthermore, many peninsulas and capes stretch out to the sea from each island, and numerous small islets dot the sea. The distance between these land areas is within hearing range. The Seto Inland Sea is as calm and fresh as a lake in the mountains. This is because the surrounding mountains protect the Sea from wind and storms, and the peninsulas, capes, and islets weaken the power of the waves.

According to Japanese mythology, one of the gods, Ninigino Mikoto, descended to Mt. Takachiho in Miyazaki Prefecture and lived at the head of the Oyodo River. Ancient civilization, the myth states, developed around that river following the descent of the god to earth, and during the era of Emperor Jimmu, our mythical first Emperor, all of the Chugoku district was unified. Be that as it may, judging from the historical background, our ancient ancestors had neither roads for marching armies nor the skills necessary for navigation on the rough open sea. We can surmise that the unification of the district was made possible by navigation on the still, calm Seto Inland Sea.

The Seto Inland Sea, with its friendly waters, provided the stage for the evolution of the Japanese people for the next 2,500 years, following the unification of the Chugoku district. It took much less time to bring Chugoku, Shikoku, and Kyushu under control than was the case in Tohoku and Hokkaido. This was because the military leaders could utilize the Seto Inland Sea to control the former districts, a conquest that provided a base from which to achieve the conquest of the whole of Japan.

If this analysis has merit, we can conclude that command of the Seto Inland Sea was a decisive factor in the extension of control over the whole of Japan. That is where the decisive battles were fought. Those who commanded the sea could dominate 16 different clans surrounding it, and from there it was but a further step to the control of the whole of Japan. Historical verification of this conclusion can be seen in the battle of Dan-no-ura between the Genji and the Heike clans, the feud between the Northern and Southern Dynasties, the unification of Japan by Oda Nobunaga (1534-1582), and others. All of these contests were decided on the Seto Inland Sea.

From Inland Seas to Open Seas

The historical record reveals that it is but one step from inland sea navigation to open sea navigation. It was not the Phoenicians, the Venetians, or other people around the Mediterranean Sea, but Spaniards and Portuguese who pioneered ocean navigation; the inhabitants of the Iberian Peninsula took the initiative. The Peninsula, located between the Mediterranean Sea and the Atlantic Ocean, was the geographical go-between for these waters. Columbus, a peninsula born Italian who was neither a Spaniard nor a Portuguese, was a seagoing pioneer. Most of the initiative in early ocean navigation, however, was taken by Portuguese or Spaniards who lived on the greatest stepping stone between the Mediterranean and the Atlantic.

The Seto Inland Sea is much smaller than the Mediterranean Sea, too small to serve as an effective training ground for open sea navigators. Furthermore, after Japan had gained control of the sea, she fell into insularism as a result of the closed-door policy of the Edo Shogunate. This policy was a major factor in the diminishing of the maritime spirit in Japan. Now, 40 years have passed since the opening of the country; nevertheless, the Japanese still fear and shrink from going to sea, their earlier history as maritime people notwithstanding.

The Seto Inland Sea was the first step toward the ocean for the Japanese people. Our second step is the Sea of Japan and other seas between the Eurasian Continent and Japan. These waters are the equivalent of the Mediterranean Sea in this part of the world: the important step from the still water of the Seto Inland Sea to the vast expanse of the ocean. This may be a gift presented by Nature. I am deeply impressed by Nature's work; the countless islands stretch in rows like stepping-stones from the southern end of the Japan Sea to the middle of the Pacific ocean. This string of islands can be valuable as footholds and guide posts for ocean navigation. The European people once ventured to the South by means of the Canary and Azores Islands, dots off the west coast of Africa, and an example of the influence of island chains in luring people to the ocean.

All things considered, Nature has provided Japan with every possible incentive to turn to the ocean. Without the limiting restrictions imposed by political leaders, Japan would have become a marine-oriented nation in the course of appreciating and using Nature's gift to us. But even so, bewailing our past isolationism is of no avail. Now, let us enjoy this natural gift and look to the ocean as a means of harmonizing our life with natural will.

In the previous chapter, I emphasized the importance, in addition to the land, of seas and oceans. In this chapter, I have described the relationship between the Japanese people and the surrounding seas, particularly the Sea of Japan, but also the Yellow Sea, the East China Sea, and the Sea of Okhotsk. These seas should be considered in Japanese geography as an appropriate sphere of activity for Japan. In the past, these seas have been treated individually in the study of physical geography, without reference to Japanese interests. That may have been appropriate before Japan obtained control of the Taiwan Strait, and therefore did not have command of the East China Sea and the Yellow Sea. Now, however, Japan commands the sea from the southern end of Kamchatka to the Taiwan Strait, a distance of 4,680 km.

From the view point of the command of the sea, these seas play an important role. Accordingly, a name that can encompass all of these seas is necessary. In fact, these seas are referred to by some scholars as "the Mediterranean Sea of the East" but I do not consider this an appropriate designation. These seas, in some respects, are more like the North Sea or the Baltic Sea area than the Mediterranean Sea. I propose therefore, the term "Oriental Inland Sea" to designate these seas surrounding Japan, and I will use this name for the sake of convenience in this book.

The Arrangement of Inland Seas in the World

After observing the role of inland seas as stepping-stones from river navigation to ocean navigation, an idea occurred to me. Is there a relationship between the arrangement of inland seas in the world and humankind? If we look closely at a world map, we can observe that three very similar inland seas are located in different parts of the world, but all of them are located in nearly the same climatic zone:

The Mediterranean Sea, Surrounded by Europe, Africa, and Asia
The Mediterranean Sea is the first inland sea which became an important means of human travel. It was the prize for which aspiring powers competed. It decided the fate of nations; that is, a country commanding it rose and, on the other hand, a country losing it fell.

The South China Sea, Encircled by the Asian Continent, the Sunda Islands, and the Philippine Islands
The South China Sea was an area in which the people of Thai-

land, Luzon, Java and other nearby areas had been active behind the historical scenes for centuries. In the 16th century, the Spaniards and Portuguese began to use the sea for transport, followed by the Dutch, and then the ships of other nations joined the race to command the sea. The Japanese, spurred by the Portuguese, also joined in the struggle. Half merchant-half pirate, the Japanese gained commercial rights and then gained control all along the coasts of Vietnam, Cambodia, Thailand, Java, Luzon and the surrounding areas.

Later, however, England replaced Japan and gained control of the South China Sea, the Mediterranean Sea, and most of the areas in between. As I have noted before, "a nation which commands the ocean can command the world," but it can also be said that "a nation which commands the sea can control the finances of the world." Now I would add one additional observation, that is, "a nation which dominates the world's inland seas can acquire the greater portion of maritime power."

The Caribbean Sea, Enclosed by North and South America and the West Indies

The Caribbean Sea is similar to the other two inland seas in several respects, and these similarities will increase after the completion of the Panama Canal. Again, the similarities will become clearer if we consult a world map. If England commands the Caribbean Sea, it will be able to command the Pacific, the Atlantic, and the Indian Oceans; or in other words, nearly all the oceans in the whole world. Obviously, the English desire to do so; however, it is not that easy. According to the far-sighted James Monroe's last wishes, the Americans are trying to maneuver so as to manage the New World all by themselves, without the interference of other nations. The more important projects in the American plan are the integration of Cuba and the building of the Panama Canal. Alfred Thayer Mahan, an American navy officer, made a revealing remark about the relationship between the Panama Canal and the United States when he observed that "The Panama Canal will be one of the greatest water routes in the world and will revolutionize worldwide trade. The Panama Canal will be to the United States what the English Channel is to England, and what the Suez Canal is to the nations around the Mediterranean Sea."

The Japan Sea and the Baltic Sea

As noted earlier, the Japan Sea is sometimes described by Western scholars as the "Mediterranean Sea of the East." I would like now to suggest that it would be more appropriate to compare the Japan Sea with the Baltic Sea. Japan is now, after several thousand years of historical development, becoming a promising, civilized nation. I hope, and I believe, that the Japan Sea can be a factor in leading Japan to become one of the strong civilized powers, just as the Baltic Sea led the nations of North Europe to become strong.

The Mediterranean Sea is a part of a past civilization, whereas the Baltic Sea and the North Sea are a part of a dynamic, present-day civilization. Japan should look to the Baltic as a model and should command the Oriental Inland Sea, including the Japan Sea. At the beginning of the 19th century, Napoleon dreamed of gaining control of the English Channel and from there controlling the entire world. But his dream never materialized because the English and other powers bordering the Baltic Sea and the North Sea were able to hold him in check due to their control of those inland seas. Japan is now the most powerful nation among the nations surrounding the Japan Sea. But are the Japanese people as prepared for assuming this kind of role as the people of northern Europe were? There is an old saying, "Start from a small place near at hand and then expand gradually." Following this path, the Japanese should establish themselves in the seas surrounding Japan, and then proceed to the South China Sea and other southern seas, just as the English people have done in their part of the world.

Straits

Straits connect two different seas. A strait is to the sea as an isthmus is to the land. While isthmuses were a convenient means of transportation for pre-civilized people, straits obstructed their movements. For civilized peoples, on the other hand, straits are a valuable aid. In recent times, ships have begun to concentrate around straits, just as people and cargo concentrate around bridges.

Nearly all the straits in this part of the world are important for us. For example, the Taiwan Strait, the Tsushima Strait, and the Tsugaru Strait are gateways to the Oriental Inland Sea, and the Bakan (Shimonoseki) Strait, the Bungo Strait, and the Kitan Strait occupy key positions in the Seto Inland Sea. Turning our eyes to the world, the Strait of Malacca is a gateway to the Pacific Ocean and the Indian Ocean; the Strait of Gibraltar, the Strait of Suez, and the Dardanelles are gateways to the Mediterranean Sea.

Straits have become of such strategic importance that they decide the fate of all the oceans which they connect. If a fleet cannot go through a strait it must take a detour, which requires much more time and travel. If the fleet is to go through a strait, it must obtain permission. Thus, controlling straits is becoming increasingly important as maritime power increases in importance. That is the reason why England has been willing to sacrifice so many lives and so much wealth to retain control of the Straits of Gibraltar and Suez. The wealth of the ocean belongs to those who command the sea, and the command of the sea belongs to those who control the straits. A strait can serve as base for a fleet, or an artillery position to defend the nation. A nation's fate depends on whether or not it can control nearby straits. It is no wonder, then, that straits are often the sites of decisive sea battles.

Likewise, straits become points of commercial importance and a focus for commercial activities. Ships and cargoes converge on straits and merchants throng them. Consequently, commerce prospers around straits and fosters the development of cities. Singapore, Penang, Aden, and Port Said are among the many examples of cities which have grown up around straits.

Chapter 13

Harbors and Ports

Harbors and Human Life

A "harbor" is a place where ships shelter from storms. Ships can operate only when they are supported by a harbor whose function is to connect the land and the ocean and make the ocean accessible. Harbors, therefore, are vital elements in the relationship between the ocean and our lives.

As civilization becomes more highly developed and interdependent, ocean navigation flourishes, and harbors become increasingly valuable as connecting points among land, ocean, and river transportation. A nation, or a district, needs a harbor, just as a house needs an entrance. Travelers and cargoes cannot enter a nation without passing through a harbor just as a person cannot enter a house without passing through the entrance. The quality and condition of its harbors determine the living standards of the people of a nation or district in the same way that the quality of the entrance reflects the character and dignity of the people living in a house. An especially important aspect of a harbor is its value as a point of defense. Thus, harbors are often fortified for military purposes.

Ports and Civilizations

A port, a town or city surrounding a harbor, functions in much the same way as a bridge functions on a river or as a mountain pass functions in the mountains. Ports facilitate transport and commerce between the two sides of an ocean just as bridges are valuable to both banks of a river and mountain passes serve both sides of a mountain. Bridges and mountain passes are interchanges for two-way traffic;

ports likewise, serve as interchanges between land transportation and ocean transportation. In other words, land routes and ocean routes concentrate at ports, as do ships, people, and cargoes.

Locations where many people throng together offer opportunities for contact with different cultures from abroad. Such locations have been the birthplaces of cultures. Port cities and their harbors enable the importing of foreign cultures to the nation or the district and exporting the local culture to foreign countries. The imported culture radiates from the port to the inland areas in all directions.

The distance from the port and transportation service to the port are decisive factors in determining the level of culture which exists in any particular district. This accounts for the fact that cultures begin on peninsulas and thrive on islands. Their harbors welcome different sorts of culture from abroad. If a peninsula or an island has no ports, it will soon become nothing more than a lump of earth. Without a port, an island or peninsula is just like a house without an entrance. People living in such places become much like caged birds. In other words, lands bordering on a sea or ocean can give birth to a new culture only when they have good ports.

Harbors also serve as a resort for seamen. After days or months of being tossed about by the waves in the vast ocean, without conveniences, leaving their fates to Heaven, seafarers can be released from the hardships of the voyage upon entering the harbor, much as a baby relaxes at its mother's breast. As soon as they arrive at the port, they desire to have fresh food, bathe, and seek for other comforts. Within this context, values, particularly as regards money, become distorted. Money circulates freely and morals tend to become corrupted. Venereal disease is common. These are some of the unfortunate developments associated with ports.

I will discuss the relationship between ports and human activities more fully in a later section. It will suffice here to recognize that all human activities are stimulated by the vitality and dynamic quality of life in port areas. The spirit of a nation or a district is inspired by its ports.

Prerequisites for a Good Port

In general, a shore location must satisfy eight basic criteria in order to qualify as the site of a good port:

A Circular Shoreline

A port must have a curving shoreline and sufficient protected water surface to provide safe haven for ships during storms. The more circular the shore is, the more protected will be its adjacent waters. On the other hand, if the shore bends in a full circle, outlet to the ocean will be too restricted and inconvenient for ships entering and leaving the port.

The Shape of the Harbor

A second prerequisite is the shape of the harbor. While every shore has some bends and curves, all shores are not suitable for a port. Some are too wide, some too narrow, others have reefs or shoals. Each of these characteristics work either for or against shipping. For example, a narrow harbor is good for anchoring but bad for entering and leaving. A wide harbor is bad for anchoring but good for entering and leaving the port.

This will become clear if we consider that whether a port is easy or difficult of access can be a matter of life or death for ships and their crews when they encounter a storm on the ocean and have need to take refuge in a harbor. This is the reason why many ships have been wrecked at ports. In one sense the most dangerous place for navigators is not in the great ocean but in a narrow harbor. To minimize the danger of such accidents, a lighthouse is essential for a modern port.

A further consideration in regard to the shape of a harbor is the depth of water along the shore. In the best ports the water along the shore is deep enough to bring a ship alongside the quay. When this is possible, the ship has direct access to the shore without being towed. Unfortunately, there are few harbors of this kind in the natural world. Therefore, at most harbors it is necessary to provide additional equipment and facilities to load and unload cargo, get passengers on and off ships, etc.

Climatic Factors in the Location of a Harbor

This is an important factor because it has a direct relation with the direction of prevailing winds. In Japan, winds blow primarily from the north or northwest in winter and from the south or southeast in summer. Use of harbors which face in those directions is difficult during stormy seasons. Most of the harbors along the Japan Sea, for example, are closed in winter due to the fact that they face north or northwest, directions from which the strongest winds blow.

Condition of the Floor of the Harbor

Mooring ships requires adequate conditions of the sea bed. Thus, it makes a difference whether the sea bed consists of gravel, solid rock, or mud. A bed of gravel is too soft and cannot hold an anchor. Solid rock, on the other hand, makes anchoring difficult because of the danger of the anchor becoming stuck in the rock. Mud makes the best sea bed for the anchoring of ships.

The Depth of the Water of the Harbor

For a good harbor, one capable of accommodating ocean going ships, the water must be neither too shallow nor too deep. The general depth for ocean liners currently uses the Suez Canal as a standard. There ships of 7.3 meters draft manage to pass through. The Canal can accommodate ships currently afloat. However, it will not be able to accept the larger ships of the future. The original plan of the Canal was that it would be 9 meters in depth on the average at low tide, and a plan is presently under consideration to deepen it up to 9 meters or more so that it will be able to handle larger ships.

I mentioned minimum depth of the harbor, but consideration must be given to maximum depth as well. When a ship moors at a port, it circles into the wind with its cable as radius. If the harbor is too deep, the ship would have to lengthen its cable according to the depth. This means that the circling ship would take up so much of the harbor space that the total number of ships which the harbor can handle at one time is too limited. In that case, the port cannot accommodate sufficient numbers of ships for its width. This is the case with the port of Kagoshima. It is circled by mountains and is blessed in this respect, but the water is too deep for good anchorage. Generally, the maximum depth of water for a good port is from 15 to 20 meters.

The Area for Moorage

Another important factor is how wide the harbor is. The best harbor has sufficient space for expansion so it will be able to keep pace with progress in ship building and, if the port handles ships engaged in world trade, it will need to accept ships in ever increasing numbers. The best ports in Japan at present are the ports of Osaka and Otaru. They are good ports because they are safe, wide, and convenient for loading and unloading.

Location for Commercial Advantage

A location which is advantageous for commercial activity, with respect both to inland trade and goods for export, is a critical factor in determining its value. The primary requirement for these two types of trade is convenience for concentrating cargo. For inland trade, a railway network or river transport service originating from the port is crucial. To be useful for foreign trade, the port must be the center of important routes for ocean liners. Hong Kong, Singapore, Shanghai, Osaka and other prosperous ports meet such requirements. Honolulu, located in the center of the vast expanse of the Pacific Ocean, has become the focus of major ship routes.

Land Forms Surrounding the Harbor

Lastly, space to develop a port town around the harbor is an essential requirement for a good port. It is difficult, however, to find potential harbor sites which combine this requirement with the first described above, a circular shoreline. For example, Ogi-no-hama meets almost all the above listed requirements, but it has little space to develop a town because the mountains rise sharply from the sea behind it. Moreover, good transport services cannot be located there because the harbor is isolated from the inland plains. Thus, though the harbor is ideal with respect to most of the requirements for a good port, it can become little more than a port of call due to space limitations of its surroundings. There are some efforts being made to compensate for this limitation by cutting through the mountains and reclaiming land from the sea, but this will involve reclamation work on a very large scale.

These are the most important prerequisites for a good port. But to really appreciate the interplay and relationships of these most important prerequisites for a good port, I would suggest a visit to Yokohama, Kobe, or some other famous port. Then one can understand first-hand why those ports are successful and why extensive reclamation projects have been undertaken to improve them. Furthermore, such visits will enable one to see the various kinds of facilities which are associated with an advanced society.

Harbor Improvement

In the last section, I listed various natural conditions needed for a good harbor and port, but, as we saw, it is extremely difficult to find sites which combine all of those features in one place. In earlier days, we could do little but be resigned to inadequate harbors provided by nature. Now, however, we are beginning to acquire the means to undertake various kinds of construction and reclamation projects to compensate for most of the limitations found in the natural environment.

Harbor Mouths

The earliest human efforts to improve harbors involved attempts to compensate for the inadequacies of harbor mouths. Most of these can be improved by means of a lighthouse and more skillful handling of ships by pilots. A more difficult problem is how to fortify the mouth of the harbor against storms. Dealing with this problem requires large scale projects which were beyond the means of ancient people. Today, we can resolve this problem by building a breakwater. Recently, there have been major advances in our ability to accomplish this. The old type breakwater consisted of gravel and stone which could only shield a small part of the harbor mouth. The new type breakwaters being built now are made of concrete and can protect most of the mouth. By this means, artificial harbors can be constructed at points of strategic or commercial importance even though in their natural state these sites do not possess all of the prerequisites for a good harbor.

Artificial protection for harbor mouths through construction of concrete breakwaters can be observed at the port of Osaka in Japan and at Madras in India. France has built a world famous breakwater at Cherbourg. While England has good, strategic ports in which ships can take refuge and obtain munitions, particularly Plymouth and Portsmouth, the French had no advantageous ports along the English Channel before they improved the harbor at Cherbourg by building an artificial breakwater. This improved harbor was an important factor in France's besting of England in some of the sea battles fought by the two countries.

There is another world famous artificial port built by the English at Colombo in Ceylon.[1] Though I have seen it only in pictures, the gigantic, monsoon waves blowing directly from the Indian Ocean, attacking the 1,273 meter-long, concrete breakwater, and splashing water toward the sky, are a magnificent sight.

Moorage

Various means have been devised for altering or adapting to the depth of water in harbors. The problem of too much depth will be solved over time by the accumulation of mud and sludge due to the action of waves and tides. To deal with cases of harbors in which the water is too shallow, we now have giant dredging machines for moving mud out of the harbor.

The area for moorage can be increased by improvement of a breakwater. Recently, also, it has become possible to build various kinds of wharves, docks, and quays which make it possible to bring ships alongside the shore, a popular method in that it is more effective than large scale projects in expanding space, and costs less money to operate. Furthermore, when ships can be brought along shore, cargo can be loaded and unloaded quickly with the use of cranes that are now being built and transported to warehouses, thus greatly reducing the time a ship needs to wait in the harbor.

In some industrial nations, comb-shaped deep-water docks and quays are being constructed. World famous facilities of this type can be seen at the port of London along the shore of the Manchester Channel and at the port of New York. In contrast to such efficient ports as these which are becoming common in the industrial countries, at ports in Japan ships must waste precious extra time being loaded and unloaded with only the use of lighters.

Land Forms Surrounding Harbors

We can now change the land form surrounding a harbor to a certain extent. For example, the fjords which line the coast of Norway leave very little room for the development of cities or towns along the shore. However, by reclaiming land from the sea and terracing mountainsides, the people of Norway have developed lots for housing and, in some cases, built towns overlooking busy harbors. The port at Otaru (in Japan) has become a prosperous port through the same process of land form expansion as the ports in Norway. We humans have developed the ability to do some marvelous things.

Location

Location is a natural factor far beyond human ability to control. And yet we can find people trying creatively to overcome the disadvantages caused by location. The tenacious Slavs, to mention one example, invented an icebreaker to navigate around Vladivostok's frozen port because of its strategic importance. Again, along the coast of Newfoundland in North America, because thick fog rising from the Labrador Current makes lighthouses useless, a system of ringing bells and the roar of artillery to warn approaching ships has been devised.

Commercial factors often provide the incentive for major harbor renovation projects. At one time, the port of Genoa was much smaller than the port of Marseilles. While the port of Genoa has only the small catchment area of the Po River and was separated from the central cities in Europe by the Alps, the port of Marseilles provided access to the cities in Switzerland via the Rhone River and transportation service to the plains along the Rhine River. Thus, the port of Marseilles became the central port city opening on to the Mediterranean Sea for most of central Europe. The relative positions of the two ports changed, however, with the construction of two big tunnels through the Alps to the port of Genoa, one at Saint Gotthard and the other at Simplon. These tunnels have made possible access from Genoa to the main cities of Europe. The Marseilles Chamber of Commerce calculated the effects of the two tunnels. After completion of the Saint Gotthard Tunnel, the distance to Basel from Marseilles is 727 km, from Genoa the distance is only 471 km. After completion of the Simplon Tunnel, the distance to Lausanne from Marseilles is 581 km, and from Genoa 471 km. The shorter travel distances for European cities to the Mediterranean provided by the construction of these tunnels reversed the positions of these two port cities.

The value of a harbor can be enhanced in other ways, also, such as building warehouses which are connected to wharves, creating fixed places for ships to enter and register, developing facilities for ship repair and maintenance with convenient means of opening and closing water gates, keeping harbors and port cities clean, and provision of fire prevention equipment. Facilities and services of this nature can compensate for disadvantages and improve the worth and value of ports.

Note

[1] Formerly Ceylon under British control, the name was changed back to its traditional name, Sri Lanka, when the island became an independent republic on May 22, 1972.

Chapter 14

The Seashore

Classification of Seashores

In the previous chapter, we considered harbors and ports, the most important aspects of shores. It remains here to consider several additional ways in which seashores are related to human life. The word "seashore" is, in fact, somewhat ambiguous. In ordinary usage, the seashore includes both the line where the sea touches the land and the land running along that line. The line itself, however, is not fixed. It fluctuates day and night because of the range of the tides. Moreover, the line is usually characterized by many slopes and curves and indentations.

For our purposes, the seashore can be divided into three main parts:

The Beach Line

This refers to the area of land between watermarks at high tide and low tide. The beach line differs in different areas depending on the shape of the shore. In other words, whereas steeper shores have a narrower beach line, about 0.3 of a meter to 3 meters, shores with a gentle slope have wider beach lines.

Land along the Beach Line

This part of the shore is sometimes called "hama" which means beach or shore. Many Japanese place names include "hama" in their names, such as Ara-hama, Taka-hama, and so on. Like the beach line, this part of the shore differs according to its shape. When the land slopes gently, this area is wide; when it is steep, the area is narrow.

Water Along the Beach Line

The area of water along the beach line is of two types: one in which the land drops away precipitously, resulting in deep water along the beach line, the other in which the sea bottom slopes gently away from the shore, resulting in shallow water along the beach line.

Characteristics of the Soil

In addition to this three-part classification of seashores, with each division consisting of different types according to the shape and slope of the land, each type differs also according to the nature of the soil and various combinations of soil type. Thus, before considering further this matter of the relationship of the seashore to our lives, we will need to note some characteristics of soil.

Sandy Beaches and Human Life

Geologically, seashores can be divided into two types, sandy beaches and rocky shores, with many gradations between sandy and rocky shores, and soft and hard rocks. Generally, the inclination of the seashore varies with the nature of the soil. In other words, most hard, rocky shores have steep precipices running parallel to the beach line and deep water along the beach line, whereas most soft, sandy beaches have flat land along the beach line and a gently sloping sea bottom.

Transportation

Sandy beaches are generally advantageous to inland transportation, but disadvantageous to overseas transportation. Most sandy beaches are situated at the end of big rivers or in the general vicinity of rivers, and the beaches adjoin flat plains in inland areas. These beaches are convenient for transporting goods on land and rivers, but most sandy beaches are shallow and therefore cannot accommodate ocean liners. Shoals and sandbars in particular are a bane for navigators. A further defect of sandy beaches from the standpoint of navigation is that most of them are either straight, bow-shaped, or fish-hook-shaped and cannot provide protection from storms.

Vegetation

The sand along sandy beaches can be easily blown by the wind. Thus, the topography of the land along sandy beaches is constantly changing, preventing growth of vegetation. Blowing sand damages crop land and buries buildings, causing major problems and inconvenience for people who attempt to live near beaches.

Marine Products

While sandy beaches harm living creatures in the ways just described, they are well suited to the production of marine products. Sandy beaches are production centers for sardines, one of the most important marine products in Japan. Such desolate sandy beaches as Kujukuri-hama, a long beach along the Boso Peninsula, and some of the beaches in the Hokuriku district are suppliers of "hoshika," a fertilizer made from sardines. It is because sandy beaches are veritable production centers for these sardine products that people live along these beaches in spite of the trouble caused by wind and sand.

In addition to sardine products, sandy beaches, especially in Hokkaido, yield scallops, clams, sea slugs, and salt. However, these can be harvested only during certain seasons of the year, making it necessary for the people who live around sandy beaches to seek other jobs in order to earn a living. This has led to various efforts to develop other kinds of industries. Several philanthropists, for example, have invested in a cotton crepe industry in Ibaraki Prefecture and a fishing net industry in Niigata Prefecture.

Recreation

A small recreation industry has developed along the sandy beaches of Niigata and Ishikawa Prefectures as wealthy people have invested in various kinds of pleasure boats and sailing ships. Some sandy beaches have also become famous for their beautiful landscapes. These beaches form over the years as granite is eroded by wind and water, and as broken pieces of granite are transported to the shore and accumulate there. This provides conditions in which pine trees can take root, drawing nourishment from deep underground. Only pine trees are able to thrive in this damp, salty environment. The sharp contrast of white sand and pine trees creates landscapes which are breath-taking in their beauty. Among these, Ama-no-Hashidate in Kyoto Prefecture, a sand jetty protruding into the water, is one of the three most famous views in Japan.

Rocky Shores and Human Life

There are various types of rocky shores: steep cliffs, bluffs which have room for houses, both sharp and gently sloping rocky shores, and shores with terraces. All of these different types can be found under the surface of the water as well as on dry land. Each type has it own peculiar influence on human activities.

Transportation

From the standpoint of transportation, most rocky shores above the surface of the water are worthless, except as superb landscapes. Rocky shores below the surface of the water, on the other hand, are useful for anchoring ships. A shore with plain fields, deep rock bottom, and curving coast line provides the best conditions in terms of transportation. However, shallow rock bottoms are hazardous for navigation, and ships often run aground along shallow rocky shores.

I would note, also, that when a rocky shore has room for residences along the coast, fishermen can settle there, making it convenient for them to travel from ports to other areas by marine transportation. Cliffs are not suitable for human residence, but they do provide an ideal environment for some kinds of birds. They also attract tourists. In Norway, for example, the world-famous fjords, consisting of steep cliffs, deep blue sea, and white birds, attract thousands of European sight-seers every year. Japan, likewise, has many beautiful rocky shores, such as both sides of the Bungo Channel, Bonotsu in Kyushu, and the Kii Peninsula.

Marine Products

Rocky shores are most valuable as the seat of the marine products industry. Rocky sea bottoms which are not too deep are especially suited for marine life. They make ideal breeding grounds for many kinds of marine algae or sea weed. And those same algae breeding grounds serve also as the spawning grounds for herring and other varieties of fish.

Forestry and Fishing

Rocky shores alone, however, do not provide the conditions necessary for a profitable marine industry. Perceptive fishermen will tell you that rocky shores with abundant forest coverage yield large amounts of fish, whereas in cases of shores with poor forestation the yield is small. This is because of the part forests play in supplying fish with good spawning grounds and food. Fish come to shore to spawn and find nourishment, and shores blessed with rich forest cover abound in the kind of plant and animal life which attract fish. The coast along the shores of Tokushima Prefecture are a case in point. In earlier times, these coasts were covered with abundant forests and yielded large catches of fish. Now the trees are gone from these coasts and very few fish are caught there any more.

Historically, there is another interesting relationship between humans and steep, rocky shores such as those surrounding the Seto Inland Sea, In-no-shima Island, the South China Sea, the Strait of Hormuz, and others. Only people who have developed a "feel" for such places can gain access to their shores. Furthermore, these rough, rugged shores offer no transport services for navigators or land travelers. They do, however, make ideal hiding places for pirates. From ancient times, they have served as dens for pirates who could dash out to plunder passing merchant ships and quickly gain refuge again in the safety of their rocky lair.

130 A Geography of Human Life

Part Two:
Nature as a Medium Between Human Life and the Earth

Taking pupils to nature. Makiguchi (back row, center): "Immediate experience with the natural and social environments of our homelands fosters compassion, goodwill, friendship, kindness, sincerity, and humble hearts."

Chapter 15

The Inanimate World

In Part I, we considered the relationship between the earth's surface and human life on the basis of topographical features. Part II examines these relationships from another perspective. Natural phenomena, both animate and inanimate, as well as the field of meteorology, are discussed in terms of their influence on the earth's surface and on human beings. In their interrelatedness with various characteristics of the earth's surface and their combined effect on human life they can be perceived as a medium between the earth and human life.

Construction Material

That rocks and minerals are important for our lives has already been noted in the section on mountains. A list of specific examples of the usage of these materials would be a long one, so in this section, an overview of the usage will be presented rather than give a detailed explanation of each example.

The use of rock in construction is widespread. Most of the buildings and houses in Japan, including my own, use stone in at least part of their structure and its importance increases with the size of the building. Stone is useful in two main ways: to protect structures from decay due to moisture and from destruction by fire.

Water-resistant Material
Foundations of houses and warehouses, steps, and columns for bridges are typical examples of the use of rock in building. Rock used for such structures is resistant to prolonged exposure to water and is

hard enough not to splinter or fracture in conditions of ice and frost. Some of the more popular types of rock currently used in building are andesite, granite, quartz, diorite, orthoclase, and basalt.

Fire-resistant Material

The rocks listed above are also fire-resistant, but since they are hard and crystalline in nature, they are not as durable against fire as they are against rain, ice, and frost. Furthermore, they are expensive because their hardness makes them difficult to quarry and carve. Thus, tuff and sandstone are more widely used in stonework, and sand itself is important in building with cement.

Material for China and Glass

Rock and stone are used in many of the objects we can observe in our homes, particularly in kitchens. China for tableware and glass for windows and lighting fixtures are indispensable for the convenience and comfort of our everyday lives. Again, we owe these products to minerals. Following are the more commonly used materials used in the manufacture of these items and utensils:

◆ Kaoline: provides material for china; consists of a fine powder produced by decomposition of feldspar.

◆ Clay: provides material for tiles and brick; similar to kaolin but contains more impurities.

◆ Marl: contains lime.

◆ Loam: contains sand.

◆ Shale: clay in a soft solid state.

◆ Slate: clay in a hard solid state.

Minerals Used for Heating, Lighting, and Other Conveniences

Needless to say, materials to generate heat, energy and light are highly important in our modern society. It is not an exaggeration to say that we owe most of what we think of as our modern civilization to mineral fuels, particularly coal and oil. Minerals are also the source of various metals which are so very important for modern life.

Gold, silver, copper, zinc and nickel are used for coins, for example. Iron is the primary material for industrial machines, but antimony, lead, tin, sulfur, platinum, and mercury are other essential minerals used in industry.

Yet other minerals are used in the production of dyes, chemical products, and pharmaceuticals, three fields of manufactures that are of vital importance for modern living. Talc, cinnabar, tin, pyrolusite, and arsenic especially are used in making these products. Finally, we must recognize the importance of rocks and minerals used for grinding and polishing, such as whetstones, polishing sands, and grindstones.

Inanimate Objects and Civilization

Every inanimate object affects human life in some way. We are dependent on some such as water. We need stone and rock not only for the foundations of our houses, but also because of their relationship to water. We too often take these elements for granted, failing to realize how essential they are for our lives. In cases when there is too much water, for example, or when there is a shortage of water, we face serious hardships. We have noted previously that civilization began in places where people could obtain water in sufficient quantity and of good quality. But the quantity and quality of water depends on the nature of the ground, so we can see that rocks and other minerals, and the distribution of specific types of rocks, have an intimate connection with our lives. They influence our culture as well. It was the discovery of certain metals and their uses that initiated new epochs in human history, the Stone Age, the Iron Age, etc.

Observations of nature reveal that there is a sort of cooperation and communal existence among living things which are at the same time competing for their own survival. This explains the fact that most living things are armed naturally in various ways which provide protection for them. For example, some life forms enclose themselves in a hard mineral shell. Observing this makes us realize what fragile, weak animals we human beings are. We have teeth and nails, but compared to the teeth and nails of other carnivorous animals, ours are useless. We do not have any natural means of protection and self-preservation. But we have found minerals, and these minerals and skill in using them provide us with the primary means for our survival.

The discovery of minerals aided human beings first, by enabling us to expand and improve our food supply, and second, by greatly strengthening our self-protective capability. There are many examples which can be cited. Fragments of ancient stoneware, such as arrowheads and other stone weapons have been found among ancient remains of human habitation, revealing how our ancestors protected themselves and came to dominate other animals in the hard struggle for existence. In later strata, the appearance of copper and other metals gives evidence of ever-greater mastery over their environment upon the part of humans.

The invention of ceramics must without doubt be considered of equal importance to the discovery of metal in extending the means of human survival and the growth of culture, though not adding measurably to the stock of weapons for combating enemies, ceramics proved highly useful in daily life as tableware and other utensils.

It was the discovery of iron which led to a major advance in the human struggle for survival. Why? Because iron is safe and practical for domestic use as in tableware, unlike copper, for example, and it was also the most effective material which had yet been found for making weapons. Furthermore, iron is easy to cast and process, compared to copper. With the later discovery of coal, the importance of iron increased. Today, iron and coal have become important elements in the life of all progressive nations.

The Origin and Distribution of Rocks and Minerals

It must now be clear that inanimate objects, particularly rocks and minerals, are deeply connected to culture and human life. Obviously, then, the distribution of rocks and minerals is an important factor in the development of any given society. While their distribution is not immediately visible, studies in geology and archeology reveal many useful minerals among the ancient strata of the earth.

I should perhaps clarify what I mean by distribution in this context. As here defined, distribution refers to the geographical distribution of *exposed* minerals. That is, it refers not to the existence of minerals, but whether or not the minerals come to crop out of the surface of the earth so as to be available for human use. The question naturally arises, then, as to how minerals crop out on the surface from deep in the earth. In general, this "cropping out" involves three interrelated factors:

◆ Volcanic activity thrusts matter from deep within the earth to the surface and folds it into numerous strata.

♦ Water erodes the earth's surface and exposes underlying strata of rocks and minerals.

♦ Useful minerals can be found more easily in mountainous areas and coastal areas, the upper reaches of streams and rivers and along rocky cliffs and coasts.

Of course, how useful the minerals found in any given area actually are depends on several other factors. Suppose, for example, that a large quantity of a particular mineral were discovered which could be developed into an excellent mine. But if the location were far removed from any form of transportation, it would be impossible to get the mineral out. Thus, the actual value of the mineral would be greatly reduced, although this would still depend on what kind of mineral it was. If the mineral in question, for instance, were gold, it would be valuable even in such a barren and inaccessible place as the upper Yukon River in North America.

On the other hand, if the mine site is far removed from rivers or ocean transportation, some nonmetallic minerals would be almost useless. In general, then, except in the case of a few precious metals, such factors as whether the site is close to human habitation, the nature of the terrain, and whether the site is accessible from rivers or other means of transportation would determine its worth. Geographical studies reveal that there are actually very few mountainous areas which meet all these conditions to produce "useful" minerals. But it is, as we shall see, at those few places that civilization has made the most progress.

Island Countries and Minerals

We have previously noted the fact that islands are most blessed with good natural conditions conducive to the development of civilization. Now we can see more reasons why this is so. If we were to view islands from the bottom of the ocean, we would see that they consist of the summits of great mountains, and as such, islands are in a much more advantageous position with respect to obtaining and transporting minerals than are continents. Islands in volcanic regions of the earth are particularly well suited to the development of civilization.

Chapter 16

The Atmosphere

The Atmosphere and Human Life

The surface of the earth is surrounded by a thick gaseous substance which we call the "atmosphere." This atmosphere, including what we simply call the "air," is generally assumed to have the shape of an oval like the earth itself. The height or thickness of the atmosphere is not precisely known. Some estimates place it at about 60 km above the earth, others as much as 300 km. My guess is that it is at least 135 km. At any rate, we humans carry on our lives at the bottom of this atmosphere.

In our time, the wireless telegraph, a marvelous invention by an Italian electrical engineer, has resulted in the atmosphere's becoming a part of our human communication network. Moreover, a machine with the ability to fly, a long time dream of humankind, has nearly been realized. Thus, we can expect that at sometime in the near future, this atmospheric region will become another busy traffic network. Still, compared to land and water, both of which are being used widely for transportation, the atmosphere is far less tangibly entwined with human life. Why is this? It is because the atmosphere is an invisible, gaseous substance which we can neither see, feel, nor touch. This may be why most people are oblivious to the atmosphere and the important role it plays in our lives.

All of us are well aware that food and drink are essential for human life, but few people realize that the atmosphere is much more essential. This explains why employers, for example, pay little attention to the fact that thousands of their workers are suffering from illnesses caused by the terrible conditions in which they work day after day, breathing dust and dirt and dampness. Likewise, theaters put hundreds of people into tiny spaces and think nothing whatever of it. Ferries and shipping companies do the same. A list of such outrages would be endless. I fear that if the members of our society continue to be ignorant and indifferent to the existence of the atmosphere, we will never be able to do anything about the rapidly increasing numbers of people who suffer from tuberculosis and other lung diseases and brain trouble. Our biggest problem in this regard is the conventional perception of the atmosphere as being nothing more than a realm for birds and insects.

I propose, in order to counteract this problem, that we give increasing attention to observations of the atmosphere. As we do so, endless thoughts and images surge up in our minds. We live here on the earth under 1,500 kilograms of air pressure. Land is limited but there seem to be no limits to human population increase. This has led to our recent construction of high-rise buildings to live in.

> *The one theme or principle that ties all of these thoughts together is this: the place where we and all other creatures live is the place where land, water, and air meet. We seem to be racing with other living things to try to occupy as much of this limited living space as possible.*

The one theme or principle that ties all of these thoughts together is this: the place where we and all other creatures live is the place where land, water and air meet. We seem to be racing with other living things to try to occupy as much of this limited living space as possible.

Air-Land-Water Interface and Civilization

In the previous chapter, we noted that coastlines and civilization have been deeply interconnected throughout human history. This chapter establishes that we humans find our living space at the point where land, water and atmosphere meet. The distinctions we have previously observed between land and water apply as well to the meeting of land and water with the atmosphere. I have found it helpful to think of this meeting point of water, land, and atmosphere as an "air-coastline." What is the significance of labeling this interface? We have already established that there is a clear relationship between coastlines and culture. Now we can observe with equal clarity the presence of a third element, the atmosphere, in the development of culture and civilization.

This three-way interrelationship can be better understood by reference to civilizations with which we are familiar. Why did Greece become such a highly advanced civilization? Why, in Europe, did civilization blossom much earlier than on other continents? Some historians believe that Greece was an early leader in the development of an advanced civilization because of that country's complex coastlines and rugged mountains. But Europe's position as the world's most civilized continent is due not only to its long coastline. Europe, like an enlarged version of Greece, is a land of complex geography: long coastlines, rugged mountains, cliffs, and valleys. This suggests that complex geographical features may also be an essential element in the development of a society. These considerations, at any rate, led me to coin the term "air coastline" as a meaningful way to express these complex interrelationships.

The Air

In conclusion, these are the aspects of air, the main body of the atmosphere, which we must note:

The Contents of Air

Air exists in a gaseous state and is transparent and resilient. The main contents of air are nitrogen (78.6%), oxygen (21%), plus traces of argon, water vapor, and carbon dioxide. Oxygen maintains all animal life. Carbon dioxide is an essential ingredient in the fixation of energy during the photosynthesis of plants. Vapor supplies fresh water to the ground and energizes living things.

The Heat of Air

The air does not obtain heat directly from the sun. Rather, the sun's rays simply go through the air and heat is radiated when they reach the ground. That radiated heat rises and heats the lower part of the atmosphere. In other words, the atmosphere accumulates heat at the bottom, providing protection for humans as well as other living things.

The Weight of Air

The weight of air changes as gravitation changes. Thus, as we would expect, air is thicker, or heavier, at sea level and becomes thinner, or lighter, at higher elevations.

Chapter 17

Climate

Climate and Geography

Human beings are, so to speak, products of climate like other living things. Of all natural phenomena, climate exerts the most powerful influence on our lives. It is true that our intellectual capabilities have made it possible to change climate a little and to adjust to changes in climate. In recent years, there has even been a tendency for human beings to try to control climate. Yet, even so, our lives are still extremely dependent on climate.

While we have already arrived at a definition of geography suitable for the purposes of this book, I would like to suggest that geography may also be thought of as a study of the causes and effects of climate. The Japanese people, whose main business is agriculture, are deeply dependent on climate and are very much aware of it. Yet we do not have scientifically correct ideas about climate. This is unfortunate. We should not leave responsibility for learning about climate entirely to meteorologists, but should engage in serious observation of the climate and climatic phenomena ourselves to learn not just about climate but also about the mutual relationship between human beings and other living things.

Is it too simple a question to ask what is climate? Consider the words which we use for daily greetings. They include references to temperature, if it is sunny or windy, or if it is raining. While there is a tendency to think of weather and climate as the same thing, actually they are not. Weather is a temporary phenomena, the combined action of temperature, wind, rain, sunshine, snow, and other factors at a given time. Climate, on the other hand, describes the average weather conditions of a particular area or region over an extended period of time.

Temperature

Temperature, moisture, and weight: these three aspects of the air are determining factors in the creation of climate. Wind, or air circulation, is based on all three factors. Air temperature controls the moisture and weight of air. Thus we see that air temperature is the key factor in the determination of climate. Since climate is a complex phenomena growing out of the interrelationships of these three factors, we must consider each factor separately before proceeding to observe the nature of relationships between climate and land and climate and our lives. Let's start with air temperature, as the most essential element in determining the climate of any given area; it influences human life not only directly but indirectly as well, particularly through the food we eat.

Temperature and Plant Life

We can observe that the growth of plants is under the control of temperature. Though some seeds have protective mechanisms enabling them to survive extreme heat or cold, most plants stop their growth or die if the temperature falls below 4 degrees C or rises above 40 C. Plants differ in regard to the lowest temperature and the highest temperature at which they can survive. In this regard, observations reveal that there are more varieties and a larger quantity of plant growth at the higher temperatures than at the lower. In other words, greatest plant growth occurs in the tropical zone, next the temperate zone, and the least in the frigid zone.

We cannot help but be amazed by the mysteries of nature. For example, in temperatures above 40 degrees C, plants preserve themselves as seeds or fruit. They form a hard, solid husk or hull and take root in the ground where the temperature is usually quite stable, and in this way fruits or seeds can endure sudden changes of temperature. When the temperature goes beyond their limit, they have only to wait and when the right time comes, they shoot out buds and grow and blossom. By the next time the temperature exceeds their limit, they are sheltered, that is, they have turned into seeds again or live in the soil to protect the survival of their species. Consider how rice, our staple food, is protected by very hard hulls, and many varieties of tropical fruit protect themselves with thick, horny, husks.

Temperature and Animals

Now let us consider temperature in relationship to animal life. Some animals dig holes in the ground and hibernate in them. Some build nests. Others rest in the shade of big trees when the sun gets too hot. Migrating birds change their habitat according to the season of the year. Some animals shed their hair or molt when it gets hot and again when it gets cold. Compared to plants, the range of temperatures animals can tolerate is more limited, but they also have greater capacity for self-protection. Thus, animals can thrive over much of the earth, but at the same time, since many of them depend on plants as their source of food, their distribution is affected by vegetation.

In ancient times we humans used to dig pits in the ground or make caves on the sides of hills to live in. Later, we built houses which could keep out heat and cold, rain and snow. In winter, we wear more clothes and in summer we dress more lightly. Recent improvements in transportation have made it easy for many people to go to warmer areas in winter and cooler areas in summer. In these ways of protecting ourselves from the elements, we have been able to develop nearly every function that plants and animals have to protect themselves.

Beyond these means of coping with temperature extremes, the acquisition of fire has made it possible for us to survive in conditions of severe cold. For example, there are over 100,000 people living in Verkhoyansk in Siberia where the temperature falls to 68 degrees below zero, and the average temperature in January is 44 degrees below zero.

On the basis of my experience and observations, I believe the optimum temperature for human beings is between 15 degrees to 20 degrees C. How does Japan compare with this? The average temperature on the southern tip of Kyushu is 17 degrees C and in the Tohoku region it is about 10 degrees C. Thus, temperatures in Japan are close to ideal.

Human beings, as we have noted before, are naturally very fragile creatures. However, we have been able to acquire means of self-protection which are far beyond the capacity of other living things, and this enables us to thrive all over the world. Even so, we soon come to realize that we are totally dependent for our lives, especially our food and clothing, on the generosity of plants and animals, and that we are deeply affected, both physically and mentally, by temperature.

In general, living in regions of extremely low temperature hinders both physical and psychological development of human beings. So much time and energy is required to provide for their basic necessities—food, clothing, and protection against cold—that little is left for intellectual and cultural development. On the other hand, extremely high temperatures such as that found near the equator tend to sap humans of energy and blunt their minds. It is possible to obtain life's necessities with little work, so people do not develop habits of working hard and cooperating with other people.

While the tropical zone is too hot for human habitation and the frigid zone is too cold, the temperate zone seems to be ideal. The seasons spring, summer, autumn, and winter alternate. While there are distinct temperature changes, the changes are not radical and this provides stimulation and incentive to work. People become accustomed to working regularly, and this helps them grow physically and mentally to a maximum degree.

If we look back in human history, we see that early human civilizations flowered in the tropical zone. A few thousand years ago such civilizations as those of India, Arabia, and India reached an incredibly high level. But then what happened? They stopped progressing and now they are stagnant. This seems to suggest that as human society progresses, the center of civilization moves toward the temperate zones.

Distribution of Temperature

The atmosphere does not get heat directly from the sun. That is, the ground first absorbs the heat from the sun and then radiates heat to the atmosphere. Therefore, the source of heat is not at the top layer of the atmosphere but at the bottom layer. This explains why the temperature goes down as the altitude goes up at a rate of one degree per 170 meters. (This figure is an average and will differ depending on the seasons and other circumstances). Furthermore, the earth is not flat but is a sphere, so the degree of heat varies from place to place depending on the amount of the sun's rays and the slant at which they strike the earth. It is these differences in degrees of heat in different locations on the earth's surface which cause wind and precipitation.

Local weather stations scattered around the country record temperature readings, air pressure, wind direction, rainfall, etc., three times a day. First, they calculate the daily mean air temperature, next the monthly mean, then the yearly mean. These calculations are then sent to the Central Meteorological Observatory which collects all the reports and makes an isothermal map. As mentioned before, the air temperature falls with altitude, and, since local weather stations are located at different elevations, the temperature is adjusted to that at sea level.

Factors Which Affect Temperature

Generally, as latitude increases, temperature decreases, but this does not occur evenly. Isothermal lines do not run parallel with latitudinal lines, nor do they necessarily run parallel with each other. If you compare the temperature in winter between the seaside and inland areas at the same latitude, you will find it is warmer at the seaside than it is further inland. This can be verified by a glance at an isothermal map. On the other hand, in summer, inland areas are warmer than the seaside. Inland areas are characterized by a wider range of temperatures between the hottest and the coldest periods of the year than is the seaside.

By referring to a copy of an isothermal map and a map of ocean currents together, you will notice a close relationship between temperature and currents. The entire coast of the Sea of Japan and the southern coast along the Pacific are influenced by the Tsushima and the Kuroshio currents and are relatively warmer than the northern coast of the Pacific, which is under the influence of the Oyashio current.

Other factors which can be observed affecting temperature are the direction of the wind, the direction and location of mountains, the land's inclination relative to the sun, and the condition of the soil. Soil which is dry, hard and with few trees, absorbs the heat from the sun quickly, but loss of heat through radiation occurs quickly also. On the other hand, soil which is wet and soft absorbs the heat from the sun slowly and loss of heat through radiation occurs gradually.

Geographers classify the earth's surface into three general categories on the basis of annual mean temperature. An Austrian geographer, Zupan (1847-1920), uses the following method of classification:

- ◆ The tropical zone—yearly mean temperature above 20° C.

- ◆ The temperate zone—yearly mean temperature 0° C - 20° C.

- ◆ The frigid zone—yearly mean temperature below 0° C.

On the basis of this classification, Japan lies in all three zones:

- ◆ The tropical zone: south of Ogasawara Island, Oshima Island, the Ryukyus (Okinawa), and Taiwan.

- ◆ The temperate zone: north of Oshima Island, south of the Tohoku District in Honshu.

- ◆ The frigid zone: north of the Honshu in Hokkaido.

Wind and Human Life

We have already observed that temperature varies from place to place. Warm air expands and rises, while cold air contracts and seeks lower elevations, just as water flows from a high place to a lower place. That is why the wind blows. We usually are not aware of the wind or of its influence over us, but there are times when we become acutely conscious of it and come to appreciate it more, as for instance, when it is hot in the summer and we suddenly feel a cool breeze. Perhaps this explains why folding fans have become so popular all over Japan. Wind not only moderates heat and cold, but also cleanses the air and makes it suitable for humans to breathe.

Some plants whose stamen and pistils grow individually wait for the wind to carry out the process of pollination. In cedar groves, for example, we can see the air turn yellow as pollen is blown in all directions by the wind. Some seeds have cilia or very thin scales which help them spread over wide areas, blown by the wind. This is truly amazing. The wind also prevents frost from settling on plants and killing them. Farmers and gardeners make good use of this knowledge.

I have heard it said that if there were no wind, the temperature would reach 55 degrees C on the equator and could go as low as -77 degrees at the north and the south poles. But actual average temperatures are 27 degrees and -18 degrees respectively. Air circulation, in combination with sea currents, results in a drop in temperature at the equator of 27 degrees and a rise of almost 60 degrees at the two poles. In short, wind moderates the temperature so that we can live almost anywhere on the earth. In our earlier discussion of sea currents, I noted the role of wind in their formation. In a sense, then, it is the wind which keeps nature in harmony.

Wind provides us with even more benefits. Until the beginning of the 19th century, when the steamboat was invented, the wind was a major means of human transportation. Thanks to wind, Christopher Columbus discovered America, Vasco da Gama opened the route to India, and Ferdinand Magellan circled the globe. Wind lost its place as the chief source of energy for human transportation after the discovery of steam power, but it looks now as if it will make a great come-back. While many people still think that vehicles that fly through the air are mere imagination, I believe they will one day be one of our most important means of transportation.

Again, wind has been used as a source of energy for industry in the form of windmills for many years. Although wind has not been considered an efficient or dependable form of energy because we are not able to control wind direction, we can look at Holland, below sea level and constantly threatened by water. In that country, windmills along the coast have been used to protect the land, with the help of the wind.

Destructive and Constructive Effects of Wind

Destruction, redistribution, construction—these are all acts of wind, just as they are the acts of water. Wind erodes the surface of mountains and makes fine soil which is essential for life to breed. It creates lakes and swamps and sand dunes. Wind is the main cause of sea currents.

The wind brings many benefits to us, but once a storm begins, it uproots trees, destroys houses, and capsizes boats. Under these conditions we do not have even a second to dwell on the benefits of the wind. A hard wind at the end of summer when the rice blossoms are in full bloom can cause extremely serious consequences for 40 million Japanese who subsist on rice.

Damage from wind and earthquakes have been the two main calamities from which Japanese people cannot escape. The damage from a major earthquake can be major, with many casualties. Still, the area affected is usually limited and major quakes do not hit the same area often. In most cases there are intervals of several decades. In contrast, powerful typhoon winds strike large areas of Japan nearly every year. Thus people fear them. Typhoon damage to the rice crop affects not only our diet but many other aspects of our lives as well.

Consider Japanese houses. Wherever you go, to the cities or to the countryside, you will notice that very few houses are more than one-story. This is especially the case on Okinawa where low, one-story houses is the general rule. That is because Okinawa is so close to the Sea of China, the birthplace of typhoons. The original reason for the custom of constructing houses with tile roofs in Japan was protection from wind damage.

There is in Japan an interesting indirect affect of the threat of typhoons as well. Where do you suppose Buddhist temples thrive most and get the most donations? These temples thrive best in agricultural areas which are so susceptible to the affects of wind on crops. Fishing areas are a close second. There is a fascinating incident involving a typhoon recorded in our history books. In July, 1281, a mighty armada carrying 140,000 Mongol fighting men attacked Japan along Hakata Bay in Kyushu. We can only conjecture what the outcome of this confrontation might have been. The Japanese forces held the Mongols off for two months. Then a major typhoon struck the coast of Kyushu, destroying most of the Mongol fleet and stranding thousands of the invaders on the shore. It is believed that less than half the Mongol forces managed to return home, in complete defeat. The Japanese interpreted this incident as evidence of divine protection of their land and the typhoon came to be remembered as "kamikaze", or divine wind.

It is strange to think of this "divine wind" and the typhoons which cause so much damage every year as being the same thing. We know that primitive people were frightened by the incredible force of wind, and in the face of such power knew of nothing to do but seek divine protection. On the other hand, this same phenomenon motivated civilized people to research this mysterious force with the result that we now have a nationwide weather observation system. So now we can at least prepare for the attack of the wind. This capability has especially proven to be a blessing for seafaring people who spend their lives on the water.

Consider other aspects of the wind; the wind as a source of beauty and inspiration, the wind as companion and friend. How elegant is the sound of the wind blowing through a pine forest! And how beautiful is the sight of a weeping willow swaying in the wind. The sound of the shakuhachi (a Japanese flute) is very similar to the sound of music composed by the wind. It is said that in some parts of Southeast Asia, the native people put flutes behind their houses during a monsoon so they can listen to the wind singing through the instruments.

Sailors who sail across the ocean with the help of the wind know the wind as their friend. Certainly one who has had the experience of being stranded in a calm sea with no wind comes to appreciate the wind deeply. In the spring, I have sometimes seen children watching with fascination a single leaf dancing in the breeze, becoming so caught up in the drama of it that the wind becomes a friend with a personality of its own. Sailors and children are not exceptions. Have we not all felt and seen the gust of wind that suddenly brushes the cherry blossoms we were admiring, scattering them far and wide?

Air Pressure

We are always surrounded by air pressure of between 1,400 kg to 1,500 kg, but we seldom think about it. We do not feel pressure at all. Why is that? It is because the pressures from all directions are even and in balance with the blood pressure of our bodies. If the air pressure suddenly changes, the change instantly affects our breathing and our pulse. In thin air, that is, when air pressure decreases, our breathing and pulse speed up and we feel difficulty in breathing. If the air pressure gets extremely low—for example, if we ascend beyond 7,000 meters above sea level—we may start having nosebleeds, and this can be very dangerous. Studies indicate that the upper limit for human

Climate   151

beings to live is about 8,600 meters. We are most comfortable between sea level and about 4,500 meters.

Distribution of Air Pressure

Wind is caused by differences in air pressure. The wind blows from an area of high pressure toward an area of low air pressure. This is one of the primary factors in weather forecasting, making it possible to predict from which direction the wind will blow at a given time and to predict the weather in general. That is why every weather station diligently gathers air pressure readings by means of a barometer.

There are isobaric maps showing isobaric lines, just as there are isothermal maps. A glance at an isobaric map reveals:

◆ In winter, the center of the highest air pressure is in the continental interior. The center of the lowest air pressure is over the ocean. For Japan, the area of high air pressure is in the north-west and the area of low air pressure is in the east.

◆ In Summer, on the other hand, the area of high air pressure is over the Pacific Ocean, and the area of low air pressure is in the interior of the Asian Continent. Why does this happen? Because air pressure changes according to temperature, altitude, and moisture in the air.

Types of Wind

Language yields clues as to those things which matter greatly in a culture. Thus, it will come as no surprise to find a variety of expressions pertaining to the wind in the Japanese language. One classification distinguishes between seven types of wind according to speed:

		speed m/1s
◆ Mufu—a dead calm.	Smoke rises straight up.	0-1.5
◆ Nanpu—a gentle breeze.	We can sense it.	1.5-3.5
◆ Wafu—a slight breeze.	It moves the leaves.	3.5-6.0
◆ Shippu—a fresh breeze.	It moves the twigs.	6.0-10.0
◆ Kyofu—a strong wind.	It moves the main branches.	10.0-15.0
◆ Bofu—a stormy wind.	It moves the trunks of trees.	15.0-29.0
◆ Taifu—a typhoon.	Violent wind.	29.0-+

We become aware of the wind when it blows with a speed faster than 0.5m/1 second. Up to Nanpu and Wafu, there is no discomfort nor does the wind become a problem to anyone. However, if the wind gets stronger than that, we sense inconvenience, even difficulty, in walking against the wind. Bofu and Taifu winds often cause serious calamities.

Wind can also be classified on the basis of pattern or regularity of movement:

Trade Winds

Trade winds blow toward the equator between the 30th parallel of north and south latitude. These winds are in movement constantly as northeasterly winds in the northern hemisphere and southeasterly winds in the southern hemisphere. Many of the ships which travel to Japan from America sail at about the 20th parallel in the northern hemisphere, because they can take advantage of this trade wind as well as the equatorial current. There is also an anti-trade wind which blows in the opposite direction, just above the trade wind. We can often see in the sky cirrus, or upper clouds, moving away in the opposite direction of the lower clouds. This phenomenon confirms the existence of an anti-trade wind. The same principles apply here as in the case of current circulation, that is, heated air rises and it comes down when it gets cooler.

Trade winds initially blow due south and due north, but as the earth rotates from west to east, they shift to the right. As the name itself implies, trade winds are directly beneficial for transportation. Furthermore, by giving birth to sea currents, they are indirectly beneficial as well.

Monsoon or Seasonal Winds

This type of wind is common in the Indian Ocean and the South China Sea. In summer (from March to October), winds blow from the Indian Ocean toward the center of low pressure on the Asian Continent. But in winter (from November to February), the winds move in the opposite direction. In April, and again in October, when the direction of the wind changes, strong monsoon and typhoon scale winds develop in the Indian Ocean and the South China Sea. Our rainy season in Japan is another consequence of this shift in air pressure and wind direction.

Sea breezes and Land Breezes

On the coast, in the daytime, wind blows from the sea, whereas during the night the wind blows from the land out to the sea. This same phenomena can also be seen in the vicinity of high mountains or valleys. This kind of wind prevents sudden changes in temperature and moderates the climate in coastal areas. It is this kind of wind also which has long been utilized by sailboats and fishing boats.

Moisture and Human Life

The surface of the sea emits vapor continuously, as do swamps, lakes, ponds and forests. When water rises high in the atmosphere, it gets cool and condenses. Then, it falls to the ground where it penetrates the earth and joins with rivers, streams, and other bodies of water. Rain, snow, clouds, frost, and dew—each is water in a different state. Thus, the atmosphere always contains water at some stage in the process of vaporizing or condensing.

There is a limit to the amount of water vapor the atmosphere can contain, however. When it reaches that limit, the atmosphere is described as at the saturation point. This means that the vapor can no longer remain as vapor and turns into a liquid. When the air temperature is high, the saturation point goes up and goes down when the temperature is low. Thus, one might feel dry even if the amount of water vapor in the atmosphere is high, or one might feel wetness even if the amount of water vapor is low. It all depends on the air temperature. If the amount of water vapor remains constant, a high temperature means being drier and a low temperature means being wetter. Humidity is the amount of water contained in the air, and is measured by its relationship to the saturation point.

The level of humidity which human beings find comfortable varies from person to person, but in general a range of from 50 percent to 70 percent is most desirable. If the humidity goes below 40, the air seems excessively dry; if over 80, we say the humidity in the air is high or that it is humid.

Humidity, like temperature, greatly influences our lives. A very hot and humid environment, as in the tropics, is not ideal for humans. Such an environment saps people's energy and makes them lethargic. Physiologically, too high humidity interferes with perspiration and hinders blood circulation. This, in turn, depresses mental and spiritual activity. Hot, humid climates are also conducive to the development and spreading of severe epidemics, such as malaria, dysentery, and cholera.

In areas of moderate humidity, on the other hand, the human body gets a proper amount of stimulation. Perspiration is normal and fresh blood circulates through the body. The proper amount of humidity is like food for human minds and bodies. People become physically strong and agile. So, in general, we find that people who live in the mountains or in the highlands are stronger than those who live in the low, humid areas.

Clouds

Countless tiny drops of water gather together and a cloud is formed. Clouds are never the same; they are always changing. Clouds can be divided roughly into four categories:

- ◆ Ken-un—a cirrus cloud.
- ◆ Seki-un—a cumulus cloud.
- ◆ So-un—a low-altitude cloud.
- ◆ Amagumo—a rain cloud.

With the exception of rain clouds, these different types are difficult to distinguish from each other because their shapes are constantly changing. Clouds floating in a clear sky give us feelings of lightness and pleasantness. Dark, rain clouds, on the other hand, can make us feel gloomy and depressed. England is described as a land of many dreary days. Japanese going there, being used to bright weather in Japan, may easily fall into low spirits. Latinos are said to be fondly attached to their homes whereas Anglo-Saxons tend to leave their country and spread all over the world wherever they can find freedom. Can it be that the gloomy weather of England has something to do with this?

Near the earth, moisture collects and forms fog or mist. Fog is formed when wet and dry atmospheres collide. The coasts of Hokkaido in Japan and the coast of Newfoundland are often shrouded in fog for this reason. In spite of recent advances in navigation, dense fog is still a very serious obstacle for fishermen and others who venture upon the sea.

Rain

As pointed out in the discussion of moisture, rain—or other forms of precipitation—falls from the clouds when moisture in the air reaches its saturation point and comes in contact with cold air high up in the atmosphere. It is water falling in separate drops. Recent studies indicate that moisture needs dust floating in the air in order to fall as rain or snow.

It would be impossible to overstate the direct and indirect importance of rain for the lives of human beings as well as other living things. From our studies of history, we know that rivers have been the great cradles of human civilization and that water makes our existence possible. At the same time, we have to recognize that rain can also be the cause of great human suffering and disaster.

What matters is the amount of rain, a relative matter about which easy generalizations are inadequate. For example, consider agriculture and the fishing industry. Farmers tend to welcome a lot of rain, whereas fishermen, on the other hand, are most satisfied when there is little rain. And people engaged in the production of salt, obviously, prefer as little rain as possible. Yet, since the main diet of human beings consists of cereals and vegetables and, especially here in Japan, rice, our major consideration is rain and agriculture. Thus, in Japan, it is farmers who are most concerned about the amount of rain, and their main concern is whether there will be enough rain and at the right time of the year.

Most of Australia, a desert area with less than 250 mm of rain a year, is almost useless. The Sahara desert and a stretch of desert in the interior of the Asian continent are known also to be among the areas of the world receiving the least rain. The southern Himalayas in India, in contrast, are known to receive more rain than any other place in the world. There, rainfall normally amounts to 12,000 mm a year. Certainly the ideal amount would be somewhere between these extremes. In Japan, we are blessed with a very reasonable range, not too much and not too little. Our range of annual rainfall is between 600 mm (in Abashiri, Hokkaido) and 3,100 mm (in Shingu, in the Kii Peninsula).

For the kind of understanding and appreciation of geography which we are seeking, we should understand in detail what causes rain to fall and how much rain falls in each part of Japan. Yet, since "rainfall" includes the total amount of moisture which reaches the earth, in this country we must include not only rain, but snow, frost, and dew as well.

Snow

Snow is water frozen into small, flat, beautiful, six-sided white flakes which fall to earth in cold weather instead of rain. Snow, like rain, influences our lives in important and unique ways. People who live in the central or northern areas of Japan have had the experience of waking one morning to find that the entire world has become white with new fallen snow. Snow makes everything appear clean and bright and moves us deeply. The sight has inspired poets to write poems about the snow, and we are inspired as we read them. In many cultures snow symbolizes purity, innocence, fidelity, and justice. Snow is fair and impartial. It falls not only on palaces but on shanties as well, and covers everything with its whiteness.

But there is another side to snow also. Too much snow creates many problems. For example, in a heavy snow area most people can not work in the winter. That is one of the reasons that many people living in the northern part of Japan go to Tokyo and other cities to work during the winter months. The people of Hokkaido, especially, are forced to live in a sort of hibernation like animals or plants for nearly half the year. At the same time, for a nation such as Norway, which has made good use of snow and has become one of the strong nations of the world, heavy snow is not necessarily a bad thing. We should remember this especially in regard to northern Japan.

I have heard that farmers in some snowy areas interpret a heavy snow as a sign of a good harvest in the future. This might be considered as no more than an old superstition, but, there could be some truth in it. Snow protects plants from severe north winds and helps fallen leaves turn into valuable humus for crops. So snow, also, has a great deal to do with agriculture.

In ancient times, there were no civilizations which prospered in snowy regions. Now, however, there are civilized countries in snowy regions of the earth, also, and this is quite natural if you think about it. Tropical climates allow people to live in ease. Food is abundant. It gives people little incentive to think about the future. In snowy regions, on the other hand, people are constantly required to think ahead. Accumulating surplus capital is one of the important factors which makes a country civilized, and preparation for the needs of a snowy tomorrow is a strong incentive toward the accumulating of surplus capital.

In considering our relationship with snow, we must also take into account the matter of war. For example, let us imagine two hypothetical countries, A in a warm climate and B in a cold climate. In the event of a war between the two, which country would be in the most advantageous position? I suggest it would be B. That is because A actually has to fight against not only country B, but also the cold, another enemy. According to history, this was the situation in the Genroku incident[1] of 1703 and the Sino-Japanese War of 1894-5. Likewise, France, led by Napoleon who seemed to be unbeatable, was put to rout by Slavs when they fought in conditions of severe cold and heavy snow. Japan should remember this.

Note

[1] The Genroku Incident refers to the incident in Japanese history known as the "Forty-Seven Ronin" (leaderless warriors).

Chapter 18

The Earth's Vegetation

Agriculture, Human Life, and the Earth

Plants, especially grains and vegetables, constitute the staple food of human beings. We also sometimes eat animals that feed on plants. Plants obtain nutrition from substances in the ground and change them into elements which are essential and useful for human beings. They are nurtured by both organic matter and inorganic matter which they obtain from the earth, and they absorb carbon dioxide from the air. The carbon dioxide dissolves into oxygen and carbon in the green cells of plants. Plants, in turn, discharge oxygen, essential to life of humans and other animals, into the air so that we can live.

The carbon in plants combines with other substances to form organic compounds such as fiber, lignin, starch, sugar, resin, protein, and gum. Each of these substances is an essential ingredient in our food, clothing, and shelter. The amount of organic compounds contained in these substances varies. Some of them store mainly starch, protein or sugar. Some store mainly fiber and fiber compounds, or resin. We know the former group as crops grown in the plains, while the latter group, consisting of trees, flourishes naturally in rugged mountain areas.

Our ancestors, over many centuries of experience, discovered various kinds of plants, cultivated them, and handed them down to us as agricultural plants, along with knowledge and practices for cultivating them. Edible plants are the base of our survival. The specific parts of plants that we eat vary. Some plants offer us their grain, some their fruit, stems, leaves, or roots. These plants have been classified by agriculturists into three groups:

◆ cereals—rice, barley, wheat, rye, millet, corn, soybeans, peas.

- vegetables—sweet potatoes, potatoes, carrots, konnyaku, cabbage.
- fruit—oranges, apples, pears, persimmons, cherries.

During the early stages of human history, our ancestors had to devote their energies to obtaining the basic essentials for survival. But with the passing of time and advances in human knowledge, we have come to use plants as raw materials in the production of an almost endless array of products such as fiber, oil, dyes, medicines, spices, paper, and many others.

Forests, Human Life, and the Earth

Direct Influences of Forests on Human Life

The close relationship between our lives and forests can be seen on every hand. Most of the trees in our forests can be used with a minimum of processing, for houses, bridges, battleships, cross-ties, electric light poles, instruments, and fuel. This close relationship between people and forests, which has existed from the beginning of human history, will almost certainly continue into the future. We sometimes hear it said that today iron and coal are the two main material factors underlying civilization. But I would point out that it is wood that brings them to life. In time, I am sure that people will use more stone, brick, or metal because they are durable and nonflammable to some degree. Yet, I cannot imagine that the demand for wood will decrease because of that. New uses are being found for wood all the time, and the demand is certain to become greater in the future. We are already experiencing shortages of some kinds of wood. Every year, the situation is becoming more and more serious.

Some people are deeply concerned about the future of the forests. Our population is increasing steadily. Earlier in our history, we used wood products in their natural state, but now wood is being processed into many other products until our demand for wood seems almost boundless. For example, I think of matches. Japan is exporting matches to most of the other Asian countries, and the amount seems to be increasing constantly. More important is the demand for paper. Paper for books, newspapers, and magazines is one of the new uses of paper, and the demand is increasing rapidly. Other products being made of wood are buttons, alcohol, tar, sugar, turpentine and tannin oil. There is almost no end to the list of wood products.

There is one other important aspect of forests which we should recognize. That pertains to soils and fertilizer. Crops need a large amount of fertilizer every year, whereas trees need much less fertilizer. The reason is that they get humus from fallen leaves which they themselves shed in the autumn, and they obtain nourishment through their roots from deep in the soil. Thus, with the exception of a few trees which require large amounts of lime and magnesium, trees can grow on relatively barren land which is not suitable for agriculture.

Indirect Influences of Forests on Human Life

In Chapter 11, I referred briefly to a relationship between forests and floods. Now I would like to discuss this relationship in more detail. According to dendrologists, 25 percent of the rain that falls to the earth evaporates from tree leaves. Their studies indicate that one kilogram of pine needles can hold five kilograms of water, and that the leaves of some trees can hold seven times their weight in water. Some kinds of moss can hold as much as 10 times their weight in water. This explains why forests have the capacity to affect the water level of rivers. When rain falls, trees retain large amounts of the moisture in their leaves, 25 percent of which evaporates into the atmosphere and the rest falls to the earth where it is absorbed by leaves and moss before gradually soaking into the soil or finding its way to a river.

We can see then that, without our awareness, forests have been modulating rainfall for us. Forests help the soil retain water and prevent it from drying out. If we cut down trees recklessly, we lose this precious water monitor. Without trees, when rain falls, the rivers overflow quickly, washing away earth and sand from the upper reaches of the river, triggering landslides, and causing major destruction. As that sand and soil accumulate in the lower reaches and the mouth of a river, the riverbed rises and causes flooding.

Droughts must also be mentioned here. Floods and droughts share the same cause. That is, without trees as a water modulator, a long spell of fine weather rapidly drains reservoirs. A terrible drought occurs, and it is agriculture which suffers most.

We have learned how important and essential forests are as regulators of rivers and in holding or releasing accumulated rainfall.

Why, then, do we not turn our attention to our forests and do something about them? The simple fact is that if we have good forests, we will not suffer from either drought or flood, and we can obtain abundant materials for construction and industry. That is why statesmen in olden times exerted great effort to protect and nurture the forests. As an old proverb puts it, "If you are making a ten-year plan, plant trees first." I have noticed that all through history, the rulers who are remembered for their wisdom were very concerned about forests.

The relationship between forests and fish should also be noted. On the surface there would seem to be little connection between them, until you look more closely. First, the forest adjusts water supply. Second, it prevents river water from becoming too muddy for fish. Forests are especially beneficial for fish which swim upstream to spawn. Forests provide a home for countless kinds and varieties of insects, and many kinds of fish gather in the shade of dense forests because of the availability of insects for food.

Seaweed and Human Life

In addition to what has been said previously about the importance of plants for human beings, we in Japan have a special attachment to seaweed. We have been eating various kinds of edible seaweed (konbu, tengusa, nori, wakame) for a long time. We dry it or soak it in salt so that we can preserve and transport it. It is also made into various kinds of processed foods. The habitat and the many uses of seaweed make a fascinating study.

Seaweed accounts for a large percentage of our marine products. Our annual export of konbu to China now exceeds one million yen, and that of kanten (Japanese gelatin) is nearly seven hundred thousand yen. It is one of our main products, and seaweed is almost limitless in quantity.

Since some kinds of seaweed are high in glutinous matter, it is useful for making glue. Also, paper, roofing material, matting, and many other things are made from it. It has been reported that chemists in America and Europe have found a way to extract sugar and a kind of rubber from seaweed. Another remarkable use of seaweed is in making seaweed ash. The ash of seaweed is rich in several very scarce substances, such as sulfate of soda, iodine, and carbonate of soda. This kind of utilization of waste materials is most encouraging.

Distribution of Plants

Plants vary in regard to the type of climate and soil in which they can achieve their maximum growth. It is natural, therefore, that greatly differing kinds and quality of plant growth can be observed throughout the world and throughout Japan. We have noted the differences in plant growth in tropical, temperate, and frigid zones of the earth. Similarly, the climate changes with altitude. Just as we can see changes in plant growth as we go from a tropical to a temperate to a frigid zone, so we can see similar changes in the vegetation on our way from the bottom to the top of a mountain.

Plant life varies not only in different climates but in different types of soil in the same climate. For our purposes we can distinguish five different soil types. First is what we might call the "sands." These are areas where the outer layer of the earth's crust is exposed and where few or no plants can be found. Generally, narrow plains along coasts, lakes, and rivers are of this type. Hard clay soil, soil built up from volcanic ash, and deserts can also be classified in this type. Although in some cases there has been experimental planting of pine and other plants in these sandy plains areas, they are generally unproductive and of little use for sustaining human life.

Another category in this classification based on soil type can be called "plains," areas where trees cannot grow because of too little moisture, too much humidity, or because the soil is too hard, and where only various kinds of grasses can be found. A third category is a "shrubbery" area where shrubs and small trees grow. Fourth are the "forests" where tall trees can grow. As has been stressed earlier, forests are extremely important to human life, both for the products derived from them and because they serve as fountainheads for river systems; they influence climate, and contribute to human well being in many ways. Finally there is what we will refer to as "reclaimed land," that is, land which has been brought under cultivation.

Means of Plant Distribution

The way in which plants spread on the earth is a manifestation of the ebb and flow between the generative and multiplicative functions of the plant and the restraining function of nature. When a plant finishes its life, it leaves a given number of descendants to continue the next generation. How they manage to survive and attempt to acquire more space for their own is an amazing story in itself. Plants increase their number by their own reproductive processes, by their seeds being carried by the wind or by rivers and oceans, by being carried by animals and by being carried, either consciously or unconsciously, by human beings.

Yet, plants confront many obstacles in their struggle to survive and spread their kind: high mountains, the ocean, climatic and natural forces which work against them, and other plants which are better adapted or more suitable for a particular area or soil type. But it is climate which most influences and affects plant growth and survival. In order to germinate, plants require a certain temperature. Most plants cannot germinate in temperatures below zero, and cannot grow if the temperature rises above 46 degrees centigrade. The various kinds of plants each have an optimum temperature at which they grow most rapidly. In our studies in human geography, we will want to inquire into the critical and optimum temperatures and the northern limits of growth for each of the different plants in our area of the earth.

The Spiritual Influences of Plants

Whether you travel or stay at home, when you feel blue or sad or depressed, and when you triumph, wherever you are, plants are a source of consolation and pleasure. Plants stimulate our sense of beauty, mitigate our primal rage, and nurture our souls. Each plant affects us in different ways. Some plants delight us with their flowers, some with their scent, others with their leaves or their fruit. Poems have been composed in praise of plants since ancient times. Among the myriad plants and flowers, it is interesting the way certain flowers endear themselves to particular cultural groups: Western people and the rose, the Chinese and the peony, the Japanese and cherry blossoms. As civilization advances and as human population increases, opportunities for spiritual contact with plants are diminishing, but even so, how precious and important for our lives are plants!

Whether you travel or stay at home, when you feel blue or sad or depressed, and when you triumph, wherever you are, plants are a source of consolation and pleasure. Plants stimulate our sense of beauty, mitigate our primal rage, and nurture our souls.

Plants and Culture

Our culture, our way of living, is very much shaped by vegetation, particularly the quantity of vegetation. For example, it was in dry highlands that nomadic cultures developed, where a living was obtained by constant movement. On the other hand, low, swampy plains and wide valleys encouraged agriculture, and induced people to settle down in one place, setting the stage for the development of human civilization as we know it today. But is a rich plant life all that is necessary for the development of a rich cultural life? I believe the answer is "No!" The reason is that if plants grow too fast and too prolifically, as in the tropics or the subtropics, growth of vegetables is hindered by the rapid growth of weeds, and farmers have to spend too much of their time and energy getting rid of the weeds. A further factor is that when plant life is prolific and abundant, making a living is relatively easy and the people do not have to struggle or make great effort. When life is too easy, there is little motivation for people to better their life or develop their culture. A land of too sparse vegetation is not good for the development of culture, but a land of too prolific vegetation is not good, either. So, at least at the early stages in the life of a of civilization, an area of rich but moderate growth of plants is the most suitable for the development of culture.

Chapter 19

Animals

The Earth as Home to Animals and Humans

Animals, more flexible than plants and much less influenced by climate, still depend on plants for food, either directly or indirectly. We, in turn, depend on animals, not only for food, but also for clothing, for tools, and for various daily necessities. Society has been shaped by animals. Where there were animals, there hunters gathered. Likewise, fishermen lived where fish were plentiful. Each group or community or tribe formed its own peculiar primitive society and embarked on its own unique development, influenced by animal life. Hunting people, discovering that what they had hunted could be tamed and raised, became cattle raising people. Gatherers who collected roots, berries, nuts, and fruit became farmers. This was the beginning of human progress, and an important factor in the overall story of human beings on earth. When people lived by hunting, for example, they might at one time have too much food, but at another time they might have no food at all for days or even longer. By raising cattle instead of depending solely on the hunt, they could obtain milk and meat regularly; a stable life became possible.

The population of a given community or tribe of hunters could not rise higher than the number of animals available to be hunted permitted. However, after the domestication of animals, each community could support many more people. In other words, for a hunting people, the food supply works as a centrifugal force, dispersing them, but following the domestication of animals, it works as a centripetal force, bringing people together. Moreover, the people themselves sense value and advantage in living in close proximity to other people and families for protection and for cooperation in breeding domestic animals. Thus, because of the role played by animals, communities come to form stronger and wider bonds.

There are also enemies of human beings among the members of the animal kingdom. Rhinoceroses, wolves, bears, tigers, crocodiles and poisonous snakes come to mind as dangerous to human life. Others, including some types of birds, damage crops and interfere with human activities in other ways, and there are insects and microbes that spread disease and destroy crops.

Today, most of the animals which pose a danger to humans have been conquered or have been driven to remote areas where they no longer constitute a threat. Knowledge enabled us to control or eradicate members of the animal kingdom which in the past have been harmful to human life. We need to be careful here, however, so that our efforts in this area do not become counterproductive. We should be careful, for example, that we do not harm birds unwisely or out of ignorance, because there are some birds which may seem to damage crops or trees but which actually help the growth of trees and crops by controlling insects which feed on them.

Animals and Human Life

Each member of the animal kingdom has something to offer human welfare: fur, wool, bones or horns, meat or milk. Birds are not only a source of delicious meat and eggs; they also give us material for brushes, feather bedding, fishing tools, and various other accessories. Birds in some cultures have been used as a means of communication by carrying messages to distant places. Mention might also be made of the crucial role of the horse in providing transportation and means of conveyance for human beings in many cultures of the world.

Vegetarianism has become a way of life for many people in recent years, and this raises important questions about our diet. Rice is, of course, our staple food, but it is my conclusion that some meat is an indispensable part of the human diet because it is one of the best sources of protein, phosphoric acid, and many other elements which the human body requires to maintain good health. In this connection, in thinking about the dietary needs of our country, I have come to feel strongly that we should develop a rabbit industry and make rabbit meat a major source of the protein we need to maintain good health.

It is fascinating to study the different kinds and classes of animals, birds, fish, and the many other members of the animal kingdom. Along with this process of classification, it will be natural to inquire into the distribution of animals around the world, their habitats, numbers, and how they adapt to changes in temperature. Do they, for example, hibernate, molt, migrate, or adapt in some other way? Such inquiries as these can contribute to our efforts to understand the earth and our relationship to it and should be an important part of our study of human geography.

Animals and Human Feelings

Animals contribute not only to our physical well being, but nurture us spiritually and esthetically as well. How fortunate is the person who comes to know an animal as a companion and friend! And how much joy and beauty the members of the animal kingdom add to human life by their many colors and shapes, their graceful dancing movements, their voices and songs! Sometimes our experience with animals, birds, or other living creatures causes us to feel deep joy and happiness; sometimes we cannot help but cry, or we feel sad or lonely. Poets and other artists among us who have experienced these feelings with animals have sought to express their feelings in their works. We can imagine, for example, the experience which led Basho to write:

> *Animals can contribute not only to our physical well being, but nurture us spiritually and esthetically as well. How fortunate is the person who comes to know an animal as a companion and friend!*

> A bird has perched on a withered branch, late in Autumn.

Or Shikyo:

> A nightingale flies up to the heavens, a fish dances in a pool.

Or Sarumarutayu's poetic words:

> When I hear the plaintive call of a deer making its way through colorful autumn leaves in distant mountains I feel nostalgic.

Or again, Gokyogoku no Sessho's:

> A grasshopper is singing. How lonely I feel when I sleep alone on a frosty night.

Thus do animals affect us spiritually and emotionally, enriching and adding beauty to our culture.

Chapter 20

The Human Species

Human Beings as Social Animals

We human beings have tended to perceive ourselves as the lords of creation. However, as we have learned more about ourselves and our history, we have come to realize that present human beings are the result of an ages long process of evolution. We can look back now and imagine how weak and helpless we were in the beginning stages of that evolutionary journey.

From the viewpoint of natural history, human beings are one of the higher mammals with vertebrae and spinal cord, with hands and feet equivalent to the forelegs and hindlegs of other animals. When we walk, we walk in an upright position, but the physical differences between us and other animals are actually rather small. What separates us from other higher animals is our mind and spirit. Self consciousness, language capability, our will or rationality, all these come from our more highly developed brains.

Now, we cannot deny the fact that animals themselves have emotions, knowledge, and awareness in some degree. It is not that humans are completely different from other forms of animal life in this regard. It is rather a matter of the stage of development we are in. It has been through using the unique characteristics which we possess that we human beings have continued to live in the face of powerful and often hostile natural forces around us. Moreover, we have made use of these natural forces and have successfully adjusted ourselves to the environment. We have multiplied, conquered other species, formed societies or nations, and achieved a significant degree of prosperity. The characteristics with which we are naturally endowed and which have enabled us to do this provide the basis for us to live in the human societies of today as social beings, but how much we owe to time and the trials nature has put us through.

Population and Human Habitats

Each living thing is restricted in some way by the realities of nature and each has its own habitat, according to its capacity for adapting to its surroundings. As members of the animal kingdom, we must expect that we will be restricted by various natural geographic conditions, as well. But actually we have fewer restrictions, compared to other living things. Look at the world. Human beings are to be seen almost everywhere on the earth. It is not because we are stronger than the others. In fact, humans are relatively weak physically. Rather, it is because of our more highly developed brains, as we have noted before. This enables us to survive and multiply in the face of harsh natural forces because it gives us the ability to adjust to changing surroundings. It may be also that because of our curiosity, our adventurous spirit, or at times by accident, we have been extending our habitats. Human beings have taken the initiative in the material world. We have taken possession of all living and non living things, we make use of them, and we are increasing in number.

Stages of Human Development

There are now on the earth about one billion and a half people who differ widely in race, culture, and stage of development. In earlier days, each of these peoples lived a separate, secluded existence. Today, however, the high development of means of transportation makes it almost impossible for any group to lead an isolated life. And so, we see these many different peoples in their different stages of development coming into closer and closer contact with each other. We have come to use such terms as "savage," "primitive," "half-civilized," and "civilized" in order to distinguish among these diverse peoples. For purposes of determining which stage a given group or people are in, I have found it useful to look closely at their relationship with their land, that is, whether they are close to their land or not, whether the land they relate to is wide and spacious or small and limited. This has led me to conceive a two-part classification of the members of the human race, those whom we will call "settled," and those we will call "unsettled." Let us consider each of these in some detail.

The Unsettled

By "unsettled," I refer to people who do not have a concept of land ownership and who simply move to a new location when food or other resources are exhausted where they are. People in this category are of two types: those who are always on the move and those who stay in one place for a period of time. Hunting and fishing people belong to the former group and nomadic people belong to the latter group. At any rate, in my classification, "savage" becomes hunting and fishing peoples (the least civilized) and "primitive" becomes nomadic peoples.

The Settled

When wandering or half-settled people discover the advantages of farming and come to settle in one place, a close relationship of love and attachment between land and people is born. Gradually the basis is formed for the development of a refined culture. Settled people, too, can be divided into two types on the basis of their activity.

What has been called "half-civilized" people are limited by the absence of good transportation facilities. They are unable to understand or deal with modern concepts and technology. As a result they tend to reject modern culture. On the other hand, the development of good transportation and acceptance of modern technology permit the people classified as "civilized" to travel long distances and to develop contacts with foreign people, increasing their country's wealth and raising their standard of living. Thus, their activities are not limited by cultural or political borders.

There are no clear divisions of the living space of people in different stages of development. Still, people in each stage tend to occupy one main type of area. So, I believe we can assume that geographical conditions have a close relationship to human development. We can observe that the two areas which are subject to extreme climate—the tropics and the frigid zone—tend to be the home of "savage" peoples, while the temperate zones are the home of the more developed peoples.

Looking more closely at the temperate zones, we can observe that "primitive" peoples occupy the dry highlands which contain little vegetation. The so-called civilized peoples, in contrast, are found to occupy the lower flatlands and coastal areas which generally have an abundance of water. These areas, too, it will be noticed, are characterized in many cases by both land and water transportation and, especially, by complex and irregular coastlines. The cultural level tends to vary in proportion to distance from the coast. We may note, in addition, that density of population of nomadic peoples differs from that of settled peoples.

We may wonder why savage peoples are found in both of the climatically extreme zones. My conclusion is that in the case of the tropics the richness of vegetation and the ease with which basic food needs can be met do not encourage people to be resourceful or exert great effort. There is no motivation to develop cultural things or to better themselves. On the other hand, life in the frigid zone is so harsh and the forces of nature so severe that it requires all of the energy and ingenuity the people possess just to make a living. Thus, they have no time or energy for cultural development and advancement.

Stages of Development in Japan

All of these various stages of development can be found here in our own country. Within our 371,367 sq km of land area, nearly 50 million people are now living. In both the north and the south ends of the country there are still some people who can be classified as "savage". In the middle part of Japan, particularly in the coastal areas, are people who have reached the "civilized" stage, and in some of the remote mountain areas, there are a few "half-civilized" people.

It is possible, even in a small village, to observe these different stages of human development. There are some people who are totally dependent on nature or on other persons, and are still not able to function independently, even though they have strong, healthy bodies. On the other hand, there are some people who take advantage of modern conveniences and natural forces, and have thousands of people under them. And, of course, between the two groups we find innumerable stages of human development.

If we apply the principles and categories described above to our own lives, we will realize that we individually go through different stages of human development during our lifetimes. Of course, there are individuals who stop growing, who stagnate mentally, but in general, we go through many stages, from the fragility of babyhood to strong, knowledgeable adulthood. Going through a series of stages in the process of coming to maturity is typical of both individual growth and the development of the human species as a whole.

Different Races and Their Futures

We can observe, even among people of the same race, different stages of human development in different geographic locations. But, in general, the black, red, and brown races tend to be the ones in the "savage" or "primitive" stages, whereas the people of the white race have reached the most advanced stage. As for the yellow race, some have reached the "civilized" stage; the rest are still outside the pale of civilization. It seems that the gradation of colors almost coincides with our spiritual development. So, perhaps there are reasons why the members of the white race claim so confidently that the world is for them.

But are the members of the white race really the sole owners of the world as they seem to think? When we consider human history as a whole, it seems that superior races do conquer inferior races, as superior individuals overtake the less well endowed.

History might lead one to think that the world is ultimately to be conquered by the white people, the superior race. Yet this is still very much open to question. There are many examples of peoples of the same race developing differently in different environments. Climate, for example, as noted previously, is a critically important environmental factor influencing human development, and it is impossible for human beings, even superior human beings, to change the climate.

Will the World of the Future See a Power Struggle between the White and Yellow Races?

Charles Pearson, a British scholar, has commented on the speed with which members of the white race have increased their influence around the world within the past one hundred years, leading to the decline or extinction of the native peoples of the Americas and Australia. He concludes, however, that it is not likely that one or two superior races will conquer and monopolize the entire world. Yet, the white race lives in the temperate zones where there are four distinct seasons. They become accustomed to changes of temperature and other conditions which enable them to be highly adaptable and flexible.

These considerations have led some people to predict a struggle for supremacy between the white and the yellow races. In a sense, the history of the world supports that theory, and even now we see instances of such a struggle in various parts of the world. Since the beginning of the modern period, white people have frequently invaded Asia and conquered yellow people. In the Middle Ages, the yellow people went deep into Europe more than once, conquering and plundering the Roman Empire and other white peoples. At present, both in America and Australia, anti-yellow race movements are growing.

Pearson concludes that it may well be the Chinese who will have the biggest influence over the future of the world. John Bachman, a biologist, suggests a similar view. In recent writings he has observed that those who have trained themselves through natural selection, have lived a frugal life, and have rich procreative powers, could take over European cultures. And it is the Chinese who best satisfy those conditions.

The Spread of World Population

I have commented in previous chapters on the various environmental and geographical factors which affect the spread of population throughout the earth. Here I will try to summarize these factors and add some further explanatory material. We have discovered, first of all, that human beings need a moderate amount of moisture (roughly between 50 percent and 70 percent) to breathe. Therefore, it is impossible for us to live in an extremely dry area. That is why fewer people live in the interior of continents where there is little or no rain. On the other hand, excess humidity is not good for our health, either, so not many people live in the over-humid tropics. Likewise, air temperature directly influences the breathing of humans as well as other living things, especially plants, upon which humans depend for their survival.

Rainfall more than anything else determines the geographical distribution of plants and, indirectly, the spread of the human population as well. Thus, the distribution of the human population coincides with rainfall distribution, with the exception of extremely humid areas. Our lives are also deeply entwined with rivers since we depend on rivers for drinking water, transportation, and in meeting many other needs. We can say, therefore, that the spread of human population generally coincides with the existence of rivers. Rivers have their source in rain. Rain originates from the ocean from which vapor rises. Oceans and seas serve as vital transportation elements in the lives of civilized peoples. Therefore, it is natural to find dense populations along coasts. The further one travels from the coastal areas, the fewer people there are.

Now, in one respect, the number of people who live in a given geographic location is also influenced by the type of people who live there. Suppose there are two geographic locations which have identical conditions. If the people who inhabit one of the locations are of a superior race and the other location is home to an inferior race, the location inhabited by the superior race will, in general, have a denser population. The reason is that the people of the inferior race depend for almost everything on the land where they live, limiting their numbers to the number which the land can support. On the other hand, the superior race is not so dependent on the land because they get most of their necessities from abroad, therefore, many more people can live in the same land area.

Part Three:
The Phenomenon of Human Life on the Earth

Shirogane Elementary School principal Makiguchi (front row, in suit and tie), an educator much loved by pupils, parents, and fellow teachers. This undated photograph was taken in the schoolyard of the original wooden schoolhouse in downtown Tokyo.

Chapter 21

Society

What Is Society?

There is no word that is used in so many ways and with such diverse meanings as the word "society." For example, consider these expressions: "for the sake of society," "punishment by society," "socialism," "socialist party." These words and expressions and numerous others are used freely in every day life and in newspapers. But when we reflect on their meaning, we find they are used so loosely and arbitrarily that we are left confused as to what the speakers or writers really mean. There is some hope that sociology, which has just recently begun to develop and promises to provide a basis for all the social sciences, may be of some help in arriving at a clearer and more precise definition of the meaning of society.

By way of some preliminary observations, we can talk about "actions" of society. For example, if a man makes a profit unjustly, society will take offense and extract appropriate penalties. On the other hand, a person who undertakes an enterprise in behalf of society and in the interests of the society, without regard for personal profit, will be honored by society. Thus, we can see that what people do is judged by society. Most people care about this and are guided in some degree by their awareness of society's expectations and judgments.

But who judges? We can't see any concrete body, but as long as there are actions and reactions to those actions, there must be an actor. We can solve this problem by recognizing that a society is a group of individuals who live in a more or less permanent relationship to each other and that we are its members.

What about the size or range of this "group"? Suppose an important lecture has been planned and advertised and a large auditorium has been filled with people who are interested in the topic. If a drunken man causes a commotion and interferes with the lecture, the audience will become angry and want the man to be expelled. Hundreds, or perhaps thousands, of people have gathered in that auditorium with a common purpose and are united into a small society with a common interest, even though for a limited time.

Or, consider a family which consists of various members who are related to each other as parents and children, wives and husbands, brothers and sisters, masters and servants. Each member plays some part in the family life and all the members live together for some generations. If one or more members neglect their roles, the family will suffer, its harmony will be disturbed, its well-being will be threatened, and it may even disintegrate. This family also is a small society.

Again, consider a school which may have thousands of students, teachers who teach them, a principal who manages its affairs, clerks who take care of its routine functions, and a janitor responsible for maintenance and cleanliness of the physical facilities of the school. This school can likewise be understood as a small society. Its various members work together to achieve a common purpose, that of carrying on the process of teaching the young.

At the upper range, villages, towns, cities, and other local bodies are also societies, and the nation is the largest and most complete society. At the same time, we should recognize that the word "society" is sometimes used to identify ethnic groups or even, more recently, to refer to the whole world. We can see, then, that there is a wide range in the size and nature of groups to which we can apply the word "society," but there are certain elements which they all share. These common elements can be listed as follows:

◆ A society consists of various individuals just as a living body consists of various cells.

◆ The members of a society share a common purpose which members hold consciously or unconsciously.

◆ There seems to be a permanent mental or spiritual relationship between the individual members of a society not unlike that between the cells of a living body.

◆ The members of a society live together in a particular geographic area.

◆ Thus,the members of a society are united into a group in a manner similar to the unity between the cells of a living body, and its various members play specified roles or functions in maintaining the welfare of the society, as do the organs of the body.

A Definition of Society

We can now define society, then, as "a group of individuals who live together in a certain area, share a common purpose and some kind of permanent psychological bond." In the interests of further clarification and preciseness, two main types or divisions of society can be identified, that is, what I will call "true societies" and "social groups" which derive from societies. Villages, towns, or nations are formed naturally and should be identified as true societies. But schools, meetings, organizations, and other social groupings are formed after the initial organization of true societies as organs to sustain the body of society and to achieve its purposes.

Specialization Within Social Groups

Sociologists call these derivative groups "social organizations," "social groups," or "functional groups" and distinguish them from the larger society of which they are specialized parts. Without society and its specialized organs, individuals had to do everything for themselves in order to live. In a developed or developing society, however, each person assumes only a small part of the social life of the whole, but receives all of life's necessities from it while contributing only a little.

A good example of this division of labor can be seen in the contemporary family. The husband goes out to work to get money, defends his family, and leads its members. The wife stays at home, manages the household, sews clothes, cooks, lets the husband work without being anxious about household affairs, and nurtures their children. If the husband's and wife's parents live with the family, they can supervise the whole household, play the part of consultants by virtue of their years of experience, help with caring for the children, and contribute to the family's prosperity.[1]

Infants, while outwardly appearing to be spongers, doing nothing for the family, actually play an important role and contribute much to the family. Single men and women can live quite freely and with little sense of responsibility, but once they get married and form a family, they acquire a new sense of responsibility, strengthened when a child is born. Parents take good care of the child and work hard for the future happiness of their offspring. The parents can experience a joy which people who never have a child cannot even imagine. Even people who are cold-hearted and irresponsible toward others can be observed to be warm and gentle to their children. In this respect, we can say that infants and children contribute to the growth of their parents' moral characters.

Children may be valued as the center of a family's social life and might very well be called the "holy spirits of peace." There is something static about a family without a child, a stillness, as in a cell that does not metabolize. As Yamanoue-no Okura is said to have observed, "Silver, gold, and jewelry are nothing in comparison to the value of children."

If the members of a family live separately, each person must do everything for himself. Even a self-sufficient person may find it difficult to live a full, rewarding life by oneself alone. Think of this not merely as bias or opinion but as an observation of single people around us and married persons who can remember their feelings and difficulties from when they were single.

Whole Societies and Partial Societies

I have previously referred to two types of society, true societies and derived social groups. True societies are not all on the same level. Small societies are included within larger ones, and upper level societies control lower ones. Each sustains the other. There are prefectures within a nation, for example, and cities, towns, and villages are within the jurisdiction of prefectures; families are under these smaller divisions. The family is the simplest and most natural society.

The Mental Life of Society

In one sense, we can describe a society as sentient. People are afraid of society's censure or punishment and are happy to receive its praise. This is not unlike the relationship between children and their parents. This observation leads me to think of a society as having an intellectual, emotional, and volitional life just like a person.

Intellectual Life

Most people do not realize it, but what we regard as our own knowledge is almost totally the property of our society. Language is the best example of this. Every nation has its own language and every district has its dialect. Each professional group or family has its peculiar terms and expressions. In each case the language is owned, not by the individual members, but by the society as a whole. It was not invented by any one person, so no one can think of it as personal property.

Individuals cannot live in a society unless they learn its language. Ideas and beliefs which are expressed and communicated through language are also owned by the society. Individuals must learn these ideas and knowledge to live in the society. The main function of school education is to offer the society's language and knowledge to children and let them prepare themselves to be members of the society.

In addition to language and ideas, ways of life such as methods of agriculture, fishing, commerce, and other activities such as cooking, sewing, clothing design, and tool making are also social property, unique to each society. All of these are the fruits of human intelligence, so in this sense we can say a society has an intellectual life. Our so called "common sense" is a condensation of the particular knowledge of a society and it becomes the standard of judgment for people's deeds.

Emotional Life

Each society or group has its own unique emotional life as well. It is always in flux, just as individual emotions are. Japanese society, just before the China-Japan War, was filled with gloom and foreboding. But after Japan won her first sea battle, gloom turned to joy, confidence, and a sense of well-being.

Emotional behavior appears most dramatically and on a large scale in panics, revolts, riots, and revolutions. In these cases, just as in personal experiences of fear, anger, and wrath, intelligent action is suppressed under the impact of strong emotion. Reason, which should control emotion, is suppressed; behavior becomes extreme, violent, and misdirected. The result is social derangement which spreads like an epidemic. Though people are aware of their emotions and their actions at first, later they get caught up in the mass hysteria and their actions become unconscious reflexes. Take the example of political meetings where members of the audience clap their hands and give vigorous applause though only a few persons may be genuinely moved to express their emotion; many others merely imitate them without thought. Or when people come across an accident, they may be upset and run away not knowing what they are doing. Soldiers have been known to become demoralized by the wind or the cries of birds. These are examples of emotional dislocation.

Such emotional epidemics will tend to attract people who are easily excited, particularly younger people. Recently there have been many incidents of violence and turmoil in our schools, almost as if they were in fashion. Students lack hope. They are impatient and seem to have no sense of responsibility when they are in large groups. They trust to numbers and think that the group is responsible for whatever they do. In such circumstances they will do what they would not do as individuals.

The Social Will

We have seen that society has both an intellectual life and an emotional life. We will naturally expect, then, to find a social will deriving from these two. Laws, policies, declarations of war, and conclusions of treaties are all expressions of the social will. Some societies give high priority to matters of domestic administration. Some are consumed with diplomacy or military operations. In others, business dominates social life. Even in the same society, the main focus of concern and activity may vary with the times.

This "spirit" of a society is not imaginary. Just as we can perceive our mental life clearly and concretely through reflection and meditation, so the spirit of a society can be recognized, and it is neither imaginary nor abstract. Then what is its origin? It comes from the mind of each individual. Individual minds are united into something like an interpersonal mental entity and it influences and shapes the will of each member.

How is this interpersonal entity formed? It evolves among people as one person imitates another or feels sympathy for someone else. Then this feeling spreads through the whole society. Just as individual mental activities come from individual brains consisting of many cells, so individual brains play the part of cells in creating the mental life or spirit of a society. Language, books, newspapers, magazines, etc., comprise the channels of communication which link or connect the individual cells of the society.

The Evolution of a Society

Each part of a living body is always subject to the metabolism of that body. Parts of the body change, but the body as a whole continues to exist, to grow, and to evolve. So it is with a society. Individuals and groups are born and die, but the society itself continues to exist and to develop, not only in size, but also in its intellectual life. Some of the intellectual attainments of a given era in the society's history will survive the deaths of the people of that era, remaining within the society as oral traditions, legends, or written documents which are handed down to succeeding generations. As generation after generation adds newly discovered treasures to this evolving intellectual life of the society, it grows in richness and breadth.

When we speak of the "expansion" of a society, we are referring to its growth in size. "Development" connotes improvement in the quality of the society; that is, organizations and organizational inter-relationships within the society become increasingly complex, and its intellectual life becomes richer and more elaborate. The concept "evolution," as borrowed from biology, includes both meanings. As a society evolves, each part becomes more specialized, the division of labor and cooperation among individuals and groups becomes more wide-spread and more closely related. In time, the society becomes one mixed body and every part is harmonized. Causes produce effects and effects lead to causes. Our own society today is a product of this process of historical evolution and is at the same time a participant.

Society as an Organic Body

Society, as a kind of living body, grows in size and develops by specialization and multiplication of its inner organs. In short, a society evolves like other organic bodies. No part can live separated from the whole of society, and the whole society cannot live without its parts. For purposes of clearer understanding, let us think of society as an organic being.

Two kinds of material can be identified in the universe: inorganic, inanimate matter such as metal, stone, or clay, and organic matter, i.e., animal and plant life. In the former case, when different specimens of material happen to exist together in the same place and the same time, there is no relationship between molecules. But in the latter case, each part has a close relationship with all the other parts, and if one component is changed, that change influences the rest. Each part has a different function and it cooperates with the others in order that all the parts and the whole body can live. For example, should the stomach or the brain be taken from a living creature, that creature will die and become inanimate, unresponsive molecular material like metal or stone.

If, as suggested above, all matter in the universe can be divided into inanimate matter and organic matter, I believe it is quite natural to think of society as organic. Herbert Spencer (1820-1903), a British philosopher, observed that animals possess three different types of systems, a nurturing system, a circulatory system, and a nervous or administrative system. Spencer suggested that this three-system model could also be used to describe social systems. Thus, every society has systems to nurture the whole, promote circulation, and administer itself.

◆ Businesses serve as nurturing organs.

◆ Commerce and transportion comprise the circulatory organs.

◆ Political or administrative bodies constitute the nervous system.

If we are to perceive society as an organic body, we must also keep in mind the important differences between a society and other living creatures. For example, an animal will die if its stomach or its brain is removed. In a society, if one or even several organizations break down, others will take over their functions, and the society itself will recover. While an animal's lifespan is limited, the life of a society endures.

Note

[1] While significant change has occurred in Japanese family structure since the time in which Makiguchi wrote, there are still, today, many people in the population who perceive male and female roles in these traditional terms. This is particularly the case with the male perception of the female role. Interestingly enough, change in role expectations has occurred much more rapidly among young women than among young men, and this is currently creating problems for young people and the families they form. At the same time, increasing numbers of young men are assuming a share of the responsibility for household tasks and caring for children.

Chapter 22

The Functions of Society

The Various Activities of a Society

That our daily lives are carried on within a social context is a given. In a society, complex phenomena depend on or respond to one another, enabling survival and progress. Thus, some individual members of the society produce needed commodities, others become administrators, scholars, teachers, police to defend the society's communities, priests, entrepreneurs, or laborers, according to their individual inclinations and abilities. Those persons who follow a particular occupation or role become a special division within the society, having their own common interests and needs. Divisions cooperate and compete, as do the individuals in each division. With time, societies develop more and more complex specializations and subdivisions. When the society is viewed as a whole, however, the divisions are seen to work in harmony and mutual interdependence, just as the ears, eyes, hands, legs, and brain of a body work together in the overall interests of that body.

The functions of a society, then, and the activities deriving from those functions, may be classified as follows:

- ◆ Business and Economics
- ◆ Politics and Administration
- ◆ Morality
- ◆ Religion
- ◆ Scholarship
- ◆ Education
- ◆ Art
- ◆ Recreation

Business and Economics

It is the role of the business sector to assure that a society will have the necessary distributable goods to meet the needs and desires of the society's members, and politics must concentrate on the survival and progress of a society. Activities related to getting food, clothing, and shelter are basic both for individuals and for the society. Thus, in the early life of a society, everyone must engage in the business of acquiring these necessities, and when an enemy appears, everyone must stop work and help defend the society. As populations increase—our own, as well as the population of enemy societies—the struggle for existence becomes more and more difficult with the result that the danger of enemy attack also increases. This leads to a need for a society to have some of its members prepared for battle and defense at all times.

The response to this producer/defender two-phase struggle for survival has been to divide people into two categories, the physically weaker who engaged in economic functions to provide for basic needs, and the stronger who concentrated on military preparedness. Actually, the sharpest division between industry and politics probably began when early societies began to use slaves. The winning warriors made the prisoners of war work and produce more food than they consumed. Once the use of slaves became widespread, their masters had the leisure to turn to other fields. Society became an increasingly complex system of interdependent parts, and human affairs developed sophisticate entanglements. Thus began the business world and human civilization.

Prior to the modern era, individuals or small tribal societies consumed what they produced themselves. There was no commerce, and products had no prices, so wealth was not accumulated. When exchanges began to occur between those who produced and those who consumed, true business activity began. This was followed by the development of business organizations and the three-fold process we know today as production, distribution, and consumption.

An old Chinese saying, "When people have enough food and clothing, they know courtesy" suggests one way in which business activities affect other social activities. It is only when we are free from fear of starvation and poverty that we can engage in higher intellectual, moral, and religious activities.

We can see from this that the level of development of a society depends to some extent on whether commerce has developed or not, and how important business activity is to the well-being of a society. To neglect business and attempt only to develop political, military, or educational organizations is to go bankrupt. All the policies of a state must be based on promoting national prosperity. Of course, it goes without saying that the good life will not be found in a society which is concerned only with the development of business organizations. Business is but the first step, the means, to the achievement of more lofty social objectives.

Politics and Administration

Political activities are also two dimensional in nature, i.e., to defend the members of the society from enemies and to protect the human rights of its members by effective legislation. In other words, the function of political organizations is to enhance national integrity and contribute to internal unity. With the achievement of internal unity, a state can devote itself to the promotion of national prosperity in competition with other states in the struggle for existence. Then it is in a position to intervene, initiate, and encourage other internal social activities.

Morality

Contemporary states encourage the development of industries and educational systems as their two main functions. Political activities are dependent on the development of business, and business can not succeed without the social stability achieved by political activities. But we must note here that the quality of political activities in a society depends on the quality of the lives and the abilities of the society's politicians. Therefore, the development of educational, scientific, and religious functions within a society to serve as the basis of character training is essential in order for the society to be able to provide a good life for its members. The political functions of a society can be understood as the fruit of all the other functions, and they serve to organize, harmonize, and unite them.

Concern with morality and attempts to elevate ethical behavior become particularly prominent when morality declines and corruption abounds. These efforts tend to result in lists of rules and prescriptions for behavior at first, but become more concerned with character formation and personal development as society puts its efforts into educational activities.

Religion

Religious activities are carried on under the direction of priests or religionists who officially represent individual religious groups or sects. According to developing international custom, governments cannot intervene in matters regarding their people's faith, but they can intervene in regard to the actions of their people. So in this sense religious activities may be considered a societal function. Because religious belief has great influence on individual minds, it clearly has a close relationship to the other institutions and activities of a society. On the other hand, the character of religious belief is also affected by the nature of particular cultures.

A first step toward understanding the relationship between religion and culture would be a study of the distribution of the world's major religions, their origins, and the history of their spreading to other areas. Having studied religious phenomena at some length, including their patterns of spreading, one conclusion I have come to is that the spread of a particular religious faith depends more on the priests or missionaries who carry it than on the character of the individual sects.

Scholarship

The role of scholars in a society is to push society forward by contributing the skills and specialties of their fields of study. Motivated by the desire to know the truth, their influence appears in the form of organizations devoted to study and sharing the results of study such as schools and the mass media. Academic activities must necessarily stand on foundations provided by business. Thus if a society is to progress, industry and scholarship must go hand in hand.

Education

As important as business is for the well being of a society, it is education which is the true basis of all the other activities of the society. Education is the key factor influencing the destiny of a society. It is education which supplies talents and abilities to all other fields, and it is education which can nurture good character, ethical behavior, and social consciousness within the members of a society. But there are several things which should be clearly understood about education. First of all, in earlier times, no difference or separation was perceived between scholarship and education. In our own country, for example, scholarship and education were once under the control of monks. Learning and teaching were religious activities. Later, following the separation of these activities from religious organizations, education was still perceived as being one with scholarship and came under the control of scholars. But in more recent years, we have begun to realize that education is very different from the responsibilities of scholars and should be seen as an independent, separate function of society.

Art
There is a natural tendency in human beings to admire beauty and a desire to express one's feelings through creating beauty from materials at hand. Thus do artistic activities emerge within a society in the form of painting, sculpture, music, and literature. Artistic activities are attempts to express the ideals and feelings inspired within the artist by the beauty of the outside world, so it is natural that they are deeply influenced by the environment. Even though we must recognize this deep relationship between artistic activities and the particular land of their origin, I have not been able to discover any laws which explain why a particular district produces a given kind of art.

Artistic efforts influence and are influenced by the other activities of a society. Artistic activities elevate the ideals and the spiritual and intellectual quality of a society. The esthetic education of ancient Greece comes to mind here, as does the apprehension that, if artistic activities grow to excess, society will become effete.

Japan is perceived as possessing a highly refined and developed art and is often described as an artistic country. This leads to speculation about the origins of art, and it has occurred to me that, in a land where there is a wide variety of land forms and beautiful scenery, the people's artistic sense will be stimulated and they will be inspired to express their experience of that variety and beauty in works of art. But in lands which lack variety in the natural environment, lands which have only dull, dreary landscapes, the inspiration and impetus to create great art may be lacking.

Sugimura Kosugi, a Meiji-era scholar of classic arts, suggests another theory about the origin and quality of art in Japan. He suggests that in ancient Japan works of art were made to be offered to gods or to the emperor, so the artists were highly motivated and inspired to create powerful and exquisite works. But in feudal times art came to be created purely for the appreciation and whims of aristocrats and men of riches. This led, according to Kosugi, to a decline in the quality of art in Japan.

> *Education is the key factor influencing the destiny of a society. It is education which supplies talents and abilities to all other fields, and it is education which can nurture good character, ethical behavior, and social consciousness within the members of a society.*

This draws to our attention the kinds of places where artists gather and where works of art are to be found. When ancient art was closely related to religion, artists gathered around temples, shrines, and palaces. This is still the case today. However, works of art can also be found in cities where aristocrats and rich people live because they create a demand and a connoisseurship which are lacking elsewhere. This same reasoning can be applied to amusements as well.

Recreation

Related to but also different from artistic activities are those activities which are for amusement and pleasure such as the theater, games, sports, and so on. The difference between these activities and artistic activities lies in the objectives of the institute or organization which arises to promote them and in their evaluation by the members of the society. Some of these amusement type activities have a good influence on the mind of the society's members, but their objectives are concerned with amusement only and any good effects are incidental. This distinguishes them from education or artistic activities. Again, recreation develops naturally within a society from the demands and tastes of its members, just like other activities, so recreation should not be regarded as without value. But when taken to excess, society will become decadent, its people degenerate.

Classes in Society

When we observe a society closely, we can see, in addition to a division of labor, division of the society into classes. Until the Meiji Restoration (1868) in Japan there was an inflexible class system of warriors, farmers, artisans, and merchants. India is still characterized by this kind of rigid class structure.

Class divisions came about as a result of competition between nations, tribes, and ethnic groups. These class lines and divisions tend to be extinguished as the people of a society become capable of clear and objective thinking. Clear thinking people realize that every function is necessary and that there should be no discrimination based on ideas of "high" or "low." This is what is meant when present civilized countries proclaim that "all people are equal." People who work in entertainment, for example—with the exception of actors—have been customarily disparaged, but they will be duly respected by people who recognize the variety of functions and responsibilities distributed within the society. Recognition of role function is incompatible with artificial class systems based on ignorance and discrimination.

On the other hand, as a society becomes more complex and as its population increases, the struggle for existence becomes more severe. Since persons differ greatly in ability, the fruits of social activity are not shared equally. Some persons are not able to earn as much income or accumulate as much wealth as other persons. This reality gives rise to another kind of social classification. Giddings identified four such classes which he labeled "real social classes."

Socialized Class

This class consists of people who have a sense of fellowship and social responsibility and who can contribute positively to the society. These are people who support, advise, lead, plan without a sense of selfish desire, have mercy, give of themselves, and can rouse public opinion. A society without this class, whether it is a monarchy or a democracy, rich or poor, will not progress in the future and will ultimately become a weak society if it does not actually destroy itself.

Unsocialized Class

These are people who are narrowly individualistic. Their sense of fellowship and social responsibility is not well developed. They cannot relate openly with other people and are absorbed with their own welfare. This class is neutral in and of itself. People of this class tend to follow whatever fad or social current develops in the society. Thus, either good or evil can come from it.

Pseudo-Socialized Class

This class consists essentially of the poor of the society. They have lost whatever sense of social responsibility or concern they may have had. They regard themselves as victims. As a class, they lack morality and motivation and want only to live as spongers.

Anti-Social Class

This class consists of the society's villains. Their sense of social responsibility has been extinguished. They hate all societies and systems. Their impulse is to resist society. They are unwilling to cooperate even to protect their rights, and seek only to avenge injuries they have received or imagine they have received.

Giddings analysis is useful, but it needs more detailed distinctions to be helpful as a concept for analyzing reality. Other scholars have suggested different class categories, such as upper class, middle class, and lower class and I have mentioned the many social specializations which really represent vertical divisions. Both vertical and horizontal divisions can be seen in every society.

For our purposes, I would like to suggest the following classification scheme to guide us in our study and research:

Upper Class in the Whole Society

The people in this class are respected by the whole society because of their positive contributions to the whole society. (Giddings' "socialized class" would be a part of this class). It consists of the compassionate rich and the virtuous poor, that is, those poor people who do not hate their poverty and who do not yearn to be rich. The members of this class are not discouraged by failures and will be final winners. Many of the heroes of history belong in this category.

Upper Class in the Divisions of Society

These people are winners only within their own class or division. Only within their own groups do they have power and respect. They are not respected by the whole society. Some of them are lower in morality than ordinary people. As one would expect, people of this nature can be found in business and amusement activities, activities which have little to do with morality. However, we can observe that not only in political society, but in religious and educational societies as well, societies which cannot exist without morality, some people climb up to this class by deceit and fraud. But this is a temporary phenomenon which can only happen in a time when social morality is not developed. To be a really successful person, one must have achieved a certain level of morality.

This phenomenon varies with the particular group. It is highest in religious and educational groups, followed by political, artistic, and business groups. Amusement groups are the lowest. This can be seen in the fact that a person who is eliminated from higher groups due to a lack of morality can act in lower groups. For example, a man who is expelled from an educational society can enter business and become a winner. But a man expelled from business due to immorality, cannot enter an educational group. Thus, the lower group the group on the social ladder, the higher the proportion of degraded members.

Middle Class in the Divisions of Society

The so-called middle or independent class is in between the upper and the lower classes. Some of its members belong to what Giddings calls the pseudo-socialized class, but it contains more members who are contributors to society. Under constitutional and democratic governments, this class constitutes the backbone of society.

Theodore Roosevelt, the president of the United States, has said that there are many kinds of social reform movements which reach in every direction and can be undertaken by anyone. But the most effective reform efforts are engaged in by people of the independent class. He defined the independent class as "people who are not in poverty, who do not fall into immorality, who are not overwhelmed by the pressures of civilization, and who are going along with the progress of society." That definition is appropriate as a description of the class I am discussing here.

Lower Class in the Divisions of Society

People who are described as "lower class" can be found in all the divisions of society. They generally are confident and hope to move into the upper ranks of the society if they have opportunity. They are almost the same as Giddings' pseudo-socialized class but not exactly the same. Many of them cling to a narrow individualism and do not receive benefits from society nor give to it. On the other hand, some of them do work for others and contribute to society.

Lower Class in the Whole Society

This lowest class consists of people who are unable to obtain any kind of position in any of society's divisions. The cause varies. Some people lack physical ability because of genetic inheritance or accidents. Some lack intelligence or morality. Some are born in poverty. But some originally belonged to upper classes. For example, the so called "desperado", or "sohshi" in Japanese, who failed in political or academic societies but still have some ambition, and do not work hard because they have some kind of superficial knowledge which they rely on. Many such persons fall into vagrancy. Some come from artistic or religious societies for similar reasons. In general, fewer people come from educational circles, and more from laborers and segments of the amusement industry. People rarely fall from authentic business circles, unless they meet some unexpected accident, because it provides the most stable livelihood.

If we relate this lowest class to Giddings' classification scheme, his anti-social class and some members of his psuedo-socialized class would be included in it. Extremely poor people are difficult to distinguish from villains when they steal or commit other crimes in order to avoid starvation, and poor people who lament their misfortune and hold grudges against society can be similar to villains who want to challenge society. Giddings's classification recognizes feelings of class identity and degree of morality, but it includes a class of "poor people" that makes it unwieldy. I believe my classification is closer to reality. I have discussed the subject of classes at some length because classes and combinations of classes greatly influence a society and are closely related to the kinds of lands they develop in.

Land, Society, and Class Combinations

The number of classes in a society and the percentage of the population in each class within the whole society varies with societies. In some societies the lower class population is larger; in some the difference between the upper and the lower classes is not very big, but in others the opposite is the case.

Once the *Jiji-shimpo Newspaper*[1] conducted a survey of the number of people in Japan who had more than ¥500,000 in property. At the time of the survey there were about 480 such persons. While the survey may or may not have been accurate, it does suggest that there are not many extraordinarily rich people in this country. In the United States, on the other hand, the incomes of some of the richest people surpass the country's national budget. In that country the very rich people and the very poor exist in a wide disparity that does not exist in Japan. Westerners are said to be surprised that in Japan they see so few very poor people.

This same contrast can be seen in comparisons of Japan and underdeveloped countries, and of cities and rural areas. The larger a city is, the more extremely rich people and extremely poor people are found. In rural areas the difference between them is not very big. The same is true not only in regard to wealth, but in knowledge, morality, and other activities as well. The social problems caused by the difference between rich and poor, which rose early in the Western countries, has risen only recently in Japan. Similarly, problems of providing relief for the poor and preventing crime are urgent in the cities, but they are not an issue in the country.

Another way of analyzing societies with respect to classes and class combinations is to graph the population, stacking up each social layer to reveal either a perfect sphere or an egg-shaped social picture. Japan, with a gap between the poor and the rich, is not the spherical type. Accordingly, I will consider here only the oval type, of which there are two variations:

Bottom Heavy Oval Societies

In a bottom-heavy oval society, people's positions are confused. Virtuous people are not where they should be because they are not accepted by people in power and are often victims of persecution. Since cunning, vicious people are in the important positions, bribery is common and justice is not served. The inevitable outcome of the bottom-heavy oval society is decline and eventual extinction unless radical change occurs by some means.

Top Heavy Oval Societies

The top-heavy oval society is a society in which the moral level is generally high. In every division of the society there are some leaders who are virtuous and morally incorruptible. Vicious, self-serving people, even if they do gain access to positions of power, are unable to have their way and are prevented from controlling and dominating the society for their own ends. A top-heavy oval society is a healthy, vibrant, ascendant society.

What, then, can we say about the combination of classes in Japan?

Is there in our country a superior class capable of providing the moral leadership which is necessary for the whole society? The answer is obvious; we have but to reflect on the recent flood of bribery cases in the country. The religious groups within society, which should be concerned about morality and moral leadership, are content to limit themselves to performing funeral services. The present educational sector, which should form the foundation of society, is confused and impotent. Of course, optimism is an admirable virtue, but when the source of enlightenment is drying up, how can we fail to be concerned?

If the privileged class in society prevents free competition artificially in an effort to unfairly further its own interests, decline is inevitable. On the other hand, observation of free competition in some Western societies shows an upwardly mobile, ascendant society.

Notes

[1] A daily newspaper which had been founded by Yukichi Fukuzawa in 1882. The paper merged with the *Nichinichi Newspaper* in 1930.

Chapter 23

The Location of Industry I

The Land and the Desire to Consume

The economic life of every society consists of a three-part process: production, trade or distribution, and consumption. Production and trade are based on the human desire to obtain and consume goods. Therefore, it is important to understand the nature and different levels of human desire if we are to understand the significance of economic activity for social life.

Kinds of Human Desire

Knowledge and intellectual activity grow together with society; correspondingly, the desires felt by individual members of society also increase in kind and quantity. Economists have suggested various schemes for classifying desires, but no one has come up with a perfect one. Roscher (1817-1894), a German economist, has proposed a three-part classification consisting of natural desire, desire stemming from one's inherent abilities, and desire for luxury.[1] Human desires being without limit, it is impossible to classify them all. However, I believe Roscher's classification covers material desires satisfactorily. In general, material desires are related both to the geographic conditions within which people live and to their level of cultural development.

Geographic Conditions and Desire

We can observe that the desires of people who are on the same general cultural level differ according to climate. In climatic zones in which there are major changes in temperature, it is natural that goods vary in kind and amount. But if we leave temperature extremes out of consideration, differences in products desired depends primarily on topographical location; that is, whether mountains or plains, coastal or inland areas, heights or lowlands, convenience or incovenience with respect to transportation.

Types of Industry

Production of any kind involves the two essential elements of natural power and human power. Economists distinguish between land, labor, and capital. Capital is a fruit of natural and human power, and natural power has been considered in earlier chapters, so I will focus here on human productive activities.

The Meaning of Production

We talk about "production," but in actuality, human beings cannot create material things. When we speak of producing something, what we really mean is that we are increasing an existing thing's utility. For example, a craftsman makes a desk of wood, a farmer harvests a crop after months of labor, a lumberjack cuts trees in a forest for lumber. They seem to be producing something but they are really just changing the form of the materials they are working with or moving a thing from one place to another in order to better utilize it or, to express this another way, to increase its value. Understood in this light, commerce, which serves only as a switchboard or exchange network for goods, also produces utility. There is no difference between agriculture and industry in this respect.

The Development of Divisions of Labor

When we observe the range of industries, many divisions of labor become apparent, just as in the larger society. These divisions of labor arise because each person has different abilities, and when means exist or can be developed for the exchange of goods, there is opportunity for the members of society to engage in that activity for which each is best suited. Obviously, possibilities for exchange of goods increase with improvements in transportation. But in ancient times, before means of transportation had developed, and even now in some of the more rural and isolated areas, people had to produce what they needed by themselves. Such a situation may be inconceivable to us who take for granted the many benefits and conveniences which the labor of others makes possible for us. Today, the development of transportation is almost at its peak and we have access to markets all around the world, so whatever the world has to offer can be made

The Location of Industry | 201

available to us. In this situation, divisions of labor have increased steadily and this increase will be certain to continue in the future.

Job Classification Based on Divisions of Labor

While it would be difficult to create a classification system which would include every kind of job, the following ten-part classification includes the most important ones which are directly related to production.

- ◆ Hunting
- ◆ Fishing
- ◆ Mining

These industries change the location and the form of natural resources. They can be called "collecting industries."

- ◆ Agriculture
- ◆ Forestry
- ◆ Stock raising

These industries involve the creative power of nature, helping and making use of nature, so they can be called "material producing industries."

- ◆ Manufacturing
- ◆ Heavy industry

These industries change the form or quality of natural resources, so they can be called "material processing industries."

- ◆ Commerce
- ◆ Transportation

These industries change the locations of goods, so they can be called "transposition industries."

The first six industries listed can be termed "primary industries" whereas the last four, which developed later, can be termed "secondary industries."

The Development of Industry

Industries emerged gradually over a long period of time, with many steps or stages in their development, each of which was characterized by specific methods and tools of production, especially regarding means of obtaining food. Historical periods provide another natural means of classification.

Classification Based on Methods of Obtaining Basic Necessities

◆ *The Hunting-Fishing Age*

How the earliest humans lived can be surmised on the basis of stone tools found in many places throughout the world. It is conjectured that people depended on food which could be obtained with hands, stones, and clubs. After the invention of metal tools, early peoples hunted animals using bows and arrows and caught fish and shellfish. During that time, they were limited to already existing things. Thus, populations had to be small. People may have gathered in larger groups temporarily, just like fish or sea-mammals, but if a group grew too large, its members had to disperse in order to obtain enough food. In such unstable societies, higher forms of social activities could not develop.

◆ *The Nomadic Age*

As knowledge and analytical skills increased in a society, people realized that as long as they depended solely on hunting and fishing for their food needs, periods of food shortage would be inevitable. This led to the taming of various animals such as cattle, sheep, goats, pigs, and chickens, thereby assuring a more stable food supply. However, this new stability which was gained through the taming of animals also had a drawback. Since their lives now depended on their livestock, they had to take them with them wherever they went, and when the grass and foliage in an area of residence had been grazed down, the group had to move on to another area where there was grass and water.

◆ *The Agricultural Age*

In time, some nomadic and hunting-fishing peoples discovered edible grains among the grasses and foliage their livestock were eating and developed methods and tools suitable for cultivating the land. Thus began a shift to agriculture as the chief source of the food supply.

We can imagine that people who were able to obtain ample food supplies from nature would not be motivated to change their way of living unless they were pressed by competition due to increasing population or other groups. The change to an agricultural lifestyle, therefore, must have occurred over a long period of time. The case of the Ainu people in Northern Japan provides an example of this process.

But once the shift to an agricultural life had occurred, the same area of land could support a much larger population than had been possible during the stock raising age. This eliminated the need for continuous movement and made it possible for the members of a group to live in fixed places, develop permanent housing, and form villages. This, in turn, provided the basis for the development of complex societies. As the members of a group of people settled into the more sedentary life of agricultural villages, they began to save and store food and supplies for anticipated future shortages caused by drought, storms, etc. In this way our present system of private property arose.

As students of human psychology, we recognize that every person has different inherent abilities and skills. Likewise, each village, due to its own unique history and location, is different and produces different products. Moreover, people could not long remain content with producing everything for themselves, so there began exchange of products between individuals and between villages. But during this stage of development, producers and consumers were the same people. Exchange was direct; the products exchanged were for the use of the receiver. So this age can also be called the age of barter.

◆ *The Commercial Age*

As more and more exchange transactions of goods occurred, the time and effort required for calculating the value of goods and effecting exchange became burdensome and increasingly complicated. It was soon realized that there were some types of goods which were exchanged frequently and which were highly prized and sought after. People who possessed these items could readily acquire whatever they wanted by offering such items. Thus, these items came to serve as a medium of exchange.

At various times, cattle, grain, salt, iron, copper, jewelry, and shells were used as media of exchange. Precious metals proved to be the most convenient medium of exchange, however, both because of their compactness and because their desirability made them immediately convertible into other forms of wealth. In this way, the use of money as we now know it came about. Once money appeared, a new class, a merchant class, arose between producers and consumers. Now, producers sold their products to merchants, and consumers had to buy what they needed from the merchants. This was the beginning of the commercial age.

◆ *The Industrial Age*

Since commerce had already developed, and as means of transportation were improved, the exchange of goods became easier, their range wider, and the variety of goods greater. Now, people did not have to produce many things for themselves, but could produce only one thing as a means of obtaining money with which they could buy other necessities. This development provided grounds for the appearance of a class of people who processed raw material into products. This was the origin of industry, and the world entered the industrial age.

As time went by, money became so widely accepted and used that capital began to accumulate. Soon centers of commerce and industry developed, giving birth to the modern city. In our day, cities are increasing both in number and in size all around the world.

Classification Based on Tools and Energy

- Stone Age
- Earthenware Age
- Bronze Age
- Iron Age

The Influence of Occupations on Mind and Body

The theory of the struggle for existence and natural selection applies well to the analysis of occupations. While it is true that people with a particular type of character and constitution tend to enter certain occupations, it is also true that the influence of occupations on individuals is enormous. This is because one's experience in an occupation is direct, continuous, and permanent. The development of physical strength depends on the nature of the work and the work environment. Spiritual development—that is, the development of intellect, the emotions, and will—depends on what can be observed while at work and the extent of our interaction with whatever is encountered at work, and on the severity of the struggle for existence.

The development of education and improved means of transportation and printing make it possible to compensate for the imbalance in physical and spiritual development caused by different occupational conditions. Even so, there will be particular problems and needs according to specific occupations. It will be important to consider these in studies of the relationship between people and land.

In regard to physical development, there is a significant difference between commerce and other occupations such as agriculture, industry, forestry, and mining that require full use of the body. Persons working in commerce, primarily a mental activity, are generally poorest in physique. This applies as well to government officials and other administrative workers. Within occupations involving primarily physical labor, industrial laborers are the most challenged.

Even in old-fashioned handcraft industries, workers need not use their whole body in their work. But the problem has become more serious in recent times as increasing job specialization and ever finer divisions of labor have created job categories which require the use of only certain muscles and parts of the body. Industrial workers, in contrast to other physical laborers such as those in agriculture, forestry, and mining, who use their whole bodies every day, tend to be poorer in overall physical development. With respect to general health, also, industrial laborers are at a disadvantage for they work mainly indoors where it is often dusty and dangerous. Miners face the worst conditions, however, because they work daily in a dark and perilous environment. Consequently, these workers tend to be poorer in health than farmers and lumberjacks who work outdoors.

Compared to lumberjacks, farmers tend to have better health because they work in open fields and their labor is steady and regular, whereas lumberjacks work in dense, dark, humid woods. Our studies lead us to conclude, then, that agriculture is the best occupation in so far as the general health of workers is concerned, followed by fishing, forestry, mining, industry, and commerce.

Commerce and Spirituality

With respect to intellect or knowledge, merchants and those engaged in similar occupations have an advantage. They live in cities where people and goods gather. They have opportunities to travel. Thus they can meet various kinds of people, come to know many areas of the world, and gain knowledge beyond that which is possible for people who remain settled in one place. The need to concentrate when bargaining may make them sensitive and shrewd. Their emotions, too, reflect their expanded knowledge and contacts with many people and make them optimistic and cheerful, enabling them to become pioneers in international concourse.

Their greater intellect and stimulated emotions, however, are superficial. Their interest centers primarily in making money. Most of them judge things by intuition and do not think logically. Rather, they tend to be content with memorizing cases of success or failure and imitating the former without recognizing or studying the underlying theoretical principles. They also tend to become nationalistic due to protectionist policies and the influence of the vagaries of goodwill between nations on trading opportunities.

Even so, merchants are less nationalistic than many other workers, because they tend to be the first to shed themselves of superstitions and because they are interested in human activities. On the other hand they tend to lack lofty ideas. They abandon traditional religious beliefs readily and convert to new religions. Christianity, as an example, came into Japan from Nagasaki, Yokohama and Sapporo, which are commercial cities.

Agriculture and Spirituality

In some respects, the spirituality of farmers is the exact opposite of merchants. Merchants live by taking risks. Their fortunes may go up and down many times during their lifetime, whereas farmers inherit the lands of their ancestors and follow old, familiar methods of cultivation. They rarely make any improvement, and it would not be too far from the truth to say that they seldom use their intellect. Their attention tends to be limited to each day's weather and their crops. Their life is dominated by legends, superstitions, proverbs and their own limited experiences.

Farmers generally live on a small piece of land, going occasionally to nearby towns to sell their crops, so their views of life are narrow. Their lives are lived out in isolated places compared to the lives of merchants which are full of stimuli. They tend to resist change. Many agricultural reformers lament this characteristic of farmers.

While the struggle for existence is not as severe as in some other occupations, farmers have to work long hours. This encourages diligence and thrift. Compared to merchants, farmers are simple and honest. They are not easily moved, but once moved they become ardent. They become deeply patriotic, but their patriotism is most often limited to their hometowns or prefectures and they have little interest in relationships with other countries. This regional patriotism means that nationalism cannot spread among farmers quickly or easily. But when their patriotism grows to include the state as a whole, it is strong and greatly strengthens the state. At the same time, farmers become self-content and conservative. If some extraordinary development makes them angry, they will sometimes rise in rebellion, regardless of the consequences, as numerous peasant riots throughout history bear record.

Since farmers live out their lives close to natural phenomena such as changes in the weather and in the seasons, they have many opportunities to sense and feel super-human power, and they become piously religious. Once they develop belief in a particular religion they are not easily converted. Missionaries of new religions exert themselves among farmers in vain. As an example, in most rural districts in Japan Buddhism has been established for centuries and Christianity cannot make headway in spite of major efforts upon the part of Christian missionaries.

Forestry and Spirituality

People who live in forest regions are narrower in outlook than farmers. Like farm people, they are deeply religious, but the struggle for existence is fierce in the forest and because of this, forest people are stronger-willed than farmers. Food and material for clothing is scarce and more difficult to obtain in the forest. Forest people are less self-sufficient than farmers. Furthermore, they always carry arms to hunt or to fight against bears and wolves. Thus, although the beauty of the forest can have a mellowing effect on the human soul, forest people tend to be ferocious and aggressive, and lack the entrepeneur spirit.

Fishing and Spirituality

Fishermen venture daily into the open sea where there are no companions except their fellow fishermen and sea birds. Moreover, they usually live in remote coastal areas where there is little opportunity for contacts and experiences which could broaden their outlook. Thus, fishermen tend to be more conservative than either farmers or woodsmen. On the other hand, fishermen come into closer contact with nature than farmers. Their very lives depend on natural phenomena such as the seasons, the wind, the waves, and the location of fish. In their work they are confined to small boats floating on the boundless ocean. If a storm comes they must be prepared for death. Like farmers, they have strong religious beliefs which lead them to leave everything to nature. This encourages a spirit of adventurousness, and these seafaring people have sometimes drifted to other countries and have become pioneers in creating new settlements.

We can see, then, that fishermen must be nimble and strong like hunters. They have to fight for fishing grounds, and they become brave, ferocious, and warlike. It is perhaps more than coincidence that all the pirates in Japan have been fishermen or their descendants. We can observe, on the other hand, that fishing people tend to have limited will power. They cannot work as steadily and continuously as farmers. They are accustomed to getting an entire year's livelihood during short fishing seasons, and they cannot understand farmers' parsimony. So when we look at history from a larger perspective, we discover that fishermen have been the pioneers who have led the way in settling new areas, but it has been the farmers and the merchants who came later who made the profits. Hokkaido, Japan's northernmost island, provides evidence of this pattern.

Industry and Spirituality

Industry is the utilization of human power to change raw material into products that are desired and needed by human beings. In this sense, industrial laborers have the power to override the reign of nature in human affairs. Laborers who work diligently and sincerely in their occupation can become highly trained and skillful. Some of them, having acquired delicate and refined technique, can produce goods more beautiful than even nature provides.

In short, industry helps people realize their own power; they tend to develop progressive ideas and a hopeful, enthusiastic outlook. But since the range and scope of their labor tends to be narrow and specialized, they often become more obstinate and narrow-minded than other laborers. This tendency has become serious in modern mechanized industries where the labor input is divided into very small segments. Laborers become highly skilled in producing specific parts but have nothing to do with other parts. Whereas crafts workers complete an entire product themselves, this highly specific type of labor provides no opportunity for independent thought or activity.

Occupations and Society

Since specific occupations influence the characters of workers in specific ways, we can judge and categorize the character of a society or state by its industry. A healthy society can only evolve when there is harmonious development of all industries. Each industry has its peculiar strengths and weaknesses, and most of those weaknesses stem from the ignorance and prejudices of the people engaged in them. I conclude, then, that this problem can only be solved through education, and urge universal education for all members of society.

Note

[1] Wilhelm Georg Roscher was one of the founders of the German Historical School of economic thought.

Chapter 24

The Location of Industry II

Primary Industies and Land

Economists identify three basic elements of production: land, labor, and capital. These elements attract industry to themselves, so industries develop where land, labor and capital exist. However, the three elements are not equally attractive to all industries. Primary industries depend largely on local natural resources. For example, a particular industry might develop because of the nature of the soil or the climate. Mining develops in the mountains where mineral veins crop out, forestry with forests, stock raising on dry plains where grasses grow, agriculture on watered plains along rivers, fishing along beaches, navigation on inland seas or along indented coastlines.

Agriculture and Land

Among the primary industries, agriculture is most influenced by land. Since agriculture depends on plants and on animals which feed on the plants, the most suitable location for agriculture is in areas which best provide for the chemical and physical processes necessary to the nurture of plants and animals. Agricultural researchers have analyzed the ingredients of plants as a step toward identifying types of land whose chemical composition is suitable for agriculture. These studies reveal that plant bodies consist mainly of organic compounds, hydrogen, oxygen, nitrogen, and carbon, which are derived from air and water. Some minerals, however, must come from the soil, so land that is to be used for growing plants must contain the elements which are essential to plant growth, and have two additional characteristics. First, the land must mechanically support plant growth. That is, it must be of a certain degree of hardness that will enable the roots of plants to grow freely, yet hold them firmly. Second, the land must contain the proper amount of water.

Some of the most important elements in plant growth are sunlight, air, rain, frost, and snow. We can think of the actions of these elements as "cultivation by nature" from which humans receive enormous benefit. Or, we can think of it in terms of humans' supporting in a small way through cultivation this vast natural process of plant growth. The functions of the sun, wind and rain can be thought of as an annuity which nature gives to land. Ownership of land is perceived as involving the right to this annuity.

The location of land has as much influence as its soil. I have already written about the significance of latitude, altitude, and inclination in preceding chapters. Another important element is economic location, or the distance from cities, which in turn has a close relation to management.

Agriculture is the most self-sufficient of all industries, providing a living without any relationship with cities. This can be seen in some mountain villages that have no contacts with other villages. But when people want to exchange products with other districts, the kind of agricultural development and the degree of development must be in relationship to the distance from cities. Thünen (1783-1850), a German agricultural economist, discussed this phenomenon in his important work on the organization of agriculture. In essence, he said that if there is a city in the center of an isolated area, the character of each surrounding district will differ according to distance from the city. He argued that decisions concerning the organization of agriculture must be based on those distance-related conditions.[1]

Mining and Land

It goes without saying that mining depends on the quantity of useful minerals which the land contains. But as minerals cannot be consumed directly, as in the cases of food and clothing, the development of mining depends far more on distance from markets than does agriculture. If the location is too far from the market, however much the quantity, it is almost useless. At the present time, only water transportation is suitable for heavy and bulky products such as iron ore. Thus, mining flourishes along rivers or coasts, or where there is rail service to a waterway.

Mining requires cheap labor just as is true of other primary industries. A mine at a very high altitude or in an extremely cold climate will be less valuable because workers will be more difficult to obtain and the cost of transporting supplies make the cost of labor excessive. This would not apply to precious metals, however, because the high prices they bring can cover the costs of labor and transportation all over the world. The quantity of the precious metal or mineral, therefore, is the determining factor regardless of the distance from markets. For example, the Klondike (on the upper stream of the Yukon in Canada, North America), an area unsuited for human life because of extreme cold, has become a flourishing mining site since gold was discovered there.

Another important factor in the case of mining is the distance from available sources of fuel needed for refining. The importance of this factor can be seen in mines and related industries in Britain and France. Both countries produce coal and iron, but these industries are more highly developed in Britain because minerals and sources of fuel are closer together there.

Marine Industries and Land

Included in this category are several industries which are very different in character, including fishing, hunting of sea mammals, collecting seaweed, and producing salt. The range of marine industries covers the animal, plant, and mineral kingdoms, so it is similar to land industries in this regard. It goes without saying that in most cases marine industries will be based in waterfront and coastal areas, so distance from markets is not as crucial a factor as is the case in some of the other primary industries. Recent developments in transportation and improvements in methods of preservation lessen the influence of distance even more. At the same time, because marine products are quick to spoil and are difficult to transport over long distances, the development of marine industries will be limited in extremely isolated areas, as Thünen has postulated.

The Character and Classification of the Manufacturing Industry

As we have noted, primary industries cannot be located far from the source of their natural resources. Therefore, labor and capital are not strongly attracted to them. The manufacturing industry, on the other hand, has a much stronger affinity with labor and capital. Land, labor, and capital are all attractive to manufacturing, but the element with the strongest affinity depends on the kind of industry. For some kinds of industry, natural resources are the most important; for others, labor is most important. Before considering the relationship between land and the manufacturing industries, then, we will need to review their different types.

Classification by Type of Product
- ◆ hunting
- ◆ marine industry
- ◆ mining
- ◆ agriculture
- ◆ stock raising
- ◆ forestry

Classification by Customers
- ◆ luxury goods for rich people
- ◆ utility goods for ordinary people

Classification According to Method of Processing
- ◆ handcraft, homemade, or small industry
- ◆ mechanical, factory made, or big industry

Craft Industries

Craft industries utilize human labor primarily, assisted by animal power. Craft work attracts labor and capital to a greater extent than primary industries, but attraction varies according to type of customer rather than type of material.

Utility Craftwork

This type of craftwork must be produced for many people, so it must be cheap, produced in large quantities, be long-lasting, and be pleasing in appearance. The work consists of sitting and using the hands, thus it is not heavy, it does not require a high level of intelligence, and it is not dangerous. This kind of work requires many low-paid laborers, so women, the aged, or persons in poor health can do it with a minimum of training. Since such workers can be found in families engaged in primary industry, utility craft work often develops as companion businesses in homes of primary industry workers, or during periods of leisure such as in winter months.

Luxury Craftwork

In the case of luxury craftwork, on the other hand, since the crafts are produced for a small number of wealthy people, the finished product must be of fine quality. The materials must be carefully selected. This kind of industry does not require many workers, but it does require skillful ones. Since only a few workers are involved who can live anywhere, population does not matter, nor is distance a major factor. Rather, the existence of demand is the only important consideration.

Luxury craft industries develop in the vicinity of large cities where aristocrats, priests, or wealthy people live, especially near capitals where castles exist. In those cities, stores selling luxury craft goods gather around castles, theaters, or big hotels. Paris, for example, has become the fashion capital of Europe because it has been the capital of a major nation for some hundreds of years and has attracted many aristocrats and wealthy people. Rome, which is not only the capital of Italy, but also the capital of Roman Catholicism, is rich in art works and is a center of luxury craft industries. The same can be said of London, Berlin, and Moscow.

The production of luxury crafts requires not only skilled workers but the discerning eyes of patrons and connoisseurs, which can only be acquired through long training. This means that these crafts will not develop in newly created cities but rather they will flourish in old, established cities, supporting old cities even in their decline. In Japan, for example, the present capital, Tokyo, is still considered inferior to the old capital, Kyoto, in this regard. Luxurious, exquisite goods can be partially manufactured by machines, but the most important, delicate parts require the skill of trained workers. These skilled craftsmen tend to remain at their homes; thus, old cities of artisans survive even in an age of mechanical industries.

Mechanical Industries

Mechanical industries had their beginnings with steam power in the late 18th century and contributed to a drastic change in the style of industry. The small, cottage industries which had previously accounted for the bulk of goods produced, gave way to giant factories employing many workers. Manufacturing no longer could be carried on as a source of additional income for people engaged in primary industries such as agriculture, fishing, and forestry when manufacturing of most products required major capital investment in large factories and machinery. Products could not be produced simply to fill orders. Now production had to be carried on continuously on a mass scale in order to keep workers busy and bring in profits for investors. Manufacturing became increasingly complex.

Modern mechanical industries must have, apart from appropriate climate and other natural conditions, at least the following elements: raw materials, energy, labor, capital, markets, and suitable land on which to build factories. These elements attract industries to locations where they exist. An analysis of factories which prosper even under severe competition reveals that their locations provide these elements most adequately. Let us take a closer look at these elements and their influence in attracting industry.

Raw Material

Raw material is the main element of industry. Most products are refined from raw materials, unnecessary parts being thrown away, reducing their weight. Supply is the most important factor. Unless other conditions are very poor, industries develop where materials can be obtained most easily and cheaply. Here there are two considerations: first, how close the location is to the source of the raw material, and second, how close the location is to waterways convenient for loading and unloading.

Energy

Fossil fuels and waterpower are the primary sources of energy used by modern mechanical industries. Their bulk and weight make it likely that industry will come to them rather than vice versa. Water power cannot be transported at all. Thus, in general, industries develop in areas close to the sources of fuel and near waterways.

At one time, only firewood and charcoal were used as fuel. But since the development of coal mines, this cheap, powerful fuel has become one of the most preferred forms of energy, and various industries have developed around coal mines. Until recently, petroleum was used only for lamps, but now heavy oil and its various by-products such as kerosene are providing energy for more and more industries. Heavy oil is more powerful, cheaper, and lighter than coal and, since it is a liquid, it is more convenient to transport and refine. Furthermore, many valuable by-products can be produced in the process of oil refining. Due to these features oil is rapidly replacing coal as an industrial fuel.

An important question, however, is how long the supply of oil can be expected to last. The formation of those fossil fuels took millions of years so we cannot expect to depend on them forever. Some economists are worried about their eventual depletion if we depend exclusively on them. This has stimulated a search for other and cheaper forms of energy. Water power, in comparison, is among the cheapest forms of energy and will not run short unless we destroy its source.

Labor

With steady improvement in machinery, our present mechanically-oriented industries require far less human labor than was required by earlier forms of manufacturing. Still, as new kinds of industry appear, and with severe competition to reduce cost, cheap labor is still an important factor. Where, then, can cheap labor be obtained? The answer is: where population is dense and living costs are low. Japanese industry can compete with more technically advanced Western industries by virtue of this condition. On the other hand, population density cannot be the only consideration. When there are many other industries in the area and workers can choose among them, labor may not be cheap even with a large population.

Wages rise in proportion to workers' intelligence. Knowledgable workers with high morale can produce better products more rapidly than workers who are uninformed and unhappy. Entrepreneurs, having noticed this, will not hire workers who have not been educated, even though they could hire such workers at much less cost. The same thing has been observed in regard to the army. Today the nature of warfare has changed and the fighting ability of soldiers differs according to their educational level.

At any rate, we can conclude that, in general, the mobility of laborers has increased with the development of transportation, and the need for labor has decreased as a result of the invention of machines. Therefore, the attractive power of labor has greatly diminished insofar as the locating of factories is concerned. The case of weavers bears this observation out. Initially, in the early years of the industrial revolution, weavers had to replace the wefts manually when they ran out, but the new weaving machine invented in America does it automatically, enabling one worker to handle 25 to 30 machines.

Capital

As noted above, the importance of capital has increased as factories have increased in size. Thus, if industry does not develop in areas where other conditions are good, it is primarily because people with capital hesitate to invest. Capitalists tend to be willing to invest only in industries they can manage where they are, and industries gather around them for a while. They are unwilling to invest in enterprises in remote areas. Even so, of all the elements of industry, capital is the least fixed to any given area. Consequently, when capitalists develop an enterprising spirit, the attraction of capital in determining the location of industry disappears.

Markets

The market is also a big factor in determining the location of industry, and industries naturally tend to develop in areas which are convenient to markets. In some special cases, location is determined primarily by the market. Products for which the market is limited, the number of customers is small, those that are bulky and difficult to transport, or products which can not be stored effectively fall in this category. In such cases industries tend to gather around the market, ignoring other elements. The Sapporo Beer Company is a good example. It was established in Hokkaido, near its source of materials, but now it has a big factory in Tokyo, the location of the major market for the company's products. From another point of view, the market exerts less power of attraction than raw materials and fuel because manufactured products are generally lighter and less bulky than the material from which they are made.

Suitable Land

The building of a large factory with complex machinery requires that the land provide good footing for building, have an abundance of water, and be close to water transportation. Although sites meeting these conditions are usually expensive, the cheapest site offering these basic conditions will naturally be selected.

The Industrial Center of the Future

We can see, then, that each of the elements attracts industries. Some exert a positive attraction; others a negative attraction. Decisions concerning location will be determined on the basis of their relative strength. At the same time, it must be realized that development in certain factors, particularly in the field of transportation, changes their relative strength. Progress in transportation reduces the attraction of capital and labor. Likewise, progress in machinery design and efficiency also reduces the importance of labor. We can anticipate, then, that in the future capital and labor will have relatively less influence on decisions about location of industry.

Land, likewise, is of limited importance in the attraction of industry, and the attraction of the market is negligible except for some special products. This means that materials and fuel are the key elements. Areas which offer the best locations are those which are close to the source of both materials and fuel or, if one or the other is distant, with access to a cheap, dependable form of transport exists to move raw material or fuel to the industrial site. While, as we have previously noted, social and technological development in a society changes the relationship between location of industry and the six elements discussed above, at present it is the latter two elements, materials and fuel, which are crucial. It seems safe to predict, as things now stand, that this relationship will continue into the foreseeable future.

In considering the relationship between industrial locations and the elements which attract industry, we should note that areas in which the attractive power of fuel and raw materials is most favorable for industry will have an advantage over other areas in terms of serving potential markets. This helps explain why, in recent years, the rapid progress of American manufacturing industries has amazed and terrified Europeans. Boyeux, a French economist, has written that:

> As American products flood into Europe, both Americans and Europeans are studying and discussing this problem, especially with respect to what will happen in the future. At first, the Americans exported only raw materials such as cotton, leather, copper, wood, and petroleum. This did not create a problem and the Europeans did not sense any trouble. But then America began exporting wheat, corn, meat, and other agricultural products. This led to drastic reductions in the prices of food in the European countries, which benefited some people but was disastrous for farmers.
>
> Since in Great Britain the majority of people were engaged in manufacturing and were strongly committed to free trade, that country continued to open its market to American agricultural products. But on the Continent, farmers sought to exclude American products, and governments tried to protect their domestic markets. Now, at the third stage, American industrial products are flooding into Europe and European industries are being severely damaged. This has become a major economic issue causing concern on both sides of the Atlantic.[2]

Commenting on this rapid development of American industries, a Bavarian economist, Von Pets, has written that:

> It is neither China nor South Africa but America that most influences Europe's future. British trade has progressed gradually. Germany has made rapid progress since unification. But as for American trade, the word "rapid" is far from an adequate description. It has progressed like a storm.

America faces two oceans and is blessed with great rivers and many lakes, so water transportation is cheap and convenient. The land is fertile and extremely rich in iron and coal. Moreover, the people, mainly of British and German stock, are hardworking, enterprising people. Their steadiness, high energy, enthusiasm, and loyalty to their jobs are their nature.

Each of these three competitors has its own burden: South Africa for Britain, China for Germany, and the Philippines for America. But the Philippines is the lightest burden, and America will soon be relinquishing it, and that will have a big influence on Europe.[3]

Individual Industries and Their Relationship to Land

Those are the general rules with respect to the relationship between industrial locations and the elements which attract industry. When we observe each field of industry individually, however, there are certain characteristics within these generalizations which will need to be taken into consideration by industrialists and by students and scholars who study these phenomena. The fishing industry in Hokkaido provides a good example. Fish spoil quickly. Accordingly, fish must be processed at fishing ports. It requires large amounts of fuel to manufacture fish meal, fish oil, smoked fish, or canned fish, so if there is not adequate fuel in the area, people will cut down the forest. That is what is happening in Hokkaido. Fishermen have cut down the forest all along the coast, and they have done nothing about replanting. Now they are suffering from a shortage of fuel.

Agricultural goods provide another example. It doesn't require big factories or much fuel to process agricultural materials to reduce their weight and bulk. But there are two kinds of agricultural crops: those whose weight and bulk are reduced through processing and those whose weight and bulk are increased by processing. The former type of product includes linen, cotton, indigo, oils, etc. They lose unnecessary bulk through processing and the unused portions are made into fertilizer. When farmers build small factories, they can work when they aren't busy in farming. Thus, these products will be processed in the producing areas.

In the case of agricultural crops whose weight and bulk are increased by processing, such as sake, beer, soy sauce and the like, the original raw materials consist of various kinds of grain which are relatively easy to transport and which can be stored for long periods. These products can be more cheaply and efficiently processed in or near cities where conditions pertaining to the other elements of industry are better. This is particularly the case in which the finished product consists of a liquid for which transport costs are much higher than for the original raw materials and lengthy storage is not feasible. The best sake in Japan, for example, is made from rice brought from a distant area, and Japanese beer companies are even importing barley from Germany.

It may be noted that when a factory is built in a given location and prospers, other industries of the same type tend to be built around it. Once an industry develops with a center as a result of this process, there is little likelihood of its shifting to another location unless a major change in the economy occurs. When new technological discoveries or organizational ideas appear in such an industrial center, they tend to be shared by all the industries and serve as the basis for further improvement. Then industry as a whole improves. Furthermore, when a trade association is formed, it leads to the development of a cartel which tries to gain more of the market and cooperate in the purchase of large machinery which individual companies could not afford alone.

As an industry flourishes, other industries using its by-products or supplying its necessities will tend to arise around it, thereby helping to further reduce costs. In general, we can conclude that the establishment of an industry in an area and the rise of supporting industries around it will promote the development of the industry and the prosperity of the area.

Notes

[1] Thünen proposed the organizing of agricultural land into five zones, based on distance from city centers:

- ◆ Zone 1: This zone consists of the area immediately surrounding the city center. Suitable for growing in this area are crops which are bulky or heavy relative to price such as milk, vegetables, and flowers so they will not need to be transported long distances.

- ◆ Zone 2: Further from the city, Zone 2 is suitable for crops which can be made into products with a minimum of processing. Examples are sugar, alcohol, oil, cotton, and hemp.

- ◆ Zone 3: This zone, where both labor and capital are more difficult to obtain, can be best utilized for growing cereals and other grain crops.

♦ Zone 4: Due to distance from the city the cost of transporting products from this zone is high. Accordingly, livestock raising is recommended in this area because costs can be kept low by making the livestock walk to market.

♦ Zone 5: Areas furthest from the city center can best by utilized for forests. However, crops for which transportation costs are low, such as tea and silk, can also be produced.

[2] From an essay entitled, "American Industry and Europe."
[3] The source of this quotation is not given.

Chapter 25

The Location of Industry III

Basic Principles of Commercial Geography

The field of commercial geography examines the ways in which land influences commerce. "Commercial geography is a study of the earth as a stage upon which trade is conducted," Macklejohn writes. What we need to know is the principles which govern the movement of goods. In other words, what standards should be considered in deciding what goods to send where in order to gain maximum profit? Such a general theory may already have been formulated by scholars in Europe or elsewhere, but I have not been able to find it. Accordingly, we will have to formulate our own theory as we study.

In an industrially advanced society, a vast quantity of goods continues to move around through a complex network. We can begin to grasp this to some extent if we visit a harbor such as Yokohama or Kobe and see at first hand the bustle of men and goods. Ships, freight trains, mail, telegraph, trade companies, banks, merchants, and workers are all engaged in the movement of goods. But what we see at the harbor is only a small part of the total involvement: activity related to the goods we observe is going on in cities, towns, villages, and even in people's houses. This observation leads us into the study of trade or commerce.

In our present society, with increasingly fine divisions of labor, products usually pass through many people's hands as they move from producers to consumers. Each time a product is shifted from one place to another or each time it is handled by a new person, its value increases. We can think of this process as the exchange of goods, but it can also be perceived as the production of value or utility. Commerce, the name we have given this process, is a means for the systematic movement of goods and a way to provide for those who help to increase the value of the goods to receive a part of that increase as profit. In this way, commerce benefits both society and the merchants themselves.

Development in Transportation and Communication

Over many centuries of time, many forms of transportation have developed. Changes in transportation led to changes in society as well. It is necessary, accordingly, to consider the order of developments in transportation if we are to understand the progress of society. For example, in a very early period, the human body served as a natural means of transport. Woodsmen, farmers, and peddlers walked along narrow paths carrying lumber, crops, or goods, making of themselves both vehicle and source of power. In the cities and in the mountains the roads they walked were natural paths, adequate as they existed in nature, requiring neither development nor maintenance by human hands.

Carrying goods on horseback was the first step in the development of transportation, but the trading areas were still small and relatively few goods were exchanged. Employing animals to pull wagons and carts, separating the vehicle from the source of power which propelled it, was a further step in development. At that point, natural paths were no longer adequate and people began to widen and smooth the paths. The invention of the wheel led to pressure to build roads, which involved major construction projects that were so difficult to carry out in that early period that road construction was limited at first. Furthermore, wheeled vehicles damaged the roads, so they were not widely used except by aristocrats. In Japan, there were wagons for aristocrats pulled by cattle and man-pulled carts for transporting goods, but the Tokugawa government prohibited their use except in limited areas. Wheels were not used widely in Japan until the beginning of the Meiji Restoration (1868).

While land transportation progressed very slowly, water transportation was a different matter. Waterways provide a much more convenient and efficient means of transporting heavy cargo, compared with land transportation. Moreover, when we make use of currents and wind we can get, in effect, free energy for motive power. Lakes are generally calm, thus large ships and advanced navigation skills are not required for navigation on them, so water transportation probably developed first on lakes. And we know that the earliest civilizations arose along rivers with water transportation playing a key role in their growth. After experience on rivers and lakes, the use of water transportation on inland seas and along coastal plains was a natural next step. On the other hand, as we saw in Chapter 14, it took a long time for ocean navigation to develop to a point at which it became a practical form of transportation.

With the invention of the compass in the 15th century, a gateway was opened to ocean navigation. Many adventurers such as Columbus, Vasco da Gama, and others appeared on the scene. Columbus reached the American continent in 1492 in his quest for a sea route to the East Indies. Vasco da Gama found his way to India via the Cape of Good Hope a few years later.

The ships used for those voyages were very small by today's standards. The biggest ship in Columbus's fleet was 17 tons. It was very dangerous to sail on the ocean in such small, primitive craft. Only highly skilled and adventurous people could sail the oceans then, so cargo transport was the only beneficiary of shipping. It was only after the invention of steam power and the development of ocean liners that human traffic plied the oceans.

The practical use of steam power, the outcome of the work of James Watt, dates from 1769. During the twenty years that followed, various kinds of machines were invented to utilize steam power, including steam-driven ships. Robert Fulton put the principles of steam power into practical use for water transportation in 1807. The first ship to cross the Atlantic Ocean entirely by steam was a British vessel, the Sirius, which made its initial voyage in 1838. Steam driven water transport has been improved steadily ever since and now the shipping business is in its heyday.

The invention of the train came at about the same time, bringing about a comparable surge of development in land transportation. The locomotive was invented by George Stephenson in 1814 and the first railway was built between Liverpool and Manchester in 1829. European countries began building railways about 1865 and they have developed rapidly in every part of the world.

Prior to the beginning of the Meiji Restoration in Japan, letters were carried by human messengers used mainly by the government and a few higher class persons. The Western mail system was adopted in 1871 and now anyone can communicate easily and cheaply via a government postal system.

Although the mail system is convenient and dependable, it cannot by nature be any faster or more efficient than the existing forms of transportation. Efforts to increase the speed of communication led to the invention of the telegraph, dividing the transportation of ideas from that of bodies and goods and making it much faster. Now we can communicate quickly with people in Europe as well as in Japan.

We can see, then, that transportation in various fields has progressed rapidly during the past two centuries, and technological developments in many other fields have been a result. People have industriously constructed railways, hung telegraph wires, built and repaired roads, dug tunnels, laid submarine cables, dredged rivers, built lighthouses, and constructed harbors. Much of this progress in transportation that has so greatly influenced our lives occurred during the 19th century, so that century can surely be called the age of revolution in transportation. But people are still engaged in strenuous efforts to make even further improvements, so it is hard to say what developments we can expect during this new century we are just beginning.

There are three main effects of these accumulating developments in transportation: increase in speed and reduction of the time required to transport; increase in transport capacity (that is, as the quantity increases, the energy required becomes less, cost decreases, and more people can afford to transport); and, improved security and accuracy. The degree of demand for these three differs depending on the specific objects being transported.

◆ Persons: the most important demands here are security and accuracy. To the extent these two demands are satisfied, people will seek rapidity and saving of time. Increased savings in cost is a crucial demand with respect to ordinary people, but not for the wealthy.

◆ Cargo: with respect to valuables the need for security and acuracy is the same as for persons. However, in the case of commodities the most important demand is increased savings in cost. Speed of movement is important for some kinds of goods, but for most it is not.

◆ Ideas and language: the primary demand is rapidity, next security, and then accuracy. Postage is very expensive but people do not seem to complain, so increase in capacity is not an important factor.

I have observed that the quality most in demand differs depending on the objects being transported. Now let us look at the means of transportation. Each type of transportation has unique characteristics which suit it for movement of particular kinds of objects. At the present stage in the development of transportation, waterways depend heavily on weather, and they are inferior, compared with land transportation, in accuracy and rapidity. At the same time, water transportation is cheaper. So, water transportation is suitable for cargo, especially materials such as fuel, while wagons and trains are more desirable for transporting persons and valuables.

In the area of communication, I wish to call attention to two types, personal and public. The telephone and the telegraph, as well as the mail system, are examples of personal means of communication. But a new, public type of communication has been invented just recently. It is called "advertising" and uses newspapers and magazines to communicate with members of society. These are open, public means of communication. As education becomes widely available and people come to read more, the effect of advertising will increase, bringing benefits to the public as well as to publishers and advertisers. This will contribute to social progress.

The Influence of Transportation and Communication on Human Life

A society is formed through communication of people with other people. It follows that the development of transportation influences every aspect of that society. Let us consider, first, influences in the economic sphere. Here improvements in transportation will normally translate into savings of production costs: they reduce the time and the cost of transporting materials, workers, products and so on. Thus, the circulation of capital is facilitated and the areas in which products are traded are enlarged. A thing which had been valueless for lack of transportation now turns out to be of value. This in turn leads to increases in the kinds and the quantity of goods we consume, adjusting the prices of goods in different districts to a common level.

Another economic effect of improvements in transportation is that when there is an oversupply of a particular kind of goods in one area, the excess can be moved to areas in which there is a scarcity. This works to prevent violent fluctuations in prices. Finally, rapid means of transportation, once dominated by the rich, enable ordinary people to move to the most convenient places to work. This, too, benefits society as well as individuals.

We can see, then, that the lives of ordinary people are greatly benefited by development of the means of transportation in a society, contributing to a rise in their standard of living. There are, however, some ill effects as well which we must be aware of. One is that large scale equipment requires large outlays of capital. This provides the opportunity and the temptation for unscrupulous persons to engage in speculative trading and manipulative pricing. But these ill effects are negligible in comparison with the benefits.

Influences on the material life of the members of a society will affect their spiritual life as well, freeing them to spend energy, which had previously been required for making a living, on their intellectual growth and development. The distribution of knowledge, like that of goods, tends to become leveled. As communication among the people of a society increases, knowledge is shared more widely, enhancing and enriching the culture.

The extensive influence of developments in communication and transportation on politics should also be noted. Most important is the accumulation of power by the central government. To unite the state, the government must be able to receive information from every district and send orders to the districts quickly. Modern channels of communication make this possible, enabling the central government to effectively control the local administrations. If there are any signs of revolt, it can dispatch troops to suppress them immediately. It is primarily progress in transportation which makes it possible to build strong states.

The kind of changes resulting from progress in transportation and communication which we have been discussing can be seen not only within individual nations but all through the world. Railways and steamers have opened the door to the creation of a world economy; the telegraph enables people to obtain information about world prices and conditions almost immediately. The world has become one market. We can conclude that developments in transportation are both the cause and the effect of the progress of civilizations.

Progress in Transportation and Changes in Social Bodies

We have observed thus far in our inquiries that progress in transportation turns oceans into channels; tunnels are dug through mountains; cables are laid on the bottom of the seas; railways cut through the wilderness. In short, almost all the geographic barriers which limit the size of social bodies have been overcome as the result of developments in transportation. When we look at this process historically, we can see that there were many steps of transition.

River Traffic Age

The first geographic barrier to fall before the advance of transportation was probably rivers because simple canoes or rafts made crossings possible. High mountains remained barriers for some time, but rivers soon ceased to be barriers and became channels for interchange between societies as primitive shipbuilding skills developed. Rivers were the sites of many battles as societies sought to use rivers as their basis for defense. But in most cases the defending side lost the battle because the rivers, no longer adequate as barriers, had become channels.

Inland and Coastal Sea Traffic Age

The second stage consisted of crossing inland and coastal seas by sailing ships. This eliminated mountains as barriers in cases in which the mountains were located at a right angle to coastlines.

Ocean Traffic Age

The third stage saw the first ocean crossings. Steamships eliminated oceans as a barrier and they, like rivers, became channels between societies. Their range became even greater with the construction of canals across isthmuses.

Inland Traffic Age

When all the barriers on water had been eliminated by developments in water transportation, the only remaining barriers were high mountains, deserts, and wildernesses. The invention of the railway finally overcame these barriers. For example, the Siberian railway has been cut through one of the great wildernesses of the world and Britain is now trying to construct a railroad through the African continent, which will negate deserts as a barrier.

Sizes of Societies at Each Stage

Trade is the basic form of economic activity, which is in turn the basis of other activities. Since trade depends directly on transportation, the sizes of societies differ according to the stages in the development of transportation as described above.

River Traffic Age

People living along a river naturally form a small society, and if the mountains between other rivers are low enough to allow crossing by animal power, people living along several rivers might unite into a larger society. The sizes of societies in this stage are generally limited to one or several river basins. Where mountains divide the basin around the upper stream from that of the lower stream, the current will be rapid and falls will often form, obstructing traffic on the river, leading to the formation of two or more small societies even on the same river. Examples of this occurred during feudal periods when local leaders had their individual domains. When a military leader or group would seek to create an artificial society by uniting these small societies, conflicts were inevitable, culminating either in the defeat of the initiator of the conflict or the uniting of small social groups into one larger one.

Since only a river and narrow paths along the river provided social connections at this stage, the size of a society depended on the size of the river. Thus, as we would expect, large societies developed along the larger rivers such as the Yellow River, the Indus, the Tigris and Euphrates, and the Nile. This phenomenon accounts for the rise of early civilizations such as China, India, Assyria, Babylonia, and Egypt. In this primitive age, heavy commodities were obtained only from within the area, rarely imported from other areas. In such situations divisions of labor were not highly developed and the society itself remained primitive.

Inland Sea Traffic Age

Small societies in river basins began to unify in this stage. Inland and coastal sea navigation connected the mouths of rivers previously divided by mountains. If a tribe was strong enough to conquer other tribes, the size of the society was enlarged and the new one would subsume many smaller bodies. This was the first step in the formation of nations, but it was not real unity. Even if a hero or military leader had brought about unification, in many cases transportation was not yet developed to a point at which it could connect the society. When districts lost touch with the central government, they would rise up and seek to become independent, making social ties easy to break. Union and secession, peace and turmoil, were repeated over and over again.

From the standpoint of politics, this is the feudal age. Central governments attempted, often in vain, to create unified societies. The Tokugawa government in Japan represents one of the most successful attempts: it maintained a unified society for over 300 years through a system of limiting the powers of local leaders.

Ocean Traffic Age

Ocean navigation linked many societies over great distances. Modern nation states were formed in this age. In the case of Japan, the country had been isolated from other countries and divided into small local societies. Then when Japanese people began to have contact with Western countries, their interests expanded and they left behind them their preoccupation with small conflicts among small societies. Thus was a nation formed. While it had been dangerous to sail even along the coasts of Japan prior to contact with the outside world, the advent of steamships reduced this danger, connections between the various regions of the country became easier, and formerly hostile feudal lords became united into a new government.

As for the larger world, many primitive, weak nations were conquered and annexed by advanced nations. Many societies saw big changes along their coasts. This is the age of the development of states into unified national governments.

Inland Traffic Age

Ocean traffic connected coastal countries, influencing them profoundly, but it could only accomplish so much. As pointed out earlier, it was the construction of railways that enabled societies to expand into the inland areas. In small island countries such as Japan, the influence was negligible. But on continents, small nations were united into bigger empires such as Germany and Italy in Europe. The United States of America could not have been formed in an earlier age, and Russian unity was promoted by the building of the Siberian Railway. In the previous ocean traffic age, the expansion of societies took the form of conquest of primitive people abroad. In this age it was directed toward inland areas.

National Power Age

Now that all the geographic barriers dividing nations have been eliminated, what is there remaining that divides nations? The only barrier between nations now is the barrier of national power. Present states are like castles without moats which can expand or shrink at any time. Now when a state increases its armaments, other states must do the same. Each state must be prepared to defeat the others in order to maintain itself. Thus, all the world powers are now under the heavy burden of armaments.

Transportation Arteries

The transportation arteries of an area are expressions of the relationship between human beings and the land. Although most of the time we pass over them without a thought as to their nature or their history, they have in some cases evolved over thousands of years. No road should ever be treated lightly.

Among the various types of land arteries, modern arteries such as railways and roads are created artificially and natural influences are less involved. But even these artificial arteries are not totally free from natural influences in their formation. For example, many modern roads are influenced by the topography, often running along old roads which may have been used centuries earlier. The following is one way of classifying transportation arteries.

Roads

When we study actual roads, or look at a map, we can see that roads connect with and intersect one another so as to form a network of transportation arteries. Main roads branch off into many smaller roads, which in turn reveal smaller branches extending from them, much as blood vessels branch into capillary vessels. Every part of the country is connected with all the other parts, thanks to its roads.

The bends and intersections of these roads and their relationship to the topography of the land are important to note. Roads run along coasts, rivers, and mountains because doing so requires the least effort and expenditure of energy. As humans increased their power over nature through technological development and by acquiring new sources of energy, they could cross rivers and mountains. But even so, it is hard to resist nature and so they tended to go roundabout as long as it was not too inconvenient. When there was no other way, they would choose the easiest point, such as the lowest point between two mountains, and make a pass there.

The shortest distance between two points is a straight line. Natural roads bend and curve, however, because of the topography. Obstacles such as mountains, rivers, forests, canyons, and deserts are reasons for bends in roads. Small bends reveal accommodation to slopes. An ordinary person, upon coming to a slope, will make a detour in spite of the increase in distance. This seems quite simple, but when we look at a map, it becomes clear that this phenomenon is highly complex.

Railways

Most railways are laid along former roads and the relationship with topography is similar to that of roads. The big difference is that railways, through the use of tunnels or by some other means, generally go straight in cases in which natural roads bend. This applies only in regard to minor obstacles, however. In the case of mountains, for instance, railways have to be curved in order to reduce slope, just as with roads. Another difference is that in most cases railways connect existing cities, whereas cities grow up at the intersecting points of roads.

Waterways

The most convenient routes for ships are called "lines." There would seem to be few obstacles to interfere with transport on the ocean, but there are some reasons for bending and curving routes here, too. These can be stated in the following general terms:

◆ Lines on the ocean coincide with the directions of prevailing winds, such as the trade winds.

◆ Lines on the ocean coincide with the directions of sea currents.

◆ Aside from the above two considerations, lines follow the shortest route between two points.

◆ When supply points for coal and water do not lie along lines established on the basis of the three above considerations, ships will go out of their way in order to obtain these necessities.

The gathering points of waterways are the same as those of roads because waterways cannot be independent of land. So they converge on ports.

Transportation Arteries and Central Markets

We can imagine how markets developed by observing community fairs and festivals. Religious festivals undoubtedly provided the earliest opportunities for the people of a geographic area to gather. At such gatherings, offerings or sacrifices for the gods came to be exchanged, and the people made use of the occasion to trade goods of various kinds. As possibilities for profitting from trade were realized, trading began to occur not only in connection with religious festivals, but at any convenient location for people to gather. For the most part, these locations coincided with the points of intersection of transportation arteries, and these points became centers of trade and the sites of towns and cities. The prosperity of any given center depended largely on the size and importance of the intersecting arteries.

Industry as the Basis of State Power

For thousands of years of human history, agriculture was the foundation of states and the basis of state power. As commerce and manufacturing developed, however, this role was taken over by industry. There has been much discussion about this displacement of agriculture by industry. Some people believe it is potentially harmful and not in the best interests of the people of a society.

As long as countries were isolated from each other, each country had to be self-sufficient; each country had to rely on its own domestic agriculture to supply food and clothing and other necessities. Now, however, all the countries of the world trade goods among themselves, divisions of work have developed, and the world has become one economic unit. Thünen's model pertaining to the relationship between industries and city centers within individual countries can now be applied to the world as a whole. This new reality can be summarized in the following manner:

♦ The coasts of the North Sea, North Germany, and a part of the Atlantic coast of North America can be perceived as the central cities of Thünen's model (District 1).

♦ Areas around those central cities and areas connected to them by waterways, i.e., Central and South Europe and most of the Atlantic coast of America, are areas of horticultural crops (District 2).

♦ Areas around the second zone, Eastern Europe, including Russia, and inland America, are grain-growing areas (District 3).

♦ Areas around the third zone and those connected by land waterways, are areas for grazing. This includes most of Asia, Latin America, and Australia (District 4).

♦ The inland parts of these continents constitute a fifth zone consisting of forests (District 5).

As we have seen, the prices of goods increase in proportion, first, to the distance they are transported and, secondly, the extent to which they are processed. The increase in cost in the former case grows in arithmetical progression, while in the latter case the increase in cost grows in geometric progression. Therefore, it is very disadvantageous for a country to import processed goods and export raw materials. It was on this basis that Britain, the Netherlands, Belgium, and other Western European countries have sought to make commerce and manufacturing the basis for their development.

In recent years, a change in this pattern can be seen emerging, however. As we noted earlier, the location of manufacturing is shifting toward areas which produce the raw materials. Thus, North America and Russia are becoming both agricultural and industrial countries. As a result, all countries are beginning to adopt protectionist policies, and nations based on commerce and manufacturing are in a disadvantageous position. First they lost their domestic agriculture and raw materials, and then lost the markets for their products. In the end they must compete with the newly developing industrial countries, which once supplied them with raw materials.

As we can see, then, the winners in international competition are those countries which produce both raw materials and industrial products. This suggests the following general considerations in regard to decisions about the basic industry of a country. First of all, if a country relies only on commerce and manufacturing, it may place itself in a dangerous position in this age of protectionism. Therefore, a country's primary industries should not be neglected. It is never wise for any country to depend on one or two industries alone, but should encourage development of a wide variety of industries.

If we apply these principles to Japan, we will notice the same pattern of zoning relationships between Japan and the Asian mainland as exists between the Atlantic coast and the Pacific coast of the United States. That is, Japan represents the first zone, the city zone. The coasts of China and Korea constitute the second zone. The interiors of those countries, along with Manchuria, Siberia, India, and the coast of Australia are the third, and the other parts of Asia and the interior areas of Australia constitute the fourth zone. This strategic position should be the primary consideration in decisions concerning our industrial development. We should realize the natural opportunity which the location of our country gives us and make full use of it.

Chapter 26

The State

The Functions of a State

A state is a society which possesses sovereignty; that is, it has complete responsibility for governing its own affairs. It is the largest communal body in the life of human beings. Through observing the activities of existing governments which are the executive agents of sovereign states or nations, we can learn about the functions which the state should perform as well as the objectives a state should pursue. Four types of functions become apparent through this kind of observation:

♦ Activities to protect itself from internal disturbances. The state must defend its own existence against internal disintegrating forces. At the same time, it must actively promote activities which strengthen its internal unity.

♦ Activities to protect itself from external disturbances. In other words, the state must establish its independence and defend itself against attacks or intervention by other states.

♦ Activities to guarantee individual freedom and protect human rights.

♦ Activities to promote the happiness and well being of its nationals.

The relative importance of these categories of activities depends on the particular time and the state's location, and they do not develop at the same rate. Some have become important only recently; others were at one time at the center of world attention.

Activities against Internal Disturbances

This type of activity can scarcely be seen now in the peaceful Meiji era in our own country. There is almost no interest in or need for criminal law. In the case of our neighbor to the west, however, we find the government there struggling to control insurgencies and scarcely able to provide for the other needs of its people. In our own history, the overwhelming part of Japan's energies has been spent on suppressing domestic conflicts and establishing sovereignty.

Activities against External Disturbances

Activities in this category have become increasingly important in modern times. Now that imperialism has become the prevailing mode of national behavior in the world community, each nation state is striving with all its might to overcome and vanquish other states. Under these circumstances, states give the highest priority to activities which establish and promote their power and position among other states. Toward this end, not only the building of strong armed forces but also active diplomacy is required.

At the same time, however, since there is no power superior to that of individual states, each nation has to defend its territory by military means. As a result of this need, Japan has equipped itself with a standing military force of 170,000 personnel, 300,000 tons worth of battleships, and nine fortresses along its coast as of 1903. In fact, the major portion of the tax money paid by Japanese citizens is being spent for military purposes. However, since such activities are necessary in order to develop the foundation of our society on which the other functions and tasks of the state can be performed, we should not decline to cooperate if we want the secure and prosperous development of our own nation.[1]

Activities for Rights and Freedoms of Citizens

This category of activity has been recognized only recently among civilized nations. Only peoples who have learned to recognize the importance of law and to observe law and order can have the privilege of enjoying them. There are two types of activities in this category. One is to protect an individual's freedom based on recognition of his/her right as an individual. The other is to protect citizen's individual rights and freedoms against acts of violation by their own government, the executive agent of the state, based on the recognition that individual freedom is a sacred and inviolable right.

Based on this same recognition, suffrage must be guaranteed for individuals. Means for the execution of rights and for enforcement are given to both state and individual for the first time in our country's recently established constitution which identifies freedoms of conscience, thought, speech, religion and association for political, religious, and educational purposes.

At this point, we should recognize three primary categories of national law: laws that stipulate individuals' relations to the state, laws that stipulate relations between individuals, and laws that stipulate the state's relations to individuals. Since the second of these defines and regulates relations between private individuals, they are called Private Laws. Civil and Commercial Laws belong in this category. The other two categories pertain to Public Laws, that is, they determine the relations between the state and individuals, or the governing and the governed, in terms of the extent of freedom of will that each party is granted to exercise. Public Law includes Constitutional Law, Criminal Law, and Parliamentary Law.

Since crime not only violates individual rights but also threatens the communal life of the state, the punishment of criminals requires power that can reach all corners of society equally. It is only natural, therefore, that such a function adheres in the nature of the state. The practice of family revenge—vendettas—that prevailed in ancient days resulted from the absence of appropriate protection upon the part of the state for individuals. The state must not only provide agencies to judge and punish criminals but also police power to arrest criminals, prosecutors to bring charges against them, and lawyers to protect their legitimate rights. These elements together constitute the judicial system of the state. The responsibility of the state also includes providing preventive measures, such as administrative police and disciplinary institutions.

In addition to protecting citizens' lives by punishing and preventing crimes, the state needs to support its citizens in the execution of their legitimate rights. Thus, the state provides the legal framework enabling citizens to execute contracts, obtain compensation for damages, guarantee trade marks, and obtain patents and publishing rights. The state also provides protection for individuals from possible damages incurred by forgery. By observing the functions of the state described above, we can now understand that safe and stable life in our society, including security of our lives and property and the freedom to execute our rights, is protected by the state.

Various definitions pertaining to the rights and freedoms of citizens have been proposed by modern jurists and political scientists:

◆ By our 'rights' is meant the pursual of the necessary conditions for promoting the betterment of human life approved by the state.

◆ A right is a pursuit by an individual approved by society and implemented by a state.

◆ Rights are abilities guaranteed for each individual in society.

◆ Freedom is a product invented by the states, just as government is a state invention.

◆ Human beings did not enjoy freedom from the very beginning. Freedom was gained only through the development of civilization.

According to some schools of thought, freedom is a natural or innate right and the state exists only to place some necessary limitation on it. Some social critics take the extreme view that the existence of states is incompatible with the intrinsic rights of human beings. Such arguments amount to a delusion which confuses freedom in its true sense and implies the right of having no commitment to others. What these critics call "natural rights" translates into activities that emerge when a state consists of a single individual or when a small group of people prevail, ignoring ethical feelings shared among the general public. Jurists renounce such arguments as harmful with respect both to public affairs and relationships between private citizens.

Activities to Promote the Happiness of Citizens

Activities of this type have only been recognized recently in European nations and only the most advanced nations are active in this field. Such activities are not only required for the progress of a people's life, but they are also indispensable for the survival and prosperity of the state itself. The fact that states can no longer secure their existence by military force alone, due to the modern development of ruthless competition among them, also contributes to the necessity for such activities.

Nevertheless, recognizing that prosperity and happiness cannot be expected to occur unless a balanced and harmonious development of all aspects of society is achieved, the state seeks to intervene in every activity of society as a means of assisting in its development, and in some cases, to take the initiative in promoting or strengthening certain activities. Some of the more important of these are:

◆ Intervention in industrial activities.

◆ Intervention in and administration of an educational system.

- ◆ Encouragement of moral activities.
- ◆ Intervention in religious activities.
- ◆ Protection of entertainment activities.
- ◆ Instituting sanctions on other social institutions.

When we turn our attention to the functions of the state in our own country of Japan, we find that activities of this nature are gradually developing following Western models. Education is the most outstanding example. Though systematic intervention in more sophisticated form has been initiated only recently, intervention in some areas has exceeded the level in European nations.

Intervention in Industrial Activities

To repeat a realization already acknowledged, industrial activity is the basis for all other social activities since it directly affects the growth and the decline of states. Large scale industries recently developed have become increasingly dependent on the protection and the incentives provided by the state. Peace and stability is a prerequisite of industrial planning.

In today's world, especially, every nation has a commercial life. No nation can survive now without competing in external trade. Under such circumstances, industrial development cannot occur unless the state provides protection to some degree. Thus, states make efforts to consolidate their economic systems into a firm structure. Enforcing of contracts, building of clearly defined currency systems, managing industries of a highly public nature (such as telecommunication, postal, telephone, and railway services, and other so called "public" enterprises such as dredging and the surveying of land and coastal areas), and protection of workers, all are examples of those activities.

Intervention in Educational Activities

The same reasoning which has led the state to intervene in and promote industrial activities led it to intervene also in educational activities. The recent rapid progress in industrial development has made it clear that no nation can succeed in international competition with an uneducated work force. The fundamental source of all the activities required to insure the future prosperity of a society is, indeed, in the education of the individuals who collectively organize it.

Educational activity, therefore, is the most fundamental work of the state with respect to the planning of its future. In the past, this field was completely left to individuals or to private organizations. Moreover, up to a certain point in history, activities designed to develop the intellectual abilities of the general public were discouraged because of distrust of a citizenry capable of independent thought. Now, however, the state has begun to involve itself in and encourage educational activities for its citizens. In addition, it controls the national education system and enforces school attendance.

It is natural that the state has come to regard education, which is the very basis of its existence, as one of its major responsibilities and functions. This awareness has led to the development of the present educational system, ranging from elementary schools to universities, to the benefit of all citizens. Needless to say, however, because education is such an important element in society, further improvement is needed.

Intervention in Moral Activities

The presence of morally corrupt people among its citizens is a threat to the existence of the state. Accordingly, educating its youth alone is not sufficient. The state is obligated also to encourage the growth of virtue and good works among its people through the presentation of awards and honors of various kinds. It must be recognized, however, that moral virtue cannot be legislated or created by external factors. Thus, enforcement activities in this field which are implemented by the state are likely to be passive in nature, such as regulations to control degradation of public morals, a ban on the publication of indecent literature, a ban on gambling, and elimination of other morally undesirable temptations.

Intervention in Entertainment Activities

Entertainment activities currently prevailing in society tend to degrade the morality of the public, though there are some which do have educational implications. But, again, state intervention is generally passive in nature, namely for control and regulation.

Intervention in Religious Activities

The attitude of the state toward religion and religious sects in our country is quite ambiguous. Freedom of faith in the sense of a person's internal beliefs is recognized. And explicit behavior accompanying membership in specific sects is not restricted in any way. What we must recognize, however, is that religious sects affect the state to the same extent as education. If the state adopts a completely laissez faire attitude toward religion, there is danger that some elements of the population may interpret this as softness and use it to their own advantage to the detriment of the state. Thus, based on the same reasoning and principles employed in other kinds of interventions, it behooves the state to intervene in this field as well.

It cannot be denied that there are some despicable religious groups which take advantage of the superstitions among less enlightened people by means of various material incentives, causing substantial physical and psychological damage. These should be strictly regulated. The need for such regulation has long been recognized by modern social critics, and there have been proposals to specify requirements for the educational qualifications of religious representatives and to establish an institute for religious research. These are commendable ideas, especially under present circumstances. State intervention in affairs of religion of this nature would not pose a threat to freedom of religious belief, just as intervention in education or in the area of morals does not violate freedom of thought.

There are agencies which correspond to each of the above described regulatory activities. In addition to the agencies listed, a Privy Council, which is responsible for answering inquiries by the Emperor, a Board of Audit, which supervises accounting of all the agencies, and a Court of Administrative Litigation, which rules on administrative lawsuits, exist together with their respective assisting agencies. Such a system is capable of handling the highly diverse and complicated political functions of modern states. The gradual expansion of state activities in each of these areas, however, reflects a corresponding increase in desire upon the part of the agencies of the state to control and dominate activities in those areas. Thus, the importance of understanding the nature of these specific political agencies in our country responsible for overseeing the various aspects of the lives of citizens cannot be stressed too much.

Objectives of States

In the very first stage of a state's founding, when the internal integration of the people and preparation for defense against external threats are of utmost importance, the single and only goal and preoccupation of the state is the consolidating of power, since it cannot afford to spread its attention and energy to other needs. When internal integration has been completed, the independence of the state assured, and the citizens of the state have accepted state established law and order, an environment in which greater freedom for the citizens is possible has been created. Then the state can proceed from merely protecting individuals from personal offenses among themselves to providing safeguards protecting individuals from violations of their rights by the state, based on the recognition that each individual has a sacred and inviolable existence. Establishing and recognizing this principle is the main objective during the second stage in the development of a state.

We have recently witnessed the emergence of a number of independent states around the world. These nations, based on the development of their industries, came into intense competition with each other for a greater share of wealth and trade. Given these competitive conditions, and in order to achieve survival and prosperity, states began to intervene in their citizens' lives, providing protection and incentives while attempting to promote development of each and every aspect of society. For states at this stage of development the objective is the creation of a strong national identity.

There is a progression in the development of a state's objectives. That is, as one stage is achieved, it becomes the platform toward the realization of the next stage. When we compare this developmental nature of state objectives with the development of human desires, we see that there is a marked similarity between the two. Since states cannot exist independent from the individuals which comprise them, the state's goals comprise the collective expression of the desires for self-realization of each individual. This can explain the similarity in the course of development of individual desires and national objectives.

Having seen that what states try to achieve and individuals desire are developmental in nature, now let us consider the phenomenon of imperialism, the ideology that underlies the efforts of the so-called "great powers" of our present world to develop their national interests to the maximum. When we ask ourselves if imperialism is the highest and the truest among the objectives of states, a clear answer is hard to obtain. It is obvious that we should not simply compare this ideology with the narrow egoism of an individual. On the other hand, the recent practices of European nations clearly reveal that most, if not all, of those practices are derived from purely selfish desires and motives.

The fact that the great powers of Europe always identify their imperialistic exploits with great and lofty causes, even when blatant abuse of power is crystal clear, provides convincing proof in support of the above observation. Thus, can we in any way believe that imperialism could be a goal that would satisfy the ideals of a class of highly developed and enlightened people? If the peoples of European nations continue to devote themselves solely to expanding their national power, by building arms and conducting armed aggression, disregarding the extent to which their conduct not only disturbs the peace and stability of other nations, but also creates crises in their own nations, ultimately they may end up witnessing the disintegration and destruction of their own nations. Such concern has, in fact, already been voiced by far-sighted intellectuals. It is because of this concern that a call for more humanity in international relations is increasingly being heard today.

Imperialism then, at best, can only be allowed as a transitional objective characteristic of the certain stage in which emphasis is on the development of national power and identity. Hegel (1770-1831), a German philosopher, said that the objectives of states are moral in nature. And Bosanquet (1848-1923) has written that the ultimate goals of the state, the society, and the individual are one and the same, and that goal is the realization of the best life for human beings.[2] Indeed, this should become the primary objective of states in the future.

In this regard, I cannot but agree with John W. Burgess (1844-1931), an American sociologist, about the nature of states' objectives.[3] His thesis is that there are three stages in the development of states and of state objectives and that at each stage the objectives of the prior stage become the means for achieving the objectives of the stage that follows. The main points of his argument are as follows:

◆ The objective of the *third stage*, or the ultimate goal of a state, is the nurturing of universal human beings. It is the stage of the perfection of humanity, of world civilization. It is a stage in which there is full development of human reason and of reason's reign in the affairs of humanity. In a sense this may also be perceived as the stage when human beings become gods. It is in this sense that Hegel's remark that morality is the goal of the state has meaning.

◆ The objective of the *second stage* is the completion of nationality, or the full development of a specific ideology of a particular national culture. A remark attributed to Bluntschli to the effect that the objective of a State is the development of its people's talents and the perfection of public life, refers to this stage.[4]

◆ In the *first stage,* the most immediate goal of a state is the establishment of order and the rule of law. This is the very first step in the development of a state. When these two things have been accomplished, the state can build upon them to develop its own national culture, and, finally, to contribute to the development of a world civilization.

The Wealth and Strengths of States

We have seen in the previous section that though we posit the ultimate goal of states and of individual human beings to be one and the same, there are a number of stages to pass through. We have concluded, further, that we are currently in the stage of imperialism, when nations forge their identities and compete. Obviously, then, we still have a long way to go before reaching an ideal society. In today's world, in which the great powers take every opportunity to expand their influence, it is clear that we should give utmost priority to the strengthening of our own nation, if we are to strive to realize the ideal goal of a state.

On the basis of the examples provided by the great powers of the present time, the elements that compose national power, wealth, and strength are summarized in the chart on the next page. Human capability has been classified into material and spiritual categories. The latter can be either encouraged or discouraged by the state. The former, however, is more basic within nature and can not be controlled beyond a limited range by current human capabilities. When we look at our own nation as well as at the Western powers, in light of the framework given above, we find that the blend of the two factors varies depending on the degree of national development of each country. In short, the more advanced the culture of the nation is, the larger the proportion of the spiritual factor becomes. Less advanced cultures tend to depend heavily on the material factor, their spiritual capacities being overwhelmed.

Though it is difficult to identify the degree of each element required for the build-up of the wealth and the strength of a state, a certain degree of development of the material element seems to be a prerequisite of its formation. In other words, unless the presence of a certain level of material development occurs, even the most culturally advanced nation can not evolve into what we refer to today as a "great power." What, then, is the minimum requirement of the material component?

The Area of National Land

One approach in seeking an answer to this question has been studies of the relationship between the land areas of major countries of the world and the size of their respective populations. In medieval Europe, for example, such small nations as Switzerland, the Netherlands and Belgium were at one time counted among the world's great powers. However, due to the development of transportation systems and other related factors, the balance of power among European nations has changed radically, creating the present situation in which there are a few great powers, leaving smaller nations dependent on their influence. Even Italy has now been eliminated from the great powers group of nations. From these data, we might conclude that the minimum requirement for a great power in terms of land area is equivalent to that of the United Kingdom. This conclusion, however, can not be considered at all absolute or certain because constant changes in the world situation are accelerating the process of the emergence of large nations (or perhaps we should simply recognize this for what it is, annexation by the great powers) and the elimination of small nations even at the present time. Moreover, this tendency is increasing, rather than diminishing.

Population

The expansion of large nations and the disappearance of small nations affect population as well as land area. Therefore, we cannot

---

Elements of Wealth and Strength of the Great Powers

Material Factors
- National Land
  - Area
  - Location
  - Other Natural Conditions
- Population
  - Physique
  - Physical Strength

Spiritual Factors
- Intellectual Ability
- Moral Life

draw final conclusions in regard to this matter, either. But a review of data on land area and size of population, considered together, reveals a significant relationship between them. Although Spain has a larger land area than the United Kingdom, it cannot compete successfully even with nations which are much smaller. There could be various factors involved here, but one in particular may be that of population size. Since Italy, in fact, provides an example of the minimum requirement for great power status, we might, perhaps, conclude that the minimum population requirement may be about thirty million.

Location in Relation to Climatic Zones

We established earlier that extremes in climate are not conducive to high development of human abilities. We have also concluded that high development of human capabilities is a prerequisite for becoming a great power. Though there are historical instances of great powers developing in areas outside the temperate zone, they could not qualify as great powers in the modern sense. Therefore we can conclude that it is only in the temperate zone that great powers can emerge. Though parts of Russia and the Scandinavian peninsula lie in the frigid zone, these are mere extensions of powerful core societies in the temperate zone. Within the temperate zone, it seems that northern latitudes provide more favorable conditions for the emergence of great powers than southern.

Location in Relation to the Ocean

The ocean, we have seen, is like a public road in the modern world. Whether or not a nation has access to the ocean, therefore, significantly affects its survival. Russia, for example, is eagerly trying to acquire an all season port directly connecting its land mass to the ocean for exactly this reason. Thus, in the near future, a nation without direct access to the ocean will lack at least one prerequisite to be a great power.

While these are the minimum requirements for a nation to become a great power, there are various other factors, such as a location favorable for national defense and for potential production and trade that also determine the strength and wealth of a state. There are some scholars who regard race to be another of these determinants. They argue, for example, that only the Aryan race is capable of forming the kind of political life and system required to create a modern state, and that therefore it is the legitimate role of the members of that race to intervene in the domestic affairs of nations other than Aryans. Whether or not this argument has any merit or basis in reality can be demonstrated only by the Japanese, a non-Aryan ethnic group which has created its own empire in the Far East. In the light of the attention from the rest of the world which our position has focused upon us, we have to be more aware of the importance of our responsibility.

Though the factors described above are prerequisites for great power status, we should not conclude hastily that a nation can be strong and rich simply if these conditions are met. The presence of many nations in the world which are still poor and weak despite the presence of all these factors, suggests that there must be something that serves to combine given factors in such a way as to produce this outcome—that is, becoming a great power—which is beyond simple addition. If a nation is endowed with all the tangible factors stated above but lacks a highly developed spiritual life, then it only serves to tempt the appetite of other great powers.

Types of States

States are usually classified on the basis of the form of government—monarchy or democracy, for example—or combinations such as absolute monarchy, constitutional monarchy, republic, aristocracy within democracy, etc. These distinctions are not as relevant from the geographical viewpoint on global relations as they may be for a political focus on the formalities of global relations.

Sovereignty, insofar as legal definitions are concerned, is still sovereignty, irrespective of forms of government. These above distinctions tend to give a wrong impression. Sometimes, for example, people make the mistake of thinking that a republic is a more advanced form than a monarchy, but this is not necessarily so. If it is necessary to distinguish differences in the extent of development of national cultures, a useful distinction could be constitutional versus non-constitutional government. Other distinctions do not indicate any relevant differences in the degree of nationhood. When it comes to a cultural geography of each nation, however, simple distinctions between forms of government are not adequate. Thus, for our purposes various other types of classification are needed which are more appropriate and useful.

Distinctions Based on National Polity[5]

In the previous section, we learned that the strength of the unity among the people of a state is an important factor determining growth or decline of national power. In the development of a modern constitutional state, the most powerful driving force has been the integration of its people. Thus, a state must always reserve a portion of its power to further and maintain its own internal integration. The strength of unity of a state varies depending on the number of ethnic groups politically integrated within it. In other words, a nation consisting of heterogeneous ethnic groups has a lower degree of integration than a more homogeneous state. Moreover, among nations composed of many ethnic groupings, the degree of integration or unity varies with the time elapsed since founding. An ethnic group is a product of natural forces as well as of the group's history in its present habitat. States are also products of nature and history. Thus, in geography, even a nation which in its early years was composed of several ethnic groups may be regarded as a single ethnic state after several hundred or several thousand years of history.

The degree of unity of a state affects its power in significant ways and, as previously stated, the degree of unity depends on the number of ethnic groups originally involved in the state's founding. This is a more useful typology in studies of geogaphy than typologies based on the form of government. We have, then, the following classification based on national polity:

◆ Ethnically Homogeneous State.

◆ Union of States (the joining of generally equal entities such as in the United Kingdom of England and Ireland).

◆ Alliance (states governed by the same monarch but involving separate territories such as Austria-Hungary, Sweden-Norway).

◆ Federation (each state of a federation has its own monarch, but are united by allegiance to a common monarch of the federation; Germany is an example).

Legally these different types cannot be clearly distinguished. However, since these categories are used in naming nations, and some relevance is found between such distinctions and certain geographical factors, this system of classification can be of some use.

Some aspects of this classification support my argument that geographic factors are at work in the formation of different types of national polity. For example, the emergence of very similar states at the extremes of East and West, that is Japan and the United Kingdom, can possibly be explained by their geographical similarity. Yet, they developed different polities because, in spite of their very similar geographical formation, there are present at the same time some marked geographical differences. The former consists of four main islands separated from each other by narrow straits, with the central island overwhelming the others in scale and, therefore, in influence. The latter consists of two major islands of comparable size and power with a strait between them which exerts a strong separating function.

Distinctions Based on National Power

This is the most relevant distinction in geography. Sanae Takada, a specialist in legal matters, has proposed the following classification system which in some respects is well suited to the needs of geography[6]:

◆ World-Powers: World Powers are states whose every action has impact on other States, affecting politics over several continents or sometimes over the entire world.

◆ Great-Powers: All World Powers are Great Powers but the reverse is not necessarily true. World Powers must have strong navies, otherwise they can not exercise influence over the destiny of the world. On the other hand, one of the requirements for a Great Power is a strong army but not necessarily a strong navy. Prussia, in the days before the integration of the German Empire, and Austria-Hungary at the present time are examples. Great Powers also exercise their influence beyond their national boundaries. Thus, any changes in the relations among continents cannot take place without their involvement.

◆ Intermediate Peaceful Powers: These states do not have influence over other states, engaging solely in domestic affairs. But though they have little power, they could be very effective in abating the dangerous currents generated by competition among the Great Powers.

◆ Petty-States: These States are very vulnerable in today's world, for the current world provides an environment favorable only for large States, not for small ones. Thus, Petty-States have to seek protection from large states in order to survive.

Dr. Takada's classification is useful for indicating distinctions based on the degree of wealth and strength of a given state. However, it still does not provide a good classification scheme for geography.

However, we can redefine this categorization for application to the current status of the world as follows:

◆ Strong Wealthy States: States which have achieved a high degree of spiritual development beyond the material requirements of a strong, wealthy state. Examples are the United Kingdom, France, Germany, and the United States. In light of the evolutionary nature of state objectives described in the preceding section, states in this category correspond to the second stage of Burgess's hypothesis. As national integration is completed and the rights and freedom of citizens become guaranteed, these states are able to devote full attention to the promotion of the happiness and well-being of their peoples.

In terms of international relations, since they have succeeded in establishing strong political and economic power in their own nations, those powers now flow out toward other nations, just as air flows out of a high atmospheric pressure system. Since political power and economic power are the two major components of real state power today, the combination of these two powers might be termed "international power potential" and states which excel in this kind of power can be called "high power potential states."

◆ Strong Poor States: These are states which possess a full range of natural requirements for wealth and strength, able to cope with foreign powers with a fair degree of national cooperation among their citizens, but not yet able to take advantage of their rich natural resources to build economic wealth due to insufficient spiritual development. Italy and Russia are examples. We may add Japan to this group as well. Rather than natural resources, the elements which are lacking in these states can be supplemented by the efforts of their people. If a nation's people recognize this and strive with diligence, then their nation will be able to become a strong wealthy state. These states, in other words, have achieved the primary national objectives. Therefore, though their power potential level exceeds the average, their creative potential is still below average. Since such states have firmly established domestic power they tend to compensate for their lack of international economic competitiveness by adopting aggressive policies. Consider, for example, Russian policies toward Siberia and Manchuria.

♦ Weak Wealthy States: This category includes two types. One type has nearly developed the spiritual capacity to become a state possessing wealth and strength but lacks the necessary natural resources. The other type has natural resources but lacks the spiritual elements among its people that are required for the effective utilization of materials. Belgium and the Netherlands are of the former type while China is an example of the latter. Particularly in the case of Belgium, the people are both intellectually capable and industrious. This has enabled the country to build up material wealth and accumulate a capital surplus, even loaning considerable amounts to other states, especially to Russia. Unfortunately, however, due to its small land area, a limitation which cannot be compensated for by human intelligence, Belgium is barely able to protect itself from encroachment by other states and occupies a relatively marginal position among modern states.

In the context of the development of state objectives, these two types correspond to the first two stages respectively. The former has passed the first stage and is entering the second. However, since these states are not able to compete with other states in pursuing expansionist goals, they work hard to create what is required through their own productivity. In terms of a political power scale, they are average but their creative potential is relatively high. The second type is still in the first stage, not yet having established enough power to govern domestic affairs. Thus, state power is expended to control insurgencies, leaving no extra power to attend to other needs. Even with strong effort, they often are not able to suppress civil strife by themselves, providing good pretexts for other states to intervene. States of this type are characterized by low potential in both productive and political power.

♦ Weak Poor States: These are states which are barely able to maintain themselves within a precarious balance of power with other states. They do not have wealth, nor do they have sufficient physical force to control domestic rebellions. Thus, they are subject to strong pressures both from within and from without, gradually approaching a point of exhaustion and extinction. On the power potential scale they are similar to the latter type in the previous category.

Distinctions Based on Location Relative to the Ocean

We have already learned that a state's location in relationship to the ocean is an important factor in its development. Therefore, a category which includes this element may be useful:

◆ Inland States: States surrounded by neighboring states, with no coastline within their own territory, are placed in an extremely unfavorable position in commerce and trade. Switzerland, Afghanistan, and Tibet are examples.

◆ Coastal States: States which possess some amount of coast line have an advantage in commerce and trade. In general, the extent of the advantage increases in accordance with the length of the coastal area. However, the type of ocean that they face also affects the degree of advantage. When these factors are considered, we have two sub-categories:

(1) States with an Inland Sea: States which have inland seas but are blocked from access to the open sea by the power of other states. These states are vulnerable because their participation in foreign trade can be curtailed by changes in the international situation. Should this happen, unless they have enough military power to prevent enclosure, they will share the same destiny with inland states. Russia is constantly trying to expand its territory in all directions precisely because of this fear. Threats to world peace that we now face also have roots in this problem. Italy, for instance, seems to have a very advantageous location. However, since both ends of the Mediterranean sea are controlled by other nations, Italy must ever be anxious. Other states on the Mediterranean coast are in a similar position.

(2) States Facing the Open Sea: States with direct access to open seas have no obstacles to their engaging in external trade. Germany, France, and Spain are examples.

◆ States Surrounded by Oceans: These can be called island states. They share the same advantages as states facing open seas. In addition, in terms of length of coastline, they have even more advantages. Japan and the United Kingdom are in this group and in a sense the United States can also be regarded in this light. Historically, there are two types of states in this category, island states and maritime states, distinctions which were discussed in Chapter 13.

Distinctions Based on Economic Life

Types of economic activity which are of central importance in the lives of a state's people can be classified as "primary industry states" and "commerce and industry states." The distinction between the two stems from the location of the state involved. Today, due to the development of transportation, the world has become the setting of all the activities shared by human beings. In the economic sphere, international obstacles to exchange of goods have become fewer and fewer. Both materially and spiritually, states have come to be interdependent in a way similar to the interdependence heretofore common within a single state. Just as one nation has both urban and rural areas, in a world system as well, some states lead a more urbanized style of life while others lead a rural type life. Thus, urban states involved in commerce and industry import raw materials from less developed states, process them into products, and sell them at considerable profit. On the other hand, primary industry states supply low cost raw materials and purchase expensive manufactured products. As a result they are always left in a disadvantageous position.

National Borders

Land is the basis of a nation's existence. The territory of each country is demarcated by national borders just as a body as a distinct organism is outlined by its outer skin. Skins protect the lives of organisms by resisting the harmful external forces trying to penetrate their bodies. In the same way, national borders serve as defense fronts that guard nations against the invasion of foreign powers. Just as the success of an organism in defending itself from external forces depends on the strength of its skin, so national borders vary in their defense capability depending on their strength or weakness.

Oceans, rivers, lakes, and mountains often serve as national borders. However, due to the development of transportation systems, these natural boundaries have become less and less effective. Thus, today, artificial lines which have been agreed upon by two or more parties through custom or the signing of treaties are drawn over natural borders. Types of such artificial lines are:

- Along coasts, a nation can claim as its territory the area up to 3 miles from the coast at low tide.

- In the case of rivers and lakes, imaginary lines are drawn in their center on the surface of the water.

- In the case of mountains, lines linking their summit points are drawn.

When there are no such geographical objects to serve as borders, a specific longitude, or a straight line passing through designated points on the ground is regarded as a boundary. Examples are the parallel serving as the boundary between the United States and Canada, and the parallel on Sakhalin island serving as a border between Japan and Russia. A similar principle is involved in demarcating administrative districts within countries.

Colonies

People tend to flow from densely populated areas to less populated areas. In the past, such flow took place within a country or between neighboring countries. However, migration at the present time must be seen within a global context. As population increases and becomes compressed in a country, it starts to pour out, seeking less populated and less developed areas, just as a swollen river breaks a dam and overflows. Moreover, the emigrants take control of the new land when they can overpower the indigenous people or when they meet with no resistance by other external forces. Even when there is resistance, they try to place the land under their influence by declaring it their dependency or colony and exploiting it in their own interests.

In this way, most of the areas once considered as nothing more than the home of primitives or savages came to have some form of international connection with western civilizations. Those lands were designated dependencies, protectorates, or colonies. While the closeness of the relationships varies depending on the category, all of them were put in a politically and economically subordinate position to the great powers. The difference among the categories, viewed from the great powers' perspective, was only a matter of degree, since "great power," by definition, meant to put all those countries under their complete control in time. In international politics the term "colonies" indicates only those areas that are politically subordinate to sovereign states.

Geographically, it makes little difference whether an area is designated as a colony or a protectorate. Whatever the title, all those subordinate areas have common characteristics which distinguish them from other areas. In the following discussion, therefore, the term colony will be used to indicate all of these areas. A "colony" is defined as a weak area or region which is subordinate to a strong state and which is clearly distinguished from that state by virtue of special rules applied in its governance.

Causes of Colonization

Giving up one's land which has been passed down through many generations and settling in a strange, unfamiliar environment requires a major decision that affects one's whole life. No one makes such a decision unless he is unavoidably forced to do so. Study of cases of such inevitable migrations suggests several causal factors. In some cases people emigrated to escape from economic destitution or political oppression (Russians settling in Siberia), religious persecution (in Europe in the past century), and strict social constraints. Again, some states have exiled condemned criminals to distant areas because they may threaten the existing ruling group within a nation. People have also migrated out of hunger to make a fortune, trying to follow the example of some successful predecessors. Even successful people sometimes migrate to expand their business abroad and to increase their capital. Close study would reveal hundreds of other reasons but in short, there are two major causes of recent migration pressure: intensified competition for survival due to population growth and intensifying desire for wealth accompanying capital accumulation within a nation. Most emigrants, therefore, have been losers in the social and economic competition within their home nation. Yet, at the same time these colonists tend to be innovative, courageous, and aggressive in nature. Such "peculiarities" of colonists undoubtedly greatly influence the nature of the colonies in which they settle.

Purposes and Means of Colonization

Just as individual colonists emigrated in order to seek a happier and easier life, states that encouraged emigration and protected settlers also sought, through colonization, a better and more prosperous life for their people. Thus, if colonists settle themselves in a new land, compete successfully in the new land and become prosperous, their home states consider that colonization to have achieved its goal. On the other hand, to achieve complete success in a given colonial undertaking, acquiring complete suzerainty upon the part of the home state is essential. Modern European nations employed various means in attempting to establish their sovereignty over colonial lands. Some were successful, others failed, and yet others were partially successful. These means, collectively, have been called "colonial policy" by political scientists and can be classified into three categories:

◆ Autonomous Policy: This approach has been employed by Britain. It grants each colony the right to form its own parliament, but the right to ultimate control, remains with the British parliament. The colonial parliament has legislative, judicial, and executive powers and is entrusted with administering the whole range of the colony's affairs. Thus, the colony organized its own army and navy, taking responsibility for both defense and offense. All expenses are borne by the colony. The colonial treasury is completely separate from that of the home state.

◆ Subordinate Policy: In ancient times, this approach was used exclusively. Even in modern times, when a great power attempts to colonize a new territory, this approach is used initially. The Netherlands still uses this policy today. Under this policy, the interests of the colony are not considered important. The colonizing state, in pursuit of its own wealth and power, grants no rights to the colony. If a specific law or policy serves the state's interests, it is indiscriminately applied to the colony. If the state needs money or wealth, it squeezes the colony, gaining as much revenue from it as possible.

◆ Assimilation Policy: France, Spain, and Portugal employ this policy. Under this system, the colonies send representatives to the legislatures of the colonizing state who participate in the legislative process of the parent state. Thus, policies and laws adopted by the legislature automatically apply to the colonies as well. Theoretically, the people of the colonies have rights equal to those granted to the people of the home state.

Each of these three types of colonial policy has advantages and disadvantages.

Regarding autonomous policy, if a colony is not able to attain a certain level of development, it will face great difficulty in the event it attempts to gain independence from the control of the colonial power. On the other hand, however, in cases in which the colonizing state's attitude toward the colony is one of laissez faire, the colony may try to become completely independent and deal with the state in the same way as with other foreign nations, offering no benefits to the original colonizing state. This means that the huge investment made by the colonizing state during the initial phase of colonization cannot be recovered.

Subordinate policy is the reverse of autonomous policy. The colony may benefit from the protection rendered by the colonial power to a certain extent. However, once the colony achieves a certain level of development, it will be increasingly painful for its people to bear willingly the oppressive measures of the home state. Thus, they will seek every opportunity to rebel and become truly independent, or they may seek the protection of another powerful state.

The policy of assimilation seems to be successful in avoiding most of the disadvantages of the two previously described types of colonial rule. However, even under this policy, since colonies and their home states are often geographically remote from each other, their interests often conflict. Colonies are often forced to obey decisions which are not to their advantage. The actual result of this type of rule, therefore, is similar to that of subordinate policy.

Notes

[1] The context within which this was written was a perceived military threat from Russia.

[2] Bernard Bosanquet was an English philosopher, political theorist, and philanthropist. His principal work was *The Philosophical Theory of the State*, published in 1899.

[3] John W. Burgess. This information is from a book by Burgess, *The Foundations of Political Science*, published posthumously (1933) by Columbia University Press.

[4] Johann Kasper Bluntschi, a Swiss jurist, 1808-1881.

[5] The distinction Makiguchi seems to be making here is between "seitai" (form) and "kokutai" (polity). The difference for him was that polity is concerned with the social composition and the relationships among the various types and categories of people and groups making up a state, whereas form of government refers to different approaches to the use of power in the state.

[6] Sanae Takada, a Japanese educator and politician, 1860-1938.

Chapter 27

The Phenomenon of Cities

Villages and the Land

The growth of cities is one of the most remarkable phenomena in human history and the study of cities is essential for geography. But first, we must look at villages, for it is there that we find the origins of the city.

Villages comprise the simplest and most primitive type of human society. The location and the shape of any particular village depends on its natural circumstances. Its location, from what we have learned from previous studies leads us to expect, is generally the most convenient place for human life in its area. We can see its origin in relation to the surrounding land when we observe the shape of a village. Inazo Nitobe (1862-1933), a scholar of agriculture, has classified villages into six general categories:[1]

- ◆ roadside villages.

- ◆ villages built around a spring or a church.

- ◆ villages built on the slope of a hill forming a stair-like shape.

- ◆ villages which develop randomly with no central focus or ordering principle.

- ◆ villages consisting of scattered two or three-house settlements.

- ◆ small houses built around a large house or mansion.

Nitobe developed his classification by observing many villages in different parts of the world. His different classes of villages can be seen and verified. However, his classification does not distinguish clearly between origin and shape, so I propose the following modification:

Classification by Shape

♦ Rows: Houses are built on both sides of a road or a stream. New houses are built on both ends of the rows and the rows often become some miles long. If one side of the road is not suitable for building, the houses are built on only one side. The distance from one end of the village to the other has limits, however, and if there are no natural obstacles at either end, the village will begin to develop in other directions.

♦ Multiple rows: With population increase, people will build new houses behind the first row because a village strung out over a long distance becomes inconvenient for its inhabitants. So more rows appear as the village grows in depth. The busiest place, or where the rich live, is at the center of the original village.

♦ Crossings: Sometimes rows develop at various angles, rather than parallel to each other. Crossroads and places where a stream flows into a sea or a lake often become the sites of villages. The center of such a village forms at the crossing.

♦ A Circle: Houses built around a fortress, a temple, a spring, or a port, may grow into a village which develops in the form of a circle. However, in the case of a port, the village will tend to develop in the form of a half circle.

♦ The Form of a Pocket: Villages of this shape develop when houses are built around an attracting element, such as a temple or a shrine which has a deep forest in the background, and later the village develops along a road leading to it.

♦ Scattered: Each house is built independently of other houses, with doorways facing in different directions. This shape is typical of villages begun by urban people who emigrate to newly opened frontier areas such as Hokkaido.

♦ Clustered: Houses are built in twos and threes which are prevented from growing into a more close-knit village due to hills or valleys which discourage growth. In this situation, each small cluster of houses becomes a kind of mini-village by itself.

♦ Checkerboard: Characteristic of villages planned in advance. Streets are straight and form right angles. This shape, which is not found in natural villages, suggests that urban people had immigrated there.

The above scheme for classifying villages can be helpful in our efforts to understand their history and origins. However, we must realize that most villages are some hundreds or even thousands of years old; their shapes may have changed over time. On the other hand, villages having undergone extensive change metamorph into large cities and are no longer villages. Thus, we can assume that most villages, barring destructive alternation by a major fire or an earthquake, have kept their original shape.

Classification by Density

Houses tend to be built close together in old, natural villages and separate and far apart in newly developed villages. Each type has strengths and limitations which tend to be opposites. The former has the handicap of distance between residence and work place. In some farming villages in the mountains, for example, people must often walk several kilometers to their farm every day. This is inconvenient, but in the past it was necessary and preferable to live close to other villagers for mutual help and to protect themselves from enemies. In more recent times, however, wild beasts have ceased to be a threat in most areas, transportation has developed, and effective policing systems have been created. Thus, there is no longer the need to live close together for purposes of protection. In Hokkaido, the Japanese frontier, pioneers lived close together at first, but later they traded properties among themselves in order to make residences and farming land closer together.

At the same time, while the need for protection has become less important, there is a growing awareness of a need for community life and the intellectual and emotional support it affords, and the population of a community should exceed some minimum number in order to more effectively provide for the growth and educational needs of children.

The City

Cities are of various sizes and some of the smaller ones can scarcely be distinguished from villages. Thus, we need to define the city. In recent years, some villages have grown to include as many as 10,000 people, but they are still called "villages." Government population statistics in 1900 defined cities as communities with more than 2,000 people. Nitobe also, referring to figures recommended by a conference of world statisticians, has defined cities as densely populated communities with more than 2,000 people.[2] So this seems an appropriate standard. However, we should note that large cities cannot develop on the basis of primary industries alone. Primary industries depend directly on natural resources, which are limited, and they cannot sustain very large populations. Thus, I would amend this definition as follows: "Cities are densely populated communities with more than 2,000 people who are engaged mainly in secondary or tertiary industries."

The Origin of the City

As commerce and manufacturing developed and became differentiated from primary industries, so cities became differentiated from villages. When we observe existing cities today, it is difficult to identify their origins because they have changed so much over time. But if we look at them carefully, we can deduce their origins from their shapes, archeological remains, names, legends, and the factors underlying their current growth and development. Thus, one possible classification scheme for cities focuses on the reasons for their development:

◆ For Protection Against Enemies: When nations are not strong enough to maintain law and order , wealthy people must protect themselves, or depend on some regional power or powerful lord, as in Korea and China. In such cases, the Lord's palace or castle affords the greatest safety and becomes a gathering point. Once aristocrats and their retainers gather to these havens of safety, they are soon followed by poorer people who seek their living by providing services for their wealthier countrymen, laborers who build the palaces and castles and the merchants who trade with them gathering first. Thus do such places grow into cities.

◆ For Religious Reasons: Religious feeling is one of man's

primitive natural characteristics. In ancient times, people engaged in worship of deities or spirits, not only to prevent natural disasters but also to protect themselves from enemies. The shrines and temples of their guardians were firmly built and came to serve as places of refuge and assurance. Monks and priests lived nearby and people came daily or gathered for special festivals. Regional leaders were sometimes attracted to these religious centers, built their houses around them, and posted their guards. Not infrequently kings and their retinues of retainers and lawyers followed with the result that religious centers grew into administrative and legal centers.

Once these upper class members of the society settled around a religious center, masses of the poorer people followed, just as in the case of development around palaces and castles. Furthermore, as the members of different tribes were drawn to the festivals and to meet each other, they brought with them the products of their land as offerings or sacrifices. This inevitably led to exchanges of cattle, grain, cloth, spices, salt, oil, and other items. Cattle markets were often organized at festivals. In time, the festivals grew into permanent markets, leading to the transformation of the former religious centers into cities.

◆ For Political Reasons: Cities originating in political activity generally developed through the same process as cities originating for religious reasons and for the need for protection. Once power had become concentrated in a central government, lives and wealth became safer, and bureaucrats and people interested in trade gathered.

◆ For Artistic Reasons: People do not live for material pleasure alone. Once the basic maintenance needs of food and clothing can be adequately met, human beings long for the deeper spiritual dimensions of living afforded by artistic and intellectual activity. It is natural, then, that places which are rich in natural beauty and works of art attract people, almost always the rich and upper classes, who build their villas and resort homes nearby. Here again, a city develops as people gather to engage in their trades and crafts and support services for the well-to-do.

◆ For Academic Reasons: People will, in some cases, gather for academic reasons. However, there are no cases in Japan of cities which began for this reason. In some Western countries, some such cities can be found. In England, for example, Cambridge and Oxford are known as names of universities, but they are also the names of cities which developed around these universities.

◆ For Economic Reasons: Most cities have their origin in economic activity. When an area has some useful product or products for manufacturing, or when a location is particularly convenient for trading, people will gather in large numbers and soon a city develops.

Where Cities Develop

As will be noted from what has been said above, the origins of cities are influenced, for the most part, by human factors which have little to do with the land. But on the other hand, geographical factors also are important in some cases, particularly those involved in native resources and products and gathering points for cargo:

◆ Special Resources and Products: When transportation is not well developed in an area or products of the area are difficult to transport over long distances, local processing is necessary if industry is to develop. This attracts various related and supporting industries to the area and a city begins to emerge. Fishery products is one example of this kind of local resource. Thus, there is a saying that "Amsterdam stands on herring." The existence of Bergen in Norway also, although it has a very bad and undesirable climate by human standards, depends on herring and cod. Even in the Arctic polar area there is a fishing town called Hammerfest. Other examples of resources of this nature are such minerals as gold, silver, and copper, earth for pottery, and salt and various types of fuel. Manchester in England, it is said, "lives on coal" and Baku, on the Caspian Sea, owes its existence to petroleum. Similarly, cities develop in areas where there is a plentiful supply of waterpower.

◆ Gathering Points for Cargo: In societies which place high value on commerce, those points at which traffic crosses become good candidates for the development of cities. As I have written earlier, in ancient times people settled along rivers because of their potential as channels of traffic and because of the richness of the soil along river banks. The potential of rivers to serve as traffic channels depends, however, on their size, and differs for different parts of the same river. Cities tend to develop at points on large rivers which can accommodate ships, particularly at the mouths of these rivers and at the uppermost points to which ships can penetrate. An interesting aside about the development of cities at river mouths is that, except for very large rivers, a distinction must be made between sea ships and river boats; that is, the river can accommodate only the river boats. Thus, cargo must be off loaded from the ships to the boats. The most convenient place for such off loading is the river mouth, so cities tend to develop there.

In large rivers, the further upstream sea ships can go before unloading or off loading to smaller river boats, the more convenient and economical it is. Thus, cities develop at these upper most points. Shanghai on the Yangtze, Saigon on the Mekong, Calcutta on the Ganges, Cairo on the Nile, Hamburg on the Elbe, London on the Thames, are examples of cities which developed for this reason. Also in regard to large rivers, the point where sea ships and river ships meet is generally regarded as the river's "mouth." This accounts for the fact that many European countries are trying to make inland cities into river ports. Glasgow, once a small village on the Clyde River, was turned into a center of ship construction by the British by excavating the mouth of the river at a cost of 20 million dollars. Now they are trying to make Manchester into a major trading port for cotton, the cost of which will be more than 70 million dollars. For the same reasons, the Germans have made the city of Hamburg into a port as big as London, and the French are trying to dig a channel from Paris to the Atlantic Ocean.

Cities also develop at points where rivers merge and where branches flow into main streams. Wuhan and Changchow in China are good examples. Likewise, the cities of the Great Plains in North America seem to be scattered randomly over the land without any plan or principle. However, if one observes the rivers, a coherent principle becomes evident in the cases of such cities as Cincinnati, St. Louis, Minneapolis, and Omaha. A similar principle can be seen at points where rivers bend, flow into or out of lakes, and at the ends of canals.

As with rivers, it is natural for cities to develop where main roads meet or cross. Tokyo, for example, was destined to become a great city, not only because of its position at the mouths of important rivers and because it had served as a political center for 200 years, but also because it is located at the center of a large plain and many main roads lead into it. We can observe, too, that in most cases large rivers have plains on both sides. Thus bridges, or ferries in the beginning, are built at points where people and cargo gather to cross the river. Evidence of the role of bridges in the origin of some cities can be seen in their names, Cambridge in England is one example. Cities develop also at such locations as the foot of mountains, which like rivers, block traffic; the narrowest point of an isthmus or channel; where caravan routes cross, such as Damascus, a meeting point of routes between Mesopotamia, Arabia, and Egypt.

As world trade develops, most goods come to be transported by sea routes. Lands separated by a sea are similar to the two sides of a river. And while bridges are built at the narrowest points of rivers, ports develop at the most convenient locations for people and cargoes to board ships for ocean travel. Many of these points are at the head of a bay or places on shores which are surrounded by plains or which have natural barriers to serve as protection from wind.

Cities develop especially at those ports selected as foreign trade ports. There the government controls trade in order to protect fledgling domestic industries, so those ports flourish. Ports where major sea routes meet also have potential to grow into large cities. Thus, Singapore has become a center of world trade because it is a meeting point for sea routes from east, west, and south. Constantinople at the entrance to the Black Sea is another example. And when the Panama Canal is built in the near future, routes from all directions will converge there.

Another kind of convergence point for sea routes is islands in the midst of large oceans. Oahu, a small island, has no special attraction in itself, but ships call at it because it is at the center of the Pacific Ocean and serves as a crossroads for sea routes between America, Asia, and Australia. Such points are important not only for trade but also for military purposes such as supply bases for coal and water, so they are always occupied by some strong power. The state which occupies and controls these points can obtain command of the sea, a significant asset in becoming a trading power.

City and Country

Cities became differentiated from the country with the birth of "merchants" who specialized in the exchange of goods. Once a city emerges, it performs special functions and it can prosper through a close relationship and cooperation with the country. Cities are based on the country and the country gets benefits from cities. So these two parts of a society help each other and develop hand in hand. Each part has its own unique character and each its own unique contribution to offer to the whole society.

One example of this symbiotic relationship between the city and the country is that of materials flowing into cities from the country, converted into products useful in the country, and then sent back to the country. In the process, unnecessary ingredients are removed or processed into other goods. In this way, every city becomes something of an industrial center. This is also true of the circulation of money. First, it flows from the city to the country for food or raw materials, then it returns in the form of payment by country people for the goods produced in the city. But the prices of those products are much higher than the materials. And while some part of the money paid for the city's products will return to the country in the form of wages, there is always some left over, so money accumulates in cities.

People and basic cultural concepts and values flow from the country to the city as well as food and materials. New lives flow into the city, constantly renewing and refreshing it. It has been said that geniuses are rarely born in cities, and the major religions of the world were born in deserts or in the mountains.[3] The country breeds people of good character, people who embody the best and highest ideals of a society's culture. When such people go to the cities or are discovered by city people, they influence the whole society. At the same time, some people return to the village after a period of sojourn in the city, bringing with them new ideas, new outlooks, and new ways of seeing the world. This two-way flow and exchange of people and ideas between the city and the country enriches and stimulates both.

Thus, as we begin to take stock of the city, we come to recognize and appreciate the greater opportunities afforded city people to become enlightened and intellectually challenged. The city brings people from various backgrounds and experiences together, providing the opportunity for the sharing and the pooling of their experiences. This not only enriches and brings stimulation into individual lives, but results also in the expansion and growth of total knowledge within the society. This is the reason that the intellectual level of city and country differ. The country is the source and origin of experiences but the knowledge which villagers have access to is fragmented and lacking in coherence. On the other hand, the intellectual stimulation of city life encourages the synthesis of concrete knowledge into abstract principles and experiences into larger contexts. People living in cities have many opportunities to broaden their intellectual horizons and to engage in activities which lead them to think.

The same process can be observed in the realm of economics. For example, in the city, business is divided into many departments and divisions, and various specialized tasks are done by persons suited to those tasks. But in the country, there is less opportunity for such a variety of individual abilities to be utilized and specialization and divisions of labor to develop. Similarly, commerce and manufacturing requiring a high degree of intellectual activity and specialized skills arise in cities, while less specialized and primitive industries are characteristic of the country. This means that the city can offer many more job and career opportunities for people, especially young people. This has led to people from the country flocking to the cities to seek work and fortune.

There is another important aspect of cities which is beneficial and constructive up to a point. That is the greater anonymity which people can find in the city. This is another factor which draws people to the city. There they are freed from the norms and rules, the restrictions and obligations of small town and village life. In the city, people can, as it were, breathe free and experiment with lifestyles and new ideas which would be unacceptable back in their hometowns in the country. In the city, the life of an individual can expand and blossom in ways which would not have been possible if the person had remained permanently in the country.

While the growth of cities, as noted above, has been one of the most remarkable developments in human history, immeasurably enriching human life and culture, they have not been an unmixed blessing. Cities have brought with them many problems which are difficult to solve and which pose a threat to the well being and survival of the very societies which gave them birth. In our study of cities, therefore, we must be alert to the positive contributions of cities, but at the same time we must face frankly the ways in which cities can undermine and destroy societies as well.

The thing we must recognize in our study of cities is that the very characteristics of cities which can add so much challenge and stimulation to human life can at the same time lead to problems, suffering, and lost opportunities. This is a mystery which many people do not understand and, failing to understand it, they become victims of the city, rather than victors. For example, people may come to the city to search for a job, to escape the seeming restrictions of life in their village, or from a desire for knowledge and intellectual challenge. But once there they find themselves facing fierce competition in their work life. They often are lonely and find it difficult to develop strong, warm relationships with other people. In such situations, people often lose confidence in themselves and hope for their future. This makes it easy for them to drift into bad company and yield to bad influences.

Another thing to recognize is that the city, because of its greater personal freedom and lack of restrictions, tends also to attract people whose lives have not developed in a balanced way. They come looking for physical pleasure and vulgar association. They may be looking for easy money through questionable or criminal behavior. People who come to the city from the country are often duped and cheated by these more experienced but unscrupulous city dwellers or are drawn into their illicit circle of acquaintances and lifestyle.

For some or all of these reasons, many people who come to the city become, as we observed above, victims and losers in life's struggle. Some may return to the country, beaten and disillusioned. Others, however, stay in the city and help to swell its numbers. They may become beggars or neurotics. Some commit suicide or fall into lives of crime.

These realities have led to a general perception of cities as crowded, unhealthy, unbalanced, and dangerous places where everyone is competing and conniving to best the next person. While this perception of cities is not justified in all cases, it is, unfortunately, very accurate in many respects. The general perception of the country, in contrast, is that of a healthful, calm environment where one can lead a less hectic and competitive life, allowing time for more wholesome emotional and spiritual experience and growth. Here, again, while this perception has been somewhat over-romanticized, it does reflect the nature and strengths of country living.

But what the holders of these contrasting perceptions fail to understand is that neither the city nor the country is complete in and of itself. Each needs the other, not only for survival, but because the most full and rich life for human beings requires the cultivation and appreciation of the strengths and qualities which each has to offer. It is just because this is not understood and is too often ignored in the mad pursuit of pleasure and personal gain alone that problems develop which diminish and threaten the well being of both the country and the city.

The Future of the City

As we have seen, the attractions of cities are a powerful lure which draws people to them. Consequently, the population of cities all over the world is increasing rapidly. In the United States, the population of cities accounted for 3.3% of the total population in 1790, but by 1880 it was 22.5%. The growth of cities is even greater in England and Scotland. Even in France, whose total population is increasing slowly, and in Ireland, whose population is declining, the population of cities is growing. In Japan, the population grew by 1.2% in 1898, but the growth of cities was much higher. Tokyo, for example, grew by 7.4% that same year.

We have observed that cities have many good features and that they are, in fact, the centers of civilization and the source of goods and ideas which have enriched human life and culture immeasurably. But cities today are also creating serious problems which as yet we do not know how to solve, problems which may, unless dealt with intelligently, destroy culture rather than enrich it.

This negative impact of cities has several interrelated elements. One, which we have considered in earlier chapters, is their severing of the ties between people and nature. Moreover, city people are often overworked, rushed for time, and easily irritated. As cities grow ever larger, people become physically unhealthy, their minds become inactive, they tend to become vulgar and lacking in moral character, and many come to feel increasingly insecure and fearful. Such conditions lead to increases in neurotic behavior and crime. To compensate for such drab, insecure lives, people rush madly after various pleasures and pastimes to make them forget their problems and their fears.

One of the most serious problems posed by cities, however, is that they lead to the decline of the industry, enterprise, and culture of rural areas. There is no greater threat to our societies than this. William Cobbett (1763-1835), an English journalist, likened the city of London and other cities like it to warts because they suck nutrition and strength from the nation, just as warts suck nutrition from a living body.

Clearly, we must face the problem of the runaway growth of cities. We can not afford to permit the decline of our primary industries. Although their decline could be compensated for by engaging in foreign trade, the loss is permanent while the compensation is unstable and temporary. Furthermore, there is no way to calculate the overall loss. If the health of the nation is jeopardized or the productivity of the land is sacrificed, the entire society will be affected, and recovery will be difficult.

Thus, while acknowledging that cities are essential and that their contribution to the enrichment of human life and culture is an important one, we must learn how to control their growth. Cities can be permitted to expand only up to the point at which they become a threat to the society's primary industries. Beyond that point they must not be permitted to grow.

Notes

[1] Included in Nitobe"s *Nogyo Honron* (Basic Agricultural Theory).
[2] From *Nogyo Honron,* Chapter 26.
[3] See Chapter 2 for a discussion of genius and the development of character and morality.

Clearly, we must face the problem of the runaway growth of cities. We can not afford to permit the decline of our primary industries.
Although their decline could be compensated for by engaging in foreign trade, the loss is permanent while the compensation is unstable and temporary. Furthermore, there is no way to calculate the overall loss.

Chapter 28

Customs, Temperament, and Geography

Temperament and Geography

Terms such as "temperament" and "character" are sometimes used to describe spiritual or psychological characteristics common to a particular region, tribe, or class. While such terms are too loose and imprecise to be of scientific value, they are widely used as figures of speech. Just as a person's mental and emotional life is influenced by his home environment, so a tribe's characteristics are influenced by the characteristics of the region it inhabits. A relationship between the characteristics of a people and that of a region is not absolute; it is a relative matter perhaps best understood through comparison of regions with contrasting characteristics. This understanding provides the basis for the following comparisons.

Islands vs. Continents

In our earlier discussion of islands in Chapter 6, we found that people living in island nations tend to be fiercely patriotic and seek to be independent of external forces. They are staunchly loyal and obedient to their own leaders. But at the same time they tend to be less ambitious, more isolation oriented, and narrower in outlook. These characteristics can be recognized more clearly if we compare island people with people living on continents. Since islands are isolated within their vast ocean, the people living on them can behave only on the basis of the experience they have gained in the islands. They have few opportunities to be exposed to other people and therefore are little influenced by things and thoughts outside the islands. This prevents them from developing wider and more flexible perspectives. People living on continents, in contrast, are in constant contact and competition with other peoples. Therefore, they have a much wider variety of experiences than their counterparts on islands. Such differences in environment produce contrasting island and continental temperaments.

Mountains vs. Plains

A similar contrast can be observed between people living in mountains and those living on plains. Societies in mountains are isolated from the outside world by ranges of mountains just as islands are isolated by oceans. Therefore, like island people, people living in mountains have few opportunities to be exposed to and influenced by outside societies. In the case of plains, however, the situation is very similar to that of people living on continents. As we may expect, then, plains people tend to be more open and broad-minded, while mountain people cannot help being somewhat narrow-minded and fearful of innovative thinking and new customs.

A comparison of mountain people and plains people reveals that it is not only the natural environment but also differences in their respective types of work or subsistence activity which accounts for differences in character and temperament. Since people in the mountains are engaged, for the most part, in forestry and hunting, they tend to be resolute and straightforward in temperament. Plains people, on the other hand, tend toward gaiety, softness, and are not so resolute. Of course, I am fully aware that there are various trades and vocations among plains people, such as farming, merchandising, various crafts, and that each tends to occupy particular locations suitable to their nature. However I will not go into detail here since this has been considered in our earlier comparisons between urban and rural societies.

Large States vs. Small States

A similar contrast can also be observed between the people of large states and those of small states. The natural conditions prevailing on continents make it possible for continental states to grow larger while island states are unable to expand. It is tempting to apply comparisons made between islands and continents to small and large states. However, due to the development of modern transportation systems, small states are not necessarily identical to island states. Since large states tend always to be aware of their strong influence over smaller states surrounding them, their people tend to become broad-minded and resolute, and they may also tend to become overconfident and arrogant toward others. In contrast, since smaller states always exist under the threat of annexation or conquest by larger states, they tend to be indecisive and hesitant in executing new projects. Since they perceive no chance of acquiring power whereby they could dominate large nations, their aspirations focus solely on acquiring wealth, as the cases of Belgium and ancient Phoenicia give evidence.

Coastal vs. Inland Areas

We have already observed that people who are born and grow up on the coast, with their dreams nourished by the vastness of the ocean and their experience of freely riding the surging waves, have a different disposition from that of people living inland. Coastal people engaged in fishing and shipping tend to be more decisive, adventurous, daring, and unrestricted in outlook than conservative inland people who are more deeply rooted in their homelands. This is because coastal people, due to their environment, are more experienced in competing with other people overseas, always playing leading roles in opening trade and colonies. Even among coastal areas there are further differences between bay areas and straight coast line areas. However, in this case, the development of cities and ports in bay areas is involved, thus the discussion of urban characteristics will be applicable for those areas.

Urban vs. Rural Areas

In urban areas there is a concentration of people in commerce and industry. Such an environment encourages quick-wittedness, decisiveness, and free-thinking, though urban people are often criticized as being soft, frivolous, and indulging in luxury. Rural people, in contrast, are usually humble, honest, and dependable, though they tend also to be rough and unsophisticated. Such differences in disposition and temperament are not due to differences in moral development, however. Rather, such differences can be compared to the contrast between civilized and uncivilized nations and attributed to the time and energy available for cultural pursuits.

Mild vs. Extreme Climates

Nature endowed different parts of the earth with different conditions, blessing some with a mild and abundantly fruitful climate while others struggle for the necessities of life in barren extremity of climate. Where nature is warm and generous, people may develop tendencies toward idleness, self-indulgence and lack of perseverance in contrast to the sterner qualities of those who must struggle to survive against the rigors of nature. In extreme conditions, the virtues of fearlessness and courage may also be taken to extremes: Ruthless cruelty, hostility and combativeness. The threat to the Netherlands posed by tidal levels and Russia's lack of ocean access are examples of nature's extremities.

Thus we can see that the different characteristics of temperament and disposition among people in different parts of the earth can be attributed in some measure to the friendliness or unfriendliness of the natural conditions of their respective environments. These contrasts in the dispositions of peoples due to differences in climate and environmental conditions can be compared to the contrasts between warm and cold regions and between civilized and uncivilized states. This is because, in general, civilization developed out of the competition for survival among human beings in different natural environments.

Customs and Geography

Customs reflect the nature and feelings of a people. Just as human temperament is influenced by the geographical features of a people's environment, so customs are also affected by geography. People who have had the opportunity to visit various regions of the world and encounter different cultures become acutely aware of this. However, the term "custom" applies to a nearly infinite variety of phenomena in human life, and it tends to be defined too loosely for our purposes. Thus, in the following discussion I will focus on customs in three basic areas of human life: food, clothing, and housing. While occupation is also an important cultural component it will not be included here because we have already considered it in depth in a previous chapter.

Food Customs

Here we will want to observe types, quality, quantity, and appearance of food in different cultures, as well as containers and the ways in which meals are prepared and served. Tracing the origins of these various customs, we find that they are the products of historical development which in turn have been greatly affected by geographic environment. Food is most affected by geographic conditions. The staple food of a given people in a given region is decided by tradition, but it is always among the natural products of the region. It is often observed that immigrants try to obtain the food of their homeland even though the foods of the new land are much easier to obtain, but of necessity, they adapt to local customs over time and accept local food for their staple diet. Since staple foods are natural products of the land, they are subject to the climate of the land. This realization provides the starting point for our study of relationships between food and environment.

To satisfy their nutritive needs people ingest several different types of food in addition to the staple food of their area. These foods, too, are usually among the natural products of the land. However, the quantity and distribution of these supplementary foods are affected by various factors such as religion, occupation, social class, poverty, and wealth as well as climate. Peoples in colder regions favor fish and meat rich in fat, while peoples in temperate or warm areas favor vegetables. These are differences related directly to climate. The Japanese custom, prior to the Meiji Restoration, of not eating meat despite a climate that allows cattle farming, was the product of Buddhist teachings. Even today the meat eating habit has not spread widely in Japan. This is because of cultural inertia and the tenaciousness of old customs. It is interesting to note, also, that intake of salt among people varies depending on the nature of labor that they are engaged in. On the other hand, the fact that salt intake is correlated with the distance between a given area and the ocean may account for the fact that mountain people, in general, are fond of salty foods.

Clothing Customs

Items of clothing and their quality, quantity, and even their shape and color, are influenced by the specific materials and products of the land, a relationship that is an indirect influence of climate. Climate also has direct impact on clothing. The Japanese custom of wearing linen clothes in summer and wool or quilted cotton clothes in winter is one example.

The direct influence of climate can be seen in the style and color of the clothes as well. People in warm regions wear light colored clothing while in cold regions darker colored clothes are worn. The clothing of people in warm regions of the earth generally have long, loose-fitting sleeves and loose sash belts, while those of the cold regions of northern Europe have tight sleeves. This is also due to differences in climate.

Climate alone cannot explain all the differences in the design of clothes, however. There are, for example, a variety of designs in the same climatic zone which stem from other factors such as differences in occupation, tradition, competition for survival, and ethnic traditions, among others. Japanese sandals are totally made of materials produced in our own land, whereas the leather shoes worn by Europeans reflect their ancestral roots in the nomadic cultures of central Asia. The custom presently becoming popular among Japanese workers of wearing tight sleeve, western style clothes is an example of the influence of occupation on clothing.

Housing Customs

Material used for housing depends almost totally on natural products of the land. Because of the quantity required it is difficult to transport such materials over long distances. Thus, farm houses have thatched roofs made from straw left after the grain has been threshed for food. In highland regions where trees are scarce, houses are built with stone or earth. In snow and ice covered lands, people use blocks of ice to build their houses. At the same time, the fact that many houses in urban areas are built of non-flammable material such as stone and brick suggests that materials chosen depend also on population density.

The structure and design of houses are directly affected by climate because houses, similar to clothes, are one of the chief means for human beings to protect themselves from the negative impact of climate. In this context, oriental houses characterized by openings on all four sides serve better for the purposes of heat diffusion than for protection from cold. In contrast, western designed houses with narrow windows and tightly closed rooms are better suited for protection from cold. Cave dwellings among Ainu people in the Kurile Islands reflect the close relationship between houses and climate. The height and roof structure of houses have a close relationship with earthquakes and strong winds. That is why we do not have tall buildings such as are commonly seen in western nations. In terms of architectural capability we certainly have highly developed technology such as that involved in the construction of our towers and pagodas. However, these tall structures are not popular for residential architecture because of our fear of natural disasters such as earthquakes and storms. The flat, low architectural style of houses in the Ryukyu islands, the area of Japan most frequently hit by typhoons, reflects this concern. In Chile in South America and in the nations of Central America which are subject to frequent earthquakes, houses are similarly built low to the ground.

There is an almost infinite variety of customs pertaining not only to these three basic components of culture, but to many other aspects of culture as well, which are fascinating to learn about: forms of association and interactions within the same culture and between different cultures, social manners and etiquette, customs pertaining to ceremonial occasions such as weddings and funerals, and many others. However, neither time nor available information will permit our inquiry into all of these areas here. Further studies must await the work of future inquirers and students of culture.

Chapter 29

Competition for Survival

The Nature of Competition

Competition for survival is common to all species. Natural selection and evolution are competition's by-products. Whatever the kind of organism, the number of offspring always exceeds that of the parents. This means that proliferation tends to be exponential, and human beings and their societies are no exception. In the proceeding chapters, competition for survival has been mentioned where applicable to social phenomena. However, the forms of competition have changed over time and there are certain relationships between competition and geography which require clarification. Thus, a brief review of this phenomenon will be useful at this point.

Changes in the Unit of Competition

A review of human history reveals that the units of competition have changed over time and in the following order as natural and social environments changed:

- individual vs. individual and family vs. family.
- village vs. village (communities).
- tribe vs. tribe (ethnic groups).
- state vs. state (nations).

We are now in the age of competition between states. Competition also takes place within a state between groups organized by human beings such as factories, banks, business corporations, schools, political parties and religious sects. Thus, competition for survival has become more complex today and each individual is subject to multiple layers of competition. Even a person who is successful in individual competition is not assured of security and well being if he belongs to a group which is unable to compete successfully. Thus, competition between states has become increasingly important today.

Changes in the Form of Competition

Along with changes in the unit of competition, the forms of competition also change over time: military, political, economic, and humanitarian. Shifts in forms of competition can be seen by focusing on the position of a specific individual or class of people within a society. In feudal Japan, the "Bushi" or warrior class, was the most privileged and respected class. During that period, skill in the military arts and ability to excel in battle was essential for survival. The winner in battle was looked upon as the undisputed master and leader of the society. Being a warrior was regarded as the greatest possible honor for an individual.

Thus had it been since the beginning of history. As Japanese society developed, however, the people came to realize there were other means of gaining power and respect. Intellectual strength also came to be regarded as a path to winning respect in society, so adventurous people sought to gain political power through intellectual measures. Still later, as various schools of thought appeared and as some degree of freedom of individual choice became possible, rulers discovered that political power by itself was not enough to gain and keep the loyalty of their people. This is what led leaders increasingly to place more importance on economic power to maintain their control of the society.

It seems, however, that there is still a final stage in the development of forms of competition that we have not yet reached. This we conclude when we realize that not even the richest billionaire can be assured of succeeding in the competition for survival in our time. But as yet only a very limited circle of people recognize that the ultimate competition will be in the field of moral character.

Similar patterns of change can be observed in the forms of competition among societies and states. The development has been slow and it is not possible to identify specific forms of competition with specific historical eras. However, I believe it is becoming increasingly clear that emphasis on the growth of moral character is gradually replacing the earlier forms of competition. Bloodstained military combat is subsiding and more peaceful forms of competition are emerging. This has been a remarkable transition to observe. On the other hand, there has by no means been a complete replacement of the earlier forms. Their relative importance has been reversed over time, but all four forms still exist together, and in highly complex ways, in the interrelationships between societies and states today.

The Era of Military Competition

Forms of military competition have also changed throughout history. Fighting has become larger in scale, more intensive in magnitude, and more cruel. The development of weapons attest to this. Swords, spears, and pikes—the most effective weapons in earlier days—were replaced by small firearms which were much faster and capable of hitting and damaging distant targets. With the steady development of artillery, it is possible now to destroy in one attack a whole regiment consisting of thousands of soldiers. In other words, face to face battles between individuals have given way to battles between groups. More recently, this form of military battle has given way to wars waged between large organized groups, each positioned miles away from the other. As wars between states became more frequent, third party states also began to intervene before settlements or treaties were concluded to prevent the victor from gaining too much power.

Thus state leaders realized that the ultimate gains of victory could not compensate for losses suffered in war, even if they won overwhelmingly in battle. People learned, furthermore, that 100 percent victory in warfare could not guarantee recovery of war-inflicted losses and that a resultant weakening of national power is unavoidable when war is prolonged. As such recognition became widespread, states became more cautious and slower to mobilize their armies and navies. Instead, they tried to gain superiority over other states by building arms, rather than actually using them. Now, states try to gain victory through the quantity and capability of their military machines before actually engaging in war.

The Era of Political Competition

In time, then, the dominant form of competition among states shifted from military action to political activity. Arms races intensified as states tried to use them as a last resort to expand their power and sphere of influence. At the same time, however, since states did not want to use their military forces except under unavoidable circumstances, they tried to negotiate as favorable conditions for survival as possible through accommodating their negotiation partners. When completely peaceful negotiations were not possible they tried to secure their own survival by demonstrating their military capability without really using it. In order to achieve success in international relations during that period, states deployed able diplomats in locations of strategic importance. They sought to take advantage of each other at every opportunity: through intimidation, enticements, bribing a close aid to the sovereign, concluding secret agreements, or intervening in the domestic affairs of another state under the disguise of a private company with the intention of colonization. The United Kingdom and other European states expanded their territories in the Orient and the South Pacific through such forms of competition.

Era of Economic Competition

State leaders gradually came to realize that expansion of territory, when not accompanied by substantial growth in income, eventually turns out to be meaningless. Moreover, since such expansion required a major investment in order to assure assimilation of the newly acquired territory's people, these leaders discovered that it was much more beneficial to seek economic rather than political objectives. Thus has the mode of competition gradually shifted.

Economic competition can be described as "peaceful warfare" in commerce and industry. It differs from military warfare in several ways. For instance, economic wars are continuous and constant in nature, whereas military wars are temporary and occasional. Militaristic wars were recognized and remembered clearly because of their sudden outbreaks and cruelty while economic wars were often not recognized because of their gradual progress. However, in terms of final outcomes, economic wars were often much more devastating than military wars. In the case of military warfare, peace could be restored through post war peace talks, but there are no cease-fires in economic warfare. Furthermore, mediation by third parties, whether individuals or organizations, is possible only in military conflicts. In economic war, the battles usually continue until winners and losers are irreversibly determined through competition.

In short, in every part of the world, constant conflicts are taking place between individuals, societies and classes. Civilized nations are seeking to overwhelm their primitive, less civilized counterparts, while developing nations are trying to protect themselves from developed nations. In earlier days, states tried to enhance their economic power in order to win in military competition. Now the priority is reversed and armaments are seen as a part of the preparation for economic warfare. In the past, military power played a dominant role, with the assistance of economic power. Today, the reverse is true. Therefore, the final outcome of competition between states is dependent on economic rather than military power. Under such circumstances, citizens are constantly exposed to both individual competition within the state and the less visible economic competition of their state with other states.

If we compare the two kinds of competition described above, military and economic, we can make the following analogies: Merchants are the infantry, the major fighting force in an economic battlefield. The products they trade can be likened to bullets. Industrialists comprise the artillery and their sites of productions are the equivalent of munitions. Farmers and those who are engaged in other primary industries constitute the supply corps. The task of the transportation system is to provide for the smooth movement of food and munitions. Governments may be likened to an imperial headquarters whose major task is to develop plans of operation. Bureaucrats and members of the professions are equivalent to various types of officers and soldiers who protect, assist, and carry out the directions of the headquarters. Ports are gates through which people and products can flow out of the state but which enemies may also break into. The tariff is the only means whereby the state can defend its people from enemy firepower, and customs offices are the fortresses. In such warfare, people trading in their own land can be likened to defense forces while those who are trading overseas are the equivalent of offensive forces. Under such circumstances states in today's world cannot ignore vocational education as preparation for this kind of economic competition. Vocational education, in turn, must be built on a firm foundation of universal education.

Humanitarian Competition

Although humanitarian competition is not yet conspicuous in the international arena, persons who have gained some level of insight are beginning to realize that the ultimate winners in the competition for survival are not necessarily the winners of the economic race. It may be reasonable, then, to expect that the next form of competition will be humanitarian in nature. But what, one may ask, is humanitarian competition? I would describe it as the endeavor to achieve individual and social goals

> But what, one may ask, is humanitarian competition? I would describe it as the endeavor to achieve individual and social goals through invisible moral influence rather than military force or naked economic power.

through invisible moral influence, rather than military force or naked economic power. In other words, instead of forcing submission through force, intimidation, and fear, humanitarian competition seeks the voluntary cooperation and loyalty of people by gaining their respect. Selfish expansion of territory and the conquest of other states are not necessary. If the leaders of a state are persons of high moral character and virtue, justice and humanity will characterize the life and affairs of that state.

It may seem unrealistic to apply such an approach to the real world of current international relations. However, the effectiveness of this approach has already been demonstrated in interpersonal relationships. Thus, I submit that it is not as unrealistic as it may seem to expect that a humanitarian approach to international relations will triumph eventually in human affairs.

It should be understood that "humanitarian approach" does not imply that there is a specific method which can be designated as such. Rather, it is an effort to plan and conduct whatever strategies, whether political, military or economic, in a more humanitarian way. The important thing is the setting of a goal of well being and protection of all people, including oneself but not at the increase of self interest alone. In other words, the aim is the betterment of others and in doing so, one chooses ways that will yield personal benefit as well as benefit to others. It is a conscious effort to create a more harmonious community life, and it will take considerable time for us to achieve.

In the real world of international competition, each state employs its own approach, depending on specific, given conditions. Russia, for example, seeks to expand its territory through old power-oriented measures, while other European states are trying to gain more substantial interests primarily through economic measures. The United States seems to give signs of moving toward a slightly humanitarian approach. But overall, we must face the fact that we are now at the stage of economic competition. Thus, in our present world the complete energy of states is focused on building wealth and military strength. Individual states cannot afford to explore a higher form of competition. Consequently, the forces which either link or separate states all derive from selfish economic interests. In this situation, there is a constant danger of military clashes erupting when conflict of interests cannot be settled through other means.

Several forms of economic competition can be identified, depending on the degree of a state's development. In cases of primary economies, such as Japan's and China's, force or labor is the major means. In these countries, workers go abroad to work for minimal wages. The United Kingdom and the United States, using their natural resources, primarily iron and fuel, and trained manpower, are manufacturing and exporting many kinds of products, which contribute to the national wealth. This means of increasing national wealth is closed to Germany and France because their domestic conditions do not allow it. However, they invest capital in other states and receive interest. Other states invest manpower.

Each state is thus prepared to take advantage of whatever opportunities it sees to expand its economic and political influence. Just as air flows from high atmospheric pressure zones into lower ones, the flow of power can be observed on the international map. Those states which are mainly dependent on economic measures also utilize political measures and vice versa. The difference is in their relative importance. However, since open, unsophisticated political power expansion is now generally recognized as being disadvantageous in comparison with the use of economic competition, most states use political power mainly for defending existing territory, while being aggressive in expanding economic influence. Today, only Russia still depends mainly on the political power approach. Thus, there is concern that Russia's aggressive policies may endanger the current world peace. Russia is now trying to expand its influence in all three directions, the Dardanelles Strait, the Persian Gulf, and the Yellow Sea, in order to become a major economic power in the world.

The Influence of the Struggle for Survival on Geography

It is now well established that competition for survival has been a major factor in the evolution of living organisms. While human development and the survival of the human organism cannot be attributed to competition alone, it is clear that competition has been a fundamental element in human progress. Thus, it can be said that the extent of cultural development in a given society is in proportion to its success in the competitive struggle. Island nations tend to cling to the ancient ways, traditions, rituals, and customs more tenaciously than their continental counterparts, which often results in their much slower progress. Cities have much more sophisticated cultures than rural areas. Western nations achieved remarkable progress while Oriental nations, including Japan, still lag behind. These realities can be explained by their relative capability and success in the competition for survival. This suggests that where competition is severe and intense, progress and development are marked, whereas stagnation, immobility, and regression occur where free competition is precluded by natural and/or man-made conditions.

According to the law of the survival of the fittest, only the few that are equipped more advantageously than others succeed in the struggle for survival, leaving the others to perish. Thus it is only the select few who advance to the next stage of development. But the effects of the competition for survival on human social development are diverse. We will need now to examine two of them which have direct relevance to the theme of this book, that is, geography.

◆ Increases in Population and Prices: Land prices directly reflect the geographical distribution of the intensity of the struggle for survival. Not only among Western nations, but also in various other nations of the world, land prices have increased steadily in recent years. This is because of the increasing intensity of the struggle to survive, due to population increase. As a result of the land price surge, houses and buildings can no longer occupy large land areas and must be expanded vertically. This phenomena can be likened in the history of the earth to the formation of mountains caused by the transverse force generated by the contraction of the earth. Because of such development, buildings in some Western cities now often extend two to three floors below ground level and ten or more floors above the ground.

◆ Migration: One of the consequences of the struggle for survival in recent years has been the migration of population. Human beings are mobile and can select their place of residence according to their respective individual desires and preferences. Nevertheless, close observation of recent human migration reveals two distinctive elements at work here, i.e., movement from densely populated areas to less populated areas and the reverse, movement from less populated areas to densely populated areas. Although these two tendencies seem to contradict each other, in fact, each has clearly established routes. The former consists of flow from densely populated regions to land which has not yet been developed, whereas the latter is a flow from less populated rural villages to densely populated urban cities.

The Intensity of Competition for Survival and Geography

Human beings, as is true of all living creatures, tend to flock to places which are most convenient for their survival. However, such habitats are limited and are not able to accommodate all who desire them. Thus, a large number of people compete to get into limited space. The intensity of competition, therefore, varies from place to place, determined by the characteristics of a given land area. From this realization, we can draw certain conclusions. First of all, competition intensifies in proportion to the increase of human beings directly involved in the competition. In other words, it correlates with the population of a given community, the members of which, directly and indirectly, consciously and unconsciously, help each other in developing their communal life. Thus, intensity is in proportion to the population density of a given area. Since large nations have larger populations, competition in those nations is more intense than that in smaller nations. In contrast, in isolated insular nations or in nations in mountainous areas, the competition for survival is much less harsh. For the same reason, competition intensifies as transportation systems develop.

A further conclusion, then, and this has been noted briefly above, is that population density is higher in places where favorable conditions for human life exist and that density varies in proportion to the degree of desirability of those conditions. The desirability of conditions for survival, in turn, varies in proportion to the abundance of resources available (for food, clothing, and shelter), appropriateness of climate, and development of transportation systems. Finally, abundance of resources, appropriateness of climate, and efficient transportation systems correlate with the geographic location of given areas in specific respects.

◆ Climatic Location: The temperate zone has advantages in terms of appropriateness for human physiology. The tropical zone is superior in terms of the abundance of resources for living, but it is less favorable for human physiological comfort. Both, however, have advantages in comparison with the frigid zone. Thus, intensity of competition for survival is highest in the temperate zone, followed by the tropical zone and then the frigid zone.

◆ Geographic Location: Competition for survival is more intense in plains areas than in highlands and mountains. In the past when transportation was less developed competition was less intense in island nations than in continental nations. Now, however, the order is reversed.

◆ Transportation Location: Within a given geographic area or in an island nation, competition is most severe at the hub of the transportation system, such as places where sea and land transport or different means of land transportation merge. Competition becomes less intense as one travels further from such centers.

Chapter 30

On Civilization and the Earth

Centers of Civilization

We have learned in our studies thus far that the development of culture and human health, happiness, and well being are closely related to the various aspects of the land. We have noted also a significant relationship between climate and geographic location and the rise of civilizations. It remains here for us to examine this relationship in further detail.

Centers of civilization, in general, develop at those locations where traffic is convenient, the very places where cities develop. Each city's sphere of influence has its own range. National cities are the centers of nations, continental cities serve as the centers of continents, and so on.

In Europe, cities with more than one million people are situated between 48° and 60° N latitude. (Constantinople is located at 41° N latitude but it should be regarded as an Asian city). Similar cities in North America are at about 42°, while in Asia large cities are between 23° and 40° (if Kwangtung, which is no longer a center of civilization, is omitted, we can say they are between 36° and 40°). Most of these cities are near water, especially along sea coasts and on the west coasts of continents. Cities of more than one million population are between 48° and 60° N latitude while those on east coasts are between 36° and 42°.

Centers Of Past Civilizations

The locations of these city centers of contemporary civilization represent a shift from the locations of ancient civilizations. Ancient civilizations originated in Egypt on the Nile, Assyria and Babylon on the Tigris and the Euphrates, India on the Indus and Ganges, and China on the Yellow River and the Yangtze. We can readily understand why these particular cities became the centers of civilizations by referring again to Chapter 24. The development of culture requires more than adequate food and other commodities; there must also be some accumulation of wealth and knowledge so that people do not have to spend all of their energy and time providing for their daily needs. Prior to the development of a certain level of human ingenuity, such accumulation was exceedingly more difficult under the climatic conditions of northern areas.

Traffic cultivates ingenuity. Travelers share their experiences with other members of their societies, and knowledge is expanded and enriched throughout society. Traffic developed first along rivers, so culture developed along the big rivers of the south temperate zone. But rich food and beautiful clothes do not provide motivation for people to work hard, and hot climates make people languid. So the adventurous spirit of the people declines; then barbarous peoples from northern areas or from the mountains can easily conquer them. They will become slaves with memories of their tradition as their only solace, or come to feel helpless about their power over reality and become apathetic. They may tend to expect happiness only in the next life. Thus did ancient civilizations stop growing and cease to be at the center of human progress and development.

As the drama of history unfolds, we find the people of the northern areas, the conquerors, being powerfully influenced by the cultures of the southern civilizations. Building upon the South's accumulated wealth and knowledge, they soon began to free themselves from the need to spend all their energy and resourcefulness on gaining daily necessities and were able to develop in other fields. Thus, the centers of civilization moved northward into higher latitudes.

In China, topography caused the drama to develop differently. There, civilization first developed on the banks of the Yellow River and spread in both directions. It seems to contradict the principle described above, and it does, because of the topography of the area. Primitive humans were born in Central Asia. When they began to multiply and feel the need for more space, the upper streams of the Yangtze were in land too mountainous to go through, so they moved eastward along the Yellow river. In general, it seems, Western civilization was formed as a result of a westward and northern shift of civilization, while Eastern civilization arose as a result of an eastward shift.

Centers of Civilizations In the Future

If we wish to anticipate the development of civilizations in the future, we must first, then, recognize the limitations of location. In the Southern Hemisphere, humans can live north of 60° S latitude. While there are people who are eager to explore the Antarctic Continent, it is extremely difficult for them to live there. Likewise, in the Northern Hemisphere, some people are living in the Arctic zone. But they must use all their energy just to live in that cold area, so the northern limitation is probably between 50° to 65° N latitude, depending on the particular continent and whether west or east coasts.

My conclusion is that it will be within this range that Western Culture and Eastern Culture will come into close and intimate contact, and the place where that occurs will become the future center of civilization. If the New Continent he discovered had been India, as Columbus expected, England would have become the center. But America was a savage land and the momentum of civilization shifted into it. So England became merely a channel of a civilization shift, rather than a center, and didn't develop further.

Island countries, as we have noted previously, are well situated for the uniting of different cultures, and we can expect, therefore, that they will be involved in the development of centers of civilization in the future. Japan, which represents the essence of Eastern Cultures, has reached almost the same level as other advanced countries just 30 years after she first came into contact with the cultures of the West.

But it is the United States which can play the most dynamic role in the uniting of civilization in the future. Europe's complicated topography and its many small nations are an obstacle to further growth. The United States is, on the other hand, very much like an island country. It can remain free from international warfare because of its distance from other countries. Although it is as large as the whole of Europe, transportation in the United States is as effective and convenient as that of Britain. Furthermore, it is free from domestic warfare and does not have to spend money on an army. The country can focus its resources and capital on business; this can be seen in the fact that big trusts and business combines are arising. This is leading to a shift of wealth from England to its former colony.

All of these considerations lead me to conclude that world peace in the future will be spearheaded and sustained by three cultures: Britain, the United States, and Japan. Then the dream of a civilization developing through humane competition can be realized. How promising and challenging is Japan's position! The question which haunts me is, Can we make good use of this natural gift and this momentous calling?

Appendix

The Concept of Geography

How I Arrived at a Definition of Geography

Formulating a definition of geography is the most difficult part of this work. There have been for many years various views as to what geography is. Even among recognized experts and scholars in the field, no clear agreement, it seems, has been reached on a definition. However, insofar as geography exists as an established discipline, has a body of knowledge which is organized to a certain extent, is generally accepted by an academic community, and is responding to demands for refinement, I believe there must be some point of agreement which these different approaches to an understanding of geography can share. If we can find where this point of agreement is, we should be able to arrive at a satisfactory definition.

This was the justification underlying the hypothesis which I formulated as a tentative guide for our studies at the beginning of this book. If, as a result of the explorations we have made on the basis of that hypothesis, our findings are consistent with the findings and conclusions of so-called traditional geography and are, at the same time, able to meet the further requirements we have outlined, the question of definition will have been satisfactorily answered. Thus, my task at this point will be simply that of stating explicitly what was earlier implicitly accepted.

Geography of Human Life and General Geography

The material we have covered thus far has been based on the overall conceptions described above. Though still rough and incomplete, we are now coming toward the end of the task we set for ourselves, that is, a systematic description and analysis of geographical phenomena in their relationships to human life. This descriptive and analytical framework is consistent with its counterpart in the field of conventional geographic studies, but, we can conclude that most phenomena in human life related to geographical knowledge are better organized by our framework. At the same time, we can now save the vast amount of energy formerly required for memorizing a great mass of separate, individual facts and direct it to more creative and productive uses. Accordingly, I believe that a fair examination of the two frameworks, the geography of human life approach and the conventional geography approach, will lead to the conclusion that they share common ground with respect to basic, underlying principles and, further, that our geography of human life framework comes close to the point where the needs of society are satisfied by geographic phenomena.

A Definition of Geography of Human Life

We can then, with confidence, define geography of human life as follows:

> Geography is a systematic body of knowledge pertaining to the relations between natural phenomena and the life phenomena of human beings observed on the surface of earth.

The life phenomena of human beings or human life phenomena will be shortened and hereafter referred to as "human life." Similarly, natural phenomena on the surface of the earth or earth phenomena will be referred to as the "earth." The definition can then be rephrased:

> Geography is that branch of science which deals with relationships between the earth and human life.

Without specific delimitation, natural phenomena may include an infinite variety of things and events existing on the earth and in space. Among these, those that geography of human life deals with are limited to natural phenomena—natural objects and natural forces—existing on the surface of the earth. And since the major goal of a geography of human life is to clarify the rules governing relations between the earth and human phenomena, the life phenomena of human beings are naturally one of the foci of study. However, not all human life phenomena are to be studied.

Things and events in human society are infinite. Thus we will limit ourselves to those directly related with "earth phenomena" as defined above. However seriously the recall of a cabinet affects a nation's life, for example, or however extensively economic fluctuations influence society, insofar as they do not directly relate to the earth, they are not dealt with in geography. The same is true with natural phenomena. Among objects and forces that are distributed on the earth's surface, only those which have direct relevance for human life will be covered by our geography of human life.

The Subject and Scope of Geography of Human Life

Now, in terms of the life phenomena of human beings, the objects to be studied are:

◆ parts of the earth that are related to the life of human beings;

◆ natural phenomena that are related to human life and the earth;

◆ human life phenomena that are related to the earth.

To consider geography in relationship to other branches of science we begin by recognizing "earth science" as a branch of science whose subject matter is the phenomena of earth, including the earth itself, and which consists of two major divisions, geology and geography. It can be distinguished from other branches of science by noting that while for both geology and geography the subject of study is the earth, all of the other sciences investigate phenomena emerging on the earth.

Our next task is to clearly distinguish between geology and geography. Geology studies and seeks to clarify the anatomy and evolution of the earth. It examines materials that compose the earth's crust, analyzes their structure, and speculates about their transitions. Thus, the interests of students of geology are directed vertically downward deep inside the earth.

Students of geography, on the other hand, seek to obtain a systematic knowledge about phenomena on the earth's surface and their interrelationships. Although it may at times study the material composition of the earth's crust, it is to supplement systematic knowledge of the earth's surface phenomena. The student's interest is always directed horizontally over the surface of the earth. Geology studies evidence deposited in the earth during an earlier period, from which it traces history backwards and speculates about the evolution of the earth. Geography concentrates mainly on analytical studies of present phenomena. When geography studies past phenomena, it is in order to interpret current phenomena.

Natural Geography and Geography of Human Life

Geography can be further divided into two major divisions: natural geography and geography of human life. Natural geography does not presuppose any relations with our life and it simply studies the earth as habitat. For example, here is a stream. When we study this stream from the standpoint of natural geography, we want to discover such things as: How did the stream originate? Why does it flow? Why does it continue to flow? What influence does it have on the land in its basin and on other elements in the natural environment? How does it affect the surrounding biosphere? In short, the interest of natural geography rests in the relationship between the stream and the natural world surrounding it. Observation is directed toward identifying common principles which can be applied to other similar phenomena. Relevance of the phenomena to human life, its usefulness, or the benefits or the harm it may cause to human life, are not considered.

When the same stream is studied in geography of human life, we seek answers to different questions: How does the stream affect human life? In affecting its natural surroundings, does it at the same time affect human life indirectly? Again, the object of study is to discover principles which can be applied in other similar occasions. Thus, both approaches study origin, course, speed, and estuary of the stream. But since the points of interest are different between the two, the handling of the material, that is, its classification, is based on completely different criteria. Likewise, in the study of a mountain, natural geography is interested in how the mountain was formed and in its relationship to other natural phenomena, while the geography of human life is interested in the mountain's relationship to human life. Thus, if the latter considers how the mountain came into existence, what type of mountain it is, etc., it is because these factors are believed to have some relevance for human life.

We can say, then, that however interesting some phenomena may seem in terms of natural geography, it is not studied in geography of human life unless it has a marked relationship with human life. And, however precisely and strictly some concepts are differentiated in terms of natural geography, if the difference between those concepts is not meaningful in terms of human life or a human geographic point of view, we do not classify them in the same way. Contrarily, if a certain phenomena or event is highly relevant to human life, it has to be clearly stated even if it is of no interest from a natural geographic point of view. For example, ports are simply points on the curves of coast lines in natural geography. However, in geography of human life, they are highly significant objects to be closely studied because of their role in the development of transportation, the economy, politics, and culture.

A further example is biological distribution. In natural geography, the distribution of various animals and plants may be studied in relationship to climate and soil quality. If quantitative distribution is studied, it is commonly described in terms of its relationship to other natural phenomena. However, in the geography of human life, quantitative distribution is of the utmost importance in the life of a given region or given nation. Thus, it is regarded as an important subject of study, and further investigation is required to discover details of quantitative distribution, especially when it comes to an animal or a plant which affects human life in an important manner. In this connection, it is my feeling that such entries under each country or nation in conventional geographic material as "products are rice, wheat, gold, silver, etc." are quite meaningless.

Since natural geography and geography of human life share common subject matter to a greater extent than any other two disciplines, they are often regarded either as the same science or as the latter's being a part of the former. But is it appropriate to say that one aspect of geography of human life is an applied study of natural geography? It is my position that it is not. Consider the aforementioned stream as an example. Suppose you formulate a rule on how water transforms land forms, based on observation of phenomena such as erosion, sedimentation, pressure and irrigation. Application of the knowledge obtained, however, belongs to various other disciplines. For example, irrigating fields and rice paddies belongs to the study of agronomy, while studies involving the building of an embankment belong to civil engineering. Likewise, hydraulic power generation is directed by engineering. Geography of human life does not concern itself with these applications. In so far as particular principles are utilized in agronomy, civil engineering, or in various industries, it implies that there is an important relationship between a given geographic environment and human life. Therefore, such phenomena or events must be described, compared, and integrated into existing knowledge so that a general principle can be formulated, suggesting that the same principle will govern other cases in other regions where a similar set of geographic circumstances are found.

In concluding this consideration of the distinction between natural geography and geography of human life, I would like to emphasize again that though natural geography provides geography of human life with an important foundation, it does not share the same principles and rules as geography of human life. Geography of human life can draw more useful knowledge from natural geography than from any of the other sciences, but the two disciplines are different in their nature and scope.

Boundaries with Other Disciplines

In addition to distinguishing it from natural geography, geography of human life must be distinguished from other sciences as well. In our definition of geography of human life, we recognized both earth phenomena and human phenomena, which presupposes definitions of those phenomena. Geography of human life bases itself on the foundation of shared understanding of what those phenomena are. However, detailed classification of those phenomena requires that we draw on a number of different sciences, each of which is responsible for elucidating a specific part or aspect of the phenomena. In other words, geography of human life shares boundaries with a number of other sciences. While it is important that these boundaries be recognized, I will not attempt to consider each of them in detail here. The distinction between natural geography and geography of human life has been dealt with at some length because it has been a major source of confusion.

Afterword

Geographic Education in the 20th Century

Tsunesaburo Makiguchi strikes a responsive chord with late Twentieth Century American geographers when he speaks of becoming "... more and more obsessed with geography and its implications for education and human development" *(Jinsei Chirigaku [A Geography of Human Life]*, 1903). This afterword to the English edition of the book will examine some of his understandings of the content and dimensions of human geography in the beginning of the past century and, perhaps more importantly, the applicability of his human geographic concepts today will be examined.

Makiguchi begins his *A Geography of Human Life* by discussing the Earth as the base for human life. It is clear from the outset that he is concerned about the relationships between Earth and human life, the appropriate observation point for gathering information, and the nature of interaction between people and the Earth.

Makiguchi's discussion of the relationships among humans and their environment is launched from a reflection on his own situation. This may appear at first glance to be a trivial materialistic concern. In fact, what he represents by his opening statements is a very clear depiction of the complexity of the web of existence and connection that we all share (perhaps even more now than when he first recorded his thoughts). It is altogether fitting that he should consider international trade of both raw materials and finished products, considering his Japanese home base. He is rightly careful to avoid generalizing from his personal experience to explain broader patterns of behavior and relationship. What he does successfully, however, is to show that an individual's understanding must proceed from a sense of personal relationship to people, places, and events that may be far distant from one's local community. But, where does one begin?

Makiguchi clearly believed that people are best advised to start their journey to understand geography in their own local communities. He argued cogently that family, friends, neighbors, and community groups give us the power to take inspiration from the natural world. He is very much in the mainstream of geographic thought, at either end of the century, to insist on the essential importance of direct observation. While books provide a frozen geographic moment or two, direct field observation and data collection epitomize the best tradition in geography, no matter in which part of the world it is practiced. It is a commonplace that excellent teachers of geography exhort their students to leave behind their armchairs for the excitement of real field experience. From those direct observations come the insights that illuminate the web of relationship between people and places.

As an academic geographer, I am fascinated with Makiguchi's contention at the beginning of the 20th Century that geography students in Japan at that time were engaged in the useless memorization of locational facts and statistics. This is an approach to geographic learning that is incredibly counter-productive. I am sure that if Makiguchi were alive today, he would agree that this kind of education is not only not challenging to students, but very likely to dissuade them from further interest in geography. At the American university level of geographic education, I have become aware that students come to college with little exposure to the kind of geography that Makiguchi recommended. Rather, they appear (with few notable exceptions) bearing the same kinds of misconceptions about the field of geography that Makiguchi tried to counter.

As recently as three years ago, I had an interesting exchange with a student in my World Regional Geography class at Eastern Michigan University. In Michigan, World Regional Geography is a state recommended course for future teachers at all levels. The class is intended to *reintroduce* students to geographic principles and expose them to various regions of the world. The reason I say reintroduce above, is because they have supposedly had exposure to geography in the public school system (Kindergarten through 12th grade). The students had taken their first exam in the course and received the results. One student, obviously disappointed in his grade, informed me that he was going to withdraw from the course. He went on to explain that he thought the course would be "straight geography" and was disappointed that it wasn't. His statement really piqued my curiosity about his conception of "straight geography." He explained to me that geography is the memorization of place-names, capitals, and countries and being able to place them on a map. Because he seemed intent on dropping the course, I confess I did not attempt to convince him to reconsider.

What I have done, however, is to incorporate this experience into my lectures. Now I tell the students of this experience and suggest to them that they consider the following analogy. If we think of place names as analogous to the letters in the alphabet, can we say that once we know the alphabet we know how to read or write words? Can we say that we know how to read or write sentences? Their answers are, of course, a resounding no! I then extend the analogy to say that when we have learned place-names and locations it is good, but that it is only the beginning of a much more interesting and complex process; that "alphabet" is essential in learning to read the geography of the world, but context and relationships between humans and the Earth's surface are the real words, sentences, paragraphs, even volumes of geography. I usually refer them to Bloom's taxonomy and recommend against memorizing the telephone directory as both boring and unproductive. Most of them get the point and take a renewed and lively interest in geography.

The American educational establishment's concern about the education of American students at the close of the century is parallel to Makiguchi's anxiety about Japanese students at the beginning of the century. The current concern has generated a cross-disciplinary dialogue of national proportions. One result of this dialogue was the passage of *Goals 2000: Educate America Act* (Public Law 103-227). The fact is that it was only after a decade of reform in geography education (in the United States), that geography was included as a core subject in *Goals 2000*. Responding to the public desire for a geographically literate population in the United States, a broad-based group including educators and parents as well as representatives from business, professional, and civic organizations produced *Geography for Life: National Geography Standards, 1994* (Washington, DC: National Geographic Research & Exploration,1994).

Six essential *elements* were identified. They are: (1) The World in Spatial Terms, (2) Places and Regions, (3) Physical Systems, (4) Human Systems, (5) Environment and Society, and (6) the Uses of Geography. In order to establish a clear frame of reference, I will reproduce the definitions of each of these elements:

Element one: geography studies the relationships between people, places, and environments by mapping information about them into a spatial context.

Element two: the identities and lives of individuals and peoples are rooted in particular places and in those human constructs called regions.

Element three: physical processes shape Earth's surface and interact with plant and animal life to create, sustain, and modify ecosystems.

Element four: people are central to geography in that human activities help shape Earth's surface, human settlements and structures are part of Earth's surface, and humans compete for control of Earth's surface.

Element five: the physical environment is modified by human activities, largely as a consequence of the ways in which human societies value and use Earth's natural resources, and human activities are also influenced by Earth's physical features and processes.

Element six: knowledge of geography enables people to develop an understanding of the relationships between people, places, and environments over time—that is, of Earth as it was, is, and might be. (*Geography for Life: National Geography Standards, 1994,* Washington, DC: National Geographic Research & Exploration,1994: 34-35).

Contained within these elements are a total of eighteen standards. Rather than reproduce all eighteen here, I will refer to several which I believe reflect the kind of education that Makiguchi was trying to promote in 1903. In *A Geography for Life* each of the standards is introduced by the phrase: "The geographically informed person knows and understands: ... ." In striving to produce geographically informed people, Makiguchi's work in human geography supports the idea that "culture and experience influence people's perceptions of places and regions" (Standard 6). His work also explored the "patterns and networks of economic interdependence on Earth's surface" (Standard 11). Much of the first twenty chapters of *A Geography of Human Life* focuses on "how human actions modify the physical environment" (Standard 14) and its near corollary, "how physical systems affect human systems" (Standard 15). In later sections of *A Geography of Human Life,* Makiguchi discusses topics related to "how the forces of cooperation and conflict among people influence the division and control of Earth's surface" (Standard 13).

It is clear that Makiguchi was an extremely well informed and original thinker, whose ideas concerning geography were both provocative and inspirational. The scope of his work was such that if he had done nothing more after *A Geography of Human Life,* he would still have established a substantial landmark in geographic scholarship. The complexity of relationships with which he grappled in his writing successfully argue against logical positivist reductionism. There are instead strong holistic overtones in Makiguchi's work putting him solidly in the international tradition of human geography. It is also clear by comparing his thought to the established standards in *Geography for Life,* that his ideas have broad applicability to geographic education today.

Spring 2002

Andrew A. Nazzaro
Professor of Geography/Geology
Eastern Michigan University
Ypsilanti, Michigan, U.S.A.

Index

A Geography of Human Life, 301, 304-305, principles applicable today, 305; as a "ship's log" or diary of a journey, xvi
abstract knowledge, futile when disconnected from tangible experience, xx
agriculture, 157; as primary industry cannot afford to let decline, 270
American industrialism, basic tenant of: nature an object waiting to be exploited, xviii
animals, and human life, 166
art, as response to beauty, 191
Basho, 167
Berman, Morris, xxviii-xxx
bioregion, importance of in education, xxi; to know is to connect to our home planet, xxi
books, people can remain ignorant even after reading thousands of, xvii, 21; danger in becoming a slave to, 21
Burton, Catherine, xxi
Carson, Rachel, xx
Chinese, global influence of in future, 173
cities, benefits of, 267-268; growth of, 260; must control growth of, 270-271; negative impact of, 268-269; origins of, 262-264; runaway growth of, 270; size of and poverty, 196;
city and country, historical relationship of, 266; symbiotic relationship between, 267
city, future of, 269-271
civilization, 117; and air-land-water interface, 140; and inanimate objects, 135; and the earth, 291
class divisions, based on ignorance and discrimination, 192
climate, and geography, 143
clouds, 154
colonies, 254
colonization, causes of, 255; European exploitation of weaker peoples, 107; not appropriate solution to problem of population growth, 108; purposes and means of, 255
community, schools sever child's ties with, xiii
competition, and class divisions, 192; consequences of privileged class preventing fair, 197; effects of large-scale, 13; for survival, 281, 287-290; forms of, 282-286; humanitarian, xxvii, 285-286; nature of, 281
cooperation, and competition, xxvii
curricula, guidelines for developing, 33

curriculum, consists of natural and social systems of environment, xix
customs, 273; and geography, 276
deforestation, as cause of drought and floods, 82
development, in transportation and communication, 222; vs. expansion, 184-189
dialogue, with nature, xxxv; among civilizations and cultures, xxxiii
direct experience learning, and books, xvii-xix; and development of moral character, xviii, xxxiv-xxxv; nurtures genius, 21
division of labor, 181
Doi, Katsutoshi, 12
drought, causes of, 159
earth, a miracle, xiv; perceived as a unity, xix; interaction with fills heart and mind with excitement, wonder, and curiosity, 43; impact of human beings on, 44; dominated and ruled by developed nations, 95; features of, 133; and animals, 165
Earthbank Association, xxi
ecological education, immerses learner in natural systems of local community, xx; an engaged way of learning, xx
ecological literacy, xx
economic life, 199
education, true factor in social advance, 190; consists of dialogue with a place, xx; deplorable state of Japanese, ix; means to personal and social transformation, xviii; organized as a journey into natural and social systems, xxvii-xxviii
elicitation, as educational process, xix
enchanted world, and disenchanted, xxix
encounter, distinguished from experience, 28
energy, danger of overdependence on fossil fuels, 214-215
Evans, Christopher, xxviii
evolution, 110
family, as a small society, 180; as simplest society, 182
feeling, more important in learning than knowing, xx
floods, causes of, 159
forests, influence on human life, 158-159
freedom of action, voluntary limitation on, xxvii
genius, 20, nurturing of, 22-23; popular misperception of, xvii, 20-21
geography, subject and scope of, 297; definition of, 295-300; as a journey, xxviii; as path to understanding, 14; new approach to study of, 15; definition of, 15; traditional discipline of fragmented and over-specialized, 15
Geography for Life, 303-305
geography of human life, definition of, 15; and natural geography, 298-300
good institutions, essential for persons of moral character to develop, xviii
Great Powers, and annihilation of native peoples, xxii
half-day school system, xix
Hobbes, Thomas, xxiv
holism, in education, xxvii
home community, can learn about every aspect of entire universe in, xvi
home environment, influence on persons, 273
homeland, 14-15; appreciation for nurtures social consciousness, 30; as base for observing the world, 17-19; as primary source of curricula, 20-22; and personal identity, xvi, 14; mysterious power of, 18-19

Index

homelands, and human life, 14
human beings, as social animals, 169
human desire, 199
human development, stages of, 170
human life, influence of transportation and communication on, 225
humanitarian competition, xxvii, xxxiii, 285-286
Ikeda, Daisaku, xxxiii-xxxvi
imperialism, as a transition stage in human development, xxiii, 243
inborn potential, discovering and actualizing the primary purpose of education, 23; every person possesses, 20; in modern societies remains undeveloped in most people, 22
indirect learning, as imported from West the height of folly, xxviii
indust reality, xviii
industrial society, Makiguchi's perception of, xiii
industrial societies, consequences of educational policies in, xiii; inevitable, xiii
industrialism, American model of, xxix
industrialism, in Japan, xxviii
industry, and crafts, 212-213; and labor, 215; and manufacturing, 211; mechanical, 213; primary, 209; and relationship to land, 218; location of, 199-233; development of, 201-204; types of, 200-201; and state power, 232
infinite, the, realization of it fills one's heart with awe, 30
insularism, 111
integrity, a rarity in modern societies, xxv-xxvi
interaction with the earth, and moral growth; xviii; physical, 25; spiritual, 25; vital for becoming fully human, 25
interconnectedness, with natural and social phenomena, xviii, xx

islands, danger of exploitation of, 56; role in trade and military campaigns, 55-56
Japan, xxvii, 108; saved from domination by European nations, 94
Japanese militarism, xxxvi
Japanese, the, xxix
Jones, Alan H., xxxvi
Korten, David, xxxi
Kyodoka (Community Study), 36
lakes, cultivator of aesthetic sensibilities, 91; and mountains, provide inspiration for art of Japanese landscaping, 91
land, and primary industries, 209
land and water, struggle between, 46-50
land, affect of on human life, 45-48
learning, as participant observation, xvi; cannot be imposed, xix
life, a miracle, xiv; vibrating and pulsating through all phenomena, xiv
Leopold, Aldo, xxvi
Makiguchi, Tsunesaburo, vii-xxxvi 2-8, 301; as scientist, xxvii
memorization focused learning, futility of, 20
Miller, Ron, xx, xxxi
modern ethics, discards virtue of integrity, xxvi
moral character, and competition, 282; develops through interaction with the earth, xviii; nurtured through direct experience, 21-23, 25-32
Mori, Koichi, xxi, xxvii; misunderstanding of Makiguchi's philosophical position, xxi
mountains, and precipitation, 64
mountains, and relationship to rivers, 64
native peoples, as wise managers of the earth, xxii
natural environment, schools sever child's ties with, xiii

natural world, interdependence and interrelatedness with, xv
nature, 105; intimate relationship with, 31; mysteries of,144; wisdom of, 82
navigation,112
Nazzaro, Andrew A., vii, 301-305
Nichiren, 39
Nitobe, Inazo, 259, n. 271
Norton, David, xxiv-xxvi, xxxi
oceans, influence on humans, 100
occupation, influence on mind and body, 204-208
ocean, vastness of nourishes the soul, 105
Orr, David, xxi
paper, growing demand for,158
peninsulas, and development of civilizations, 58; as transmitters of culture, 58
people/earth relationship, 11
philosophy, Eastern, xxv; classical, xxxi; modern vs. classical xxiv; oriental, xxv
place, fundamental organizing concept for education, x; importance of in human experience, 17-18
plants, distribution of,160; special influence of,162
population,107; and human habitats;170
primary industries, must protect, 270-271
rain, 154
region, importance of, 273
rivers, consequences of failure to appreciate wonders of, 80-83; influence on human life, 79-80; to land what blood vessels are to human body, 70
scholars, role in society,190
scientific industrialism, moral and spiritual bankruptcy of, xxix
sense of wonder, once crushed rarely blossoms again, xx-xxi
Shiga, Shigetaka, vi, 4, 6, 18

social life, dimensions of, 32
social responsibility, nurture of, xv
social structures, within which people live must be human scale, xx
societies, greatest threat to, 270
societies, nature of human beings to form, 29
society, our indebtedness to, xv; common elements of,180; evolution of,184; as organic body,185; functions of,187; and morality,189; definition of,179, 181;
society-individual antagonism, source of, xxiv
Soka Gakkai, 10
specialization,181
spirit, of a society;184; of a nation,118
spiritual interaction with the earth, and personal growth, 30
spirituality, and cultural advance, 244
states, objectives of, 241; functions of, 235; national borders of, 253; types of, 247; wealth and strength of, 245
sun,104; and the Japanese, 38;
sun, pervasive influence on human life, 37
symbiosis, xxvii
sympathetic feelings, universalization of, xv
teacher as guide, xix
temperament, 273
temperature, and animals,144
temperature, and wind,144
Toffler, Alvin, xviii, xxxi
traditional values, sacrificed in pursuit of profits, xiii
true sociality, a whole to be won by fulfillment of parts, xxiv
Tsuboi, Kumazo, 7
Yoshida, Shoin, 21
water, and human life, 46-50,153
wind, and human life, 145
wood, and civilization, 158